Pursuing THE Pearl

Pursuing THE Pearl

A Comprehensive Resource for Multi-Asian Ministry

Ken Uyeda Fong

Judson Press

Valley Forge

Library of Congress Cataloging-in-Publication Data

Fong, Ken Uyeda.
   Pursuing the pearl : a comprehensive resource for multi-Asian
ministry / Ken Uyeda Fong.
      p.   cm.
   Includes bibliographical references.
   ISBN 0-8170-1304-0 (pbk. : alk. paper)
   1. Church work with Asian Americans.   I. Title.
BV4468.2.A74F66 1999
259'.089'95073 – dc21   99-35734

Printed in the U.S.A.
08 07 06 05 04 03 02 01 00 99
5   4   3   2   1

To Janessa Akemi Fong

You were born the same year that this book was born.
This book, my life, my ministry are all dedicated to your future
and to those generations that will come after you
long after I am gone from this earth.

You are God's gracious gift to your mommy and daddy.
As you grow up, may you, too, pursue Jesus
and his precious pearl.

CONTENTS

PREFACE

Being born and reared in Sacramento, California, and finding my faith in Christ in a bilingual Chinese American Baptist church, I can remember wondering from an early age where I fit in the larger societal scheme as well as in the more specialized realm of the church. Although my parents overtly stressed a Western identity for us children, there definitely was a subliminal emphasis on some of the core values from our Chinese culture. Later I learned to label this a bicultural upbringing, but this did nothing to quell my inner sense of not truly belonging to either of the two cultures. Why was I not comfortable just being Chinese or just being American? Why this ambivalent identity?

And more specifically, in regard to the church and ministry, where might people like me fit without having to be untrue to who we are? This book is a chance for me to formulate responses to questions like these.

The question of whether there was a Christian church that would embrace ambivalent Asian Americans like me became much more crucial for me in 1976, shortly after I graduated from college. Through a maze of different influences, I felt that God was challenging me to consider the pastorate, a pursuit that had never been one of my aspirations. As much as I was receiving immense encouragement to follow this calling, the lingering uncertainty of where I would fit caused me to balk at the prospect of being a pastor. Even if there were American-born Chinese (ABC) pastors who were as westernized as I was (and I had yet to meet them), would they be serving churches that matched who they were?

Having never been encouraged to learn to speak Cantonese, I found that my experience with Chinese American churches had thus far caused me to expect one of two options for people like me. Either I would be pegged as a perennial youth pastor, or I would serve under an overseas-born Chinese (OBC) senior pastor as I ministered to the English-speaking segment of the church. Though neither option seemed to match my still-forming vision for ministry, I nevertheless accepted the Lord's invitation and entered into theological training. I had to trust that the Lord would not call someone with my particular cultural ambivalence unless he had plans to match me with a corresponding ministry.

Growing up as an uncertain Chinese American and completing my first seventeen years in ministry clarified for me the emerging need for ministries that specialized in reaching, teaching, and unleashing Americanized Asian Americans (AAAs). Since 1995, however, God's Spirit began to show me that there was yet another evolutionary stage beyond reaching AAAs, a strategy that would not only embrace more of the biracial relationships and offspring of such unions but also be more multi-ethnic. If you have not learned this already, both in clothing and ministry paradigms, one size does not fit all. What some of us have seen and done in the last five years has only underscored the ongoing importance of having a variety of churches to match the dizzying array of Asian Americans, all at different stages in their acculturation to life in America. This latest book affords me the opportunity to share with you some of the practical insights gleaned in the process of keeping Evergreen Baptist Church of Los Angeles on the leading edge of fruitful ministry to and with Asian Americans.

God has used countless people to inform me and forge my current philosophy of ministry, and thus many people have contributed to this work.

First, I want to thank my parents, James and Emilie Fong, not only for supporting my decision to enter the ministry but also for being my perennial cheerleaders. Mom, more than you'll ever know, your belief in me and my creative gifts all these years has emboldened me to pioneer new things, to believe in my calling, even when things are difficult. Dad, it took you a while before you verbalized your blessing of me, but even before you did, your example of courage and perseverance gave me the courage and boldness I have needed to pursue God's mission and vision for his church.

Being a part of the staff of Evergreen-LA since 1978 has played a crucial role in the fruition of my concepts of Asian American ministry.

I truly thank the Lord for placing me under the guidance of my friend and former senior pastor Cory K. Ishida, a person of great vision who has been lavish in giving people like me opportunities to mature and ripen. Thank you for having the foresight to allow me to stay at the current location and establish myself as the new senior pastor of a good-sized portion of the congregation. I pray that by the time this book is on the shelves, God will have established the church you lead in a new permanent location. I am also indebted to the members of my Ministerial Relations Team who have been tireless in their support of me. A special thank you goes to Frances Tsuneishi, who in 1978 quickly sold other members of the Diaconate Board on the idea of creating a pastoral internship on the spot for a young man known only to her who had just materialized in Los Angeles. I am especially grateful to God that I serve such a loving and generous congregation. Not only have you supported my studies, but also, more importantly, you have been willing to grow and change along with me. Thanks for being God's guinea pigs with me.

Over the past twenty years, many of you have served as a sounding board for my theories and queries about Asian American ministry. Thank you, Rev. Drs. Sam Chetti and Ralph Moore, Rev. Dave Gibbons, Stan Inouye, Arlene Inouye, Mark Sakanashi, and the members of our Lil' Rascals pastors' group. A special thank you to the marvelous current and former members of my staff team at Evergreen Baptist Church of LA: David Fukuyama, Jonathan Wu, Todd Nakata, Melvin Fujikawa, Jetty Fong, Peter Huang, Carolyn Iga, Dave Martyn, Ezer Kang, Michelle Samura, and Sherwin Sun. I am especially grateful for Wendy Saito Lew, my special assistant, who bird-dogged all the publishers for their permission and always manages to simplify my life. A special thank you to her brother, Dr. Leland Saito, University of California San Diego, who sent me pertinent articles and statistics to refresh my data. I am also grateful to Victoria M. McGoey at Judson Press for being available in my times of need, to Rebecca Irwin Diehl, also at Judson Press, for being such a constant source of encouragement, and to Linda Triemstra, my copy editor, who made my writing more coherent.

Of course, I must thank my wonderful wife and lab partner, Sharon

(Snoopy), most of all, for you have been with me every step of the way, consoling, critiquing, and contributing key insights. You have made the discovery of our cross-cultural chemistry in the laboratory of our marriage both fascinating and fun. Much of this material comes just as much from you as it does from me.

Finally, I truly thank the Lord for calling me into this venture and for graciously providing me with the rich fabrics out of which this work has taken shape. You are truly the Master Designer.

INTRODUCTION

The first version of this book, my self-published dissertation *Insights for Growing Asian American Ministries,* was the culmination of two overlapping strands of my life: my growing up as a third-generation American of Chinese heritage and my first ten years in pastoral ministry. Nearly ten years have transpired since I wrote and then revised my doctoral dissertation. In the ensuing years, the Lord has seen fit to intertwine a third strand of experiences, one that has caused me to view my original work from a slightly different perspective. Once I could only envision a church that consisted of a relatively narrow band of acculturated, English-speaking Asian Americans. Today I lead a congregation that is broadly multi-Asian (encompassing more than ten Asian Pacific American groups as well as spanning five generations) and that is becoming more intentionally more multi-ethnic.

Some of my long-time allies are puzzled by what they interpret as a dramatic shift away from my career-defining emphasis on AAA (Americanized Asian American) ministry. They wonder if I am dropping my efforts to reach AAAs. All I can say is that this seems to be the next natural chapter in this unfolding story. I never thought that significant numbers of first- and second-generation Asian Americans would be attracted to the Evergreen-LA model, but ones who are fluent in English are showing up in droves. Contrary to what I used to think, this has not been a deterrent to the influx of AAAs. Thus far, our growing diversity seems to be part of what is attracting all kinds of Asian Americans and others.

Ten years ago, I was reluctant to describe the demographics of the phase of the church that would eventually grow out of an emphasis on AAAs. By God's grace, I am witnessing at least one type of evolutionary outgrowth. It is my prayer that this book will be a significant and practical tool for my many comrades who share a vested interest in the future of Asian American ministries.

This is by no means the last or best word on this new subject; at most, this is an overview of a ministry still under construction. However, this is a chance for me to share with you what we have been learning at the level of one local church situated at ground zero for Asian America in Southern California. I sincerely hope that this book will provide you with a clearer perspective of what the future may hold for many Asian American ministries.

Chapter One

WHY SPECIFICALLY TARGET ASIAN AMERICANS?

Slowly and surely, a strong Asian American culture is coming of age. It's a bold culture, unashamed and true to itself. It's a culture with a common destiny, a community of mind and soul. Instead of conforming to prefabricated images and stereotypes, we must define our own successes, our own personalities, our own images. [W]e must find a new common ethos, a new aesthetic, a new psychology.

— EDWARD IWATA[1]

No doubt there are those Christians, even among Asian Americans,[2] who do not believe there is any need to single out unconvinced[3] Asian Americans as a target audience for particular churches or ministries. To do so strikes these colleagues as inherently unnecessary, even unthinkable. To do so would only perpetuate the sad fact that there is not one Christian church in America, but five: red, white, black, brown, and yellow.

As you will discover, I am not in favor of maintaining this status quo. However, it has been my experience that some people who think they have the solution are blind to their own cultural biases. When I was in seminary, my systematic theology professor loudly proclaimed to our class that "the ethnic church in this country is an abomination to the all-encompassing gospel message. Eleven o'clock on Sunday mornings is the most segregated hour in America. We should all go to the same church." During the break I asked him, since our respective churches no doubt read the same Bible and worshiped the same God, if he was going to start attending our Asian American church. "Why, no," he replied, "I meant for you to come to our church." This fine Christian gentleman and world-class theologian could clearly imagine

3

the cultural peculiarities of our church, but he was blind to those of his own. If many Christians still cannot ignore these, how can we expect those who are not Christians to disregard such distinctives?

I am positive that these same critics of Asian American ministries would be among the first to promote missionary efforts to specific people groups in Asia. Other than the fact that one group of Japanese lives across the ocean and the other lives across the street, what's the difference? In both cases, more than 95 percent of these people are not Christians. Clearly, uninformed and nonspecific evangelistic efforts are not accomplishing mission goals on either side of the Pacific. There is definitely a need for more Asian-specific approaches.

ANOTHER BOOK PROMOTING
THE HOMOGENEOUS UNIT PRINCIPLE?

In 1990 I was a conspicuous disciple of the church growth movement pioneered by the late Donald McGavran[4] and popularized by C. Peter Wagner,[5] both of Fuller Theological Seminary in Pasadena, California. Although today I am less a proponent of this movement, there are still some aspects of it that merit our consideration as we think about Asian American and/or multi-Asian ministries.

According to this school of thought, guiding and furthering the growth of churches is a matter of identifying the right ingredients that the Holy Spirit will use to produce more fruit from evangelistic efforts.

> [W]hen you get the right "mix," the right proportion of concern, biblical authority, attractive witness, caring for people, speaking the common language, addressing the message within the culture, and many other factors, you have effective evangelism. Church growth principles are part of the mix.... To be effective, evangelism must produce results; otherwise, as Paul said, "It is beating the air," only shadowboxing. The right "mix," however, produces effective evangelism. People will respond to Christ and the church will grow.[6]

Early on, McGavran observed that one of the essential ingredients for this mix is "the kind of people we are," for we naturally attract the kind of people most like ourselves. A worship service designed around Gen-Xers (the generation that came after the Baby Boomers, born from 1964 to 1980) will not typically attract many senior citizens. A ministry that emphasizes intact nuclear families will not attract large numbers of single-parent families or single adults. Borrowing a label from sociologists, McGavran dubbed this ingredient the *homogeneous unit principle* and declared this to be one of the axiomatic tools for effectively growing churches.

The homogeneous unit principle was born out of the observation that all groupings of human beings are governed by certain social structures, structures that McGavran believed can be utilized to win many new people to Christ. "Social structure is a broad reality comprising many factors, each of which has bearing on how the Church can reconcile men to God."[7] A person is not an isolated unit but part of a whole which makes him or her what he or she is. For example, you did not choose what language you speak or whatever accent you have. Rather, those were determined by the society in which you were born, the mother who reared you, and the children with whom you played. In fact, society plays a powerful role in determining or influencing every aspect of what you think, say, and do.

So by understanding the social structure of a particular segment of the total population, McGavran believed we would know what ingredients are called for in order to make churches increase through evangelism.

In chapter 10 of *Understanding Church Growth*, McGavran identified the following eight components of every social structure:

1. Unique self-image

2. Marriage customs

3. Elite or power structure

4. Land-ownership rights (neighborhoods in America)

5. Sex mores

6. People consciousness

7. Where people live

8. Language[8]

These eight components can serve as guidelines for discerning a homogeneous unit, which the Lausanne Committee on World Evangelization defines as "a significantly large sociological grouping of individuals who perceive themselves to have a common affinity for one another."[9] Take the United States of America. Contrary to the popular myth, this nation is not the great melting pot of peoples. Even within the same country, where the majority of the people identify themselves as Americans, the above eight components exist in a dizzying array of combinations. The result, instead of a melted population of one language and one nonspecific, national culture, is more like a dynamic mosaic in which each piece has a separate life of its own that seems strange and often unattractive to men and women from other pieces. These different pieces of the mosaic can be called homogeneous units. It is the church growth movement's conviction that the gospel message must be sensitively introduced into each homogeneous unit if we are to fulfill the missions mandate of the Great Commission, namely, to go and make disciples of all people groups.[10] This conviction is held because it is believed that people "like to become Christians without crossing racial, linguistic, or class barriers."[11]

The homogeneous unit principle is but an imperfect tool, a missiological instrument found to be valuable in spreading the gospel in cross-cultural settings. It is a way to give different social groupings of people a chance to encounter Christ authentically, in their own language, setting, customs, and culture. Only recently have we begun to realize that much of the resistance put up by people we have tried to reach was not to the gospel per se but to our requiring them to cross too many boundaries to get to Christ. People deserve to receive the Christ who has come to "make his dwelling among them" (John 1:14).

But for all of the claimed benefits of the homogeneous unit principle, it can also be used to validate and perpetuate sinful human tendencies that should be uprooted by new life in the kingdom of God. Author William Abraham believes this to be a dangerous way to think because

> the legitimate attempt to respond to the particularity and integrity of cultural diversity becomes, through use of the homogeneous unit principle, a subtle way of ignoring the radical demands of the gospel with regard to repentance from social and corporate sin; it is also a means

of riding rough-shod over the radically inclusive character of the people of God. The way in which church growth theorists introduce and discuss the matter, given the history and continued prevalence of racism in America, is astonishing. They seem to have no sense of how the advocacy of such a principle will almost inevitably be used to keep the social status quo in place, they make no attempt to explore and explicate other options, which is necessary if the deep problems related to racism and cultural diversity are to be resolved. Church growth theorists are not so much wrong in some sort of absolute way; they are somewhat blind, insensitive, and unrealistic.[12]

The aforementioned individual and corporate sins have no place in the kingdom of God. Since each of us continues to be a sinful person even after accepting Christ, we must guard against the tendency to find excuses for the continuation of sinful practices. Even worse, we must not disguise these practices by dressing them up as solid Christian attitudes and procedures. McGavran himself addressed this liability as he defended the viability of the homogeneous unit principle.

> In applying this principle, common sense must be assumed. The creation of narrow Churches, selfishly centered on the salvation of their own kith and kin only, is never the goal. Becoming Christian should never enhance animosities or the arrogance which is so common to all human associations. As men [and women] of one class, tribe, or society come to Christ, the Church will seek to moderate their ethnocentrism in many ways. She will teach them that persons from other segments of society are also God's children. God so loved the world, she will say, that He gave His only Son that whosoever believes in Him might have eternal life.[13]

All this is to say that specifically designing ministries to reach Asian Americans has a place in the grand scheme of how the Spirit is drawing various people to Jesus. The fewer cultural and sociological barriers they have to cross to get to know Jesus, the better. But I also agree that emphasizing only those things that they have in common runs the risk of ignoring the eschatological call for the church to become a preview of coming attractions. For there is still coming a time when persons from every nation, tribe, people, and language will be gathered around the throne of the Lamb to worship him.[14] Not only that, but I believe that pursuing a strict homogeneous unit approach blinds us to how an incredibly diverse Christian fellowship that is united around Christ can stimulate the curiosity of unconvinced persons, particularly Asian Americans. Our experiences of the last three years at Evergreen Baptist Church of LA is that there are mounting numbers of unconvinced Americanized Asian Americans who are drawn to churches that display an uncommon sense of community amid a complex amalgam of generations, cultures, combinations, and accents. We must do all that we can to introduce more Asian Americans to Jesus. Sometimes the barriers are cultural or sociological. But sometimes the barrier is the lack of evidence of Christ's undeniable presence among us.

AMERICANIZED ASIAN AMERICANS: A SPECIAL CALLING

Innumerable people in this country have a great burden to reach Asian Americans for Christ. It is a great need that could certainly benefit from more resources and insightful applications of the homogeneous unit principle. But probably 95 percent of these efforts[15] are to evangelize specific groups of Asian American immigrants and their offspring. Worship services are being added in new dialects to accommodate some of the newest groups, English classes are being offered, and new churches are being planted in their communities.

With Asian immigrants arriving daily from all over the Pacific Rim, the demographics for this diverse group are becoming increasingly complex.[16] Most effective evangelism must recognize the existence of many distinct homogeneous units here, for it would be foolhardy to expect this eclectic mass of people to fit into one type of church simply because most have black hair and brown eyes! Seeing the myriad distinctions that these new Americans from Asia and the Pacific Islands bring with them, workers have established ministries that aim to reach these separate homogeneous units. Many of these immigrant-centered churches are attempting to offer ministries to retain and attract those Asian Americans who represent the second generation and beyond of their particular ethnic strain. While there definitely are those from succeeding generations who feel a part of these homogeneous units, there are expanding numbers of more marginal Asian Americans who do not. Quite possibly they may comprise emerging new forms of Asian American homogeneous units that will require appropriate churches.

Even if you feel that the homogeneous unit approach to church growth ultimately promotes segregation, you surely cannot disagree with the philosophy that states, "We proclaim Christ in the 'heart language' of the person, in his or her dialect, vocabulary, way of thinking, income, and education."[17] This continues to characterize the missionary efforts to bring salvation to Asians in their homelands and in their ethnic enclaves here, but it is strangely not the case when it comes to reaching the steadily increasing numbers of more Americanized Asians in this country.

Why is this? Here are three possible reasons.

Americanized Asian Americans Are Virtually Invisible

People blindness is the malady that prevents us from seeing the important cultural differences that exist between groups of people living in geographical proximity to each other, differences that tend to create barriers to the acceptance of our message of salvation through Christ.

Instead of utilizing cross-cultural modes of evangelism, those with people blindness employ monocultural methods, since they fail to see how these targeted people are quite different than themselves.

At least two major groups are blind to the unique requirements of the more Americanized Asian Americans. The first group is made up of predominantly white American Christians who belong to churches that consist mostly of people of European descent. They assume that more acculturated Asian Americans must want to blend into their Euro-American culture rather than affirm any aspects of their Asian cultural status. The second group consists of immigrant-oriented Asian American Christians who believe that the majority of Asians in this country will always identify most closely with cultural roots from the countries of their forebears. Of course there are always exceptions to every rule. Some Asian Americans do view themselves as

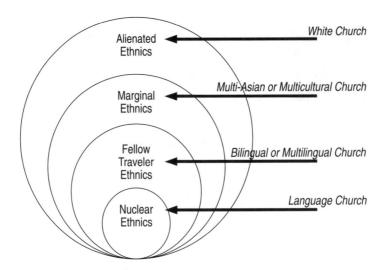

Figure 1.1
Assimilation Guide to Church Planting
(Modified from C. Peter Wagner)

white Americans and have virtually no desire to emphasize any dimensions of their ethnic identities. They feel completely assimilated[18]
and accepted (fig. 1.1, Alienated Ethnics). Then there are those who,
despite the fact that they are the fourth generation here, feel at home
in a mono-Asian, bilingual or multilingual church. For a variety of
reasons, they do not have a strong desire to incorporate more of the
Euro-American culture. These could be classified as Fellow Traveler
Ethnics.

These exceptional people will always exist and in theory should
be covered by existing churches because they have made a conscious
decision to embrace their church's prevailing cultural paradigm. However, there is an ever-expanding and increasingly complex demographic
that identifies with a subculture for which there are presently very
few churches. We must open our eyes to the existence of those who
see themselves as a combination of both Asian and American, people
who, if they were asked, would refer to themselves as Asian Americans
as much as they would call themselves Chinese Americans or Vietnamese Americans or even Eurasians. These are what Wagner would
call the Marginal Ethnics, and they will not be reached in meaningful numbers through anything less than new multi-Asian and/or
multi-ethnic ministries.

Asian Americans Find Americanized
Asian Americans Enigmatic

Asians have been immigrating to the United States in significant numbers since the mid-nineteenth century. There have been many injustices perpetrated against these pioneers, especially in the first one hundred years of their immigration, aimed at keeping them from enjoying all the freedoms and opportunities promised by the Constitution to all Americans.

Anti-Asian sentiments have always been present in this society, due in part to a curious double standard that pervades much of the thinking of many white Americans. To characterize this attitude, only those with ethnic roots in Europe are considered to be true Americans, while all others are viewed as ethnic or hyphenated Americans. In an opinion piece that ran in the *New York Times*, an Asian American put it this way: "We're still not fully integrated into the mainstream because of our yellow skin and almond eyes. Much has changed in 100 years (since the exclusion act [of 1882]), but we still cannot escape the distinction of race."[19] Asian Americans, along with some other nonwhite Americans, are frequently asked "Where are you from?" when they may have a much longer history in this country than does the typically white American posing the question. An article in *Time* underscored the continuing presence of racism aimed at Asian Americans:

> Racism in one form or another, subtle or blatantly obvious, plagues many Asian Americans. . . . As late as 1985 and 1986, violence against Asians jumped 50% in Los Angeles County. Says Henry Der of Chinese for Affirmative Action: "We're still vulnerable because of what we look like."
>
> While Asians are often thoroughly assimilated into American culture after a generation, many say that no matter how integrated they become, they will never be considered bona fide Americans because of an "otherness" factor based entirely on race. . . . Says Dr. Stanley Sue, director of the National Research Center on Asian American Mental Health: "Some people want you to be American, but then they treat you differently. Why, then, would you want to assimilate?"[20]

An accompanying article spoke of this persistent problem as being one in which white Americans are struggling against the gradual redefining of what "American" means. As such,

> The deeper significance of America's becoming a majority nonwhite so-
> ciety is what it means to the national psyche, to individuals' sense of
> themselves and their nation — their idea of what it is to be Ameri-
> can. People of color have often felt that whites treated equality as a
> benevolence granted to minorities rather than as an inherent natural
> right. . . .
>   [I]t seems all too predictable that during the next decades many more
> mainstream white Americans will begin to speak openly about the na-
> tion they feel they are losing. There are not, after all, many nonwhite
> faces depicted in Norman Rockwell's paintings.[21]

Even if one were so disposed, it is not easy to blend in to the fabric of
American society if you are not white.

But there are those Asian Americans who would much prefer to see
themselves and their progeny enjoy the many benefits of this country without losing hold of their central ethnic roots. These would be
the Nuclear Ethnics and some of the Fellow Traveler Ethnics (see fig.
1.1). To them, acculturation is undesirable and should be resisted,
not pursued. As much as they are fighting prejudice and discrimination, they are conversely struggling against the momentum of this
invisible force that exerts greater influence over each succeeding generation. They would prefer that their children marry within their own
ethnic group and carry on all of the traditions brought over from
the old country. Even the idea of the blending of various Asian ethnic groups (e.g., Chinese with Japanese, Japanese with Korean) is
frowned upon.

Although there are those who would deny having this attitude, it
is my contention that many of the Nuclear Ethnics and Fellow Traveler Ethnics in non-English-speaking and multilingual Asian churches
in America do possess this. This is not a criticism; rather, I see it as
another possible reason for their not dealing with the growing presence of Marginal Ethnics, oftentimes in their own families. To admit
that these people exist and have different needs is to concede that
acculturation is inevitable. For some, this is too threatening, for acculturation strikes at one of the fundamental tenets of Asian-cultured
people: the protection and perpetuation of the extended family's unity.
When your grandchildren cannot speak to you in your heart language,
when your family's heritage is being diluted and engulfed daily, when

your entire family can no longer attend the same church, you may begin to wonder if coming to America was worth it.

In many cases the Asian church in America that is heavily influenced by overseas elements is seen as one of the last bastions of one's essential heritage and culture. So Marginal Ethnics are pushed to become less marginal and more ethnic, a choice that increasing numbers apparently are not willing or able to make. More and more, they are conspicuously absent from immigrant-focused churches, even those that offer English-speaking ministries.

Americanized Asian Americans Are a High-Maintenance Group

Finally, I submit this third interpretation of the widespread failure to evangelize multicultural Asian Americans as a valid homogeneous unit. Too many church leaders believe that each local church is supposed to reach out to as many different kinds of people as possible. Contrary to the church growth movement, they feel that the biblical mandate for every church is to be heterogeneous, not homogeneous. Their conviction is grounded in an admirable commitment to model the new life of relational harmony in the kingdom of God. But they usually succeed only in attracting the Alienated Ethnics. Scant progress is made into the still-unreached groups, especially the group that we are most concerned with here, the Marginal Asian Ethnics.

Then there are those who are part of churches with a large constituency of immigrants. Although they usually limit their attention to their specific ethnic group, they attempt to meet the needs of all the different language groups within their target population. This is not to say that this is inappropriate. However, by trying to care for too many homogeneous units at the same time, there tends to be a diluting of the church's overall effectiveness. The Marginal Ethnics, who were born here, are fluent in English as their native tongue or preferred language and already are more settled. But they tend to be shortchanged when it comes to energy and staff resources.

Like children who have long experienced neglect, even benign neglect, Americanized Asian Americans are tired of being overlooked by the majority of churches, of being seen as cultural mongrels by their predecessors, of being fed the scraps from the banquet. They will make deep commitments to Christ and invest in the life of the church when those of us already in the church will do the same for them. We must be prepared to concoct and shape ministries that fully embrace Americanized Asian Americans and that take seriously the effects of acculturation.

THINGS TO THINK ABOUT

1. What is your interest in the subject of this book (i.e., Americanized Asian American ministries)? What do you hope to gain by reading this book?

2. In your own words, what is the homogeneous unit principle? What are some of the advantages and pitfalls to building a ministry around this principle?

3. How intentional has your ministry been at targeting a homogeneous unit? How would you describe it? Does it include or exclude more Americanized, English-speaking (Marginalized Ethnics) Asian Americans? How does it do this?

4. Do you agree that most existing marginalized Asian bilingual and marginalized Asian multilingual churches and Asian church leaders as a rule ignore Americanized Asian Americans (AAAs) as a distinct homogeneous unit? Can you think of additional reasons for this oversight?

Chapter
Two

PURSUING THE PEARL THROUGH THE FLOW OF GENERATIONS

Again, the kingdom of heaven is like a merchant looking for fine pearls. When he found one of great value, he went away and sold everything he had and bought it. —MATTHEW 13:45–46

But Jesus' own gospel of the kingdom was not that the kingdom was about to come, or had recently come, into existence. If we attend to what he actually said, it becomes clear that his gospel concerned only the new accessibility of the kingdom to humanity through himself.
—DALLAS WILLARD[1]

PURSUING THE PEARL

Like the nameless pearl merchant in this parable, most Asian immigrants journey to this country at great cost to themselves because they believe that life in America is the pearl of incalculable value. Leaving behind almost all things familiar and beloved, they embark on a pilgrimage to possess the jewel of incomparable opportunities for themselves and their progeny.

Have Asian Americans found that pearlescent prize? That depends on which ones you ask. According to a recent article in the *Los Angeles Times*, even in California, where some Asians first arrived 150 years ago, the contrast is stark. For a group that until several decades ago could not own land, testify in court, become naturalized citizens, or marry freely, the record is striking. Asian Americans' affluence and achievements have challenged the notion that to be a minority is to be disadvantaged.

They are the largest student group on top UC campuses and have the highest rate of obtaining advanced college degrees. They have started hundreds of high-tech firms, and own some of the biggest banks in the Los Angeles area. Their contributions to everyday life range from Play-Doh and Prozac to daisy-wheel printers and Bing cherries, from the music of Yo-Yo Ma to the novels of Amy Tan.

But greater numbers also have brought greater problems: Asian Americans have the fastest-rising welfare population and persistent gang activity. An undercurrent of racial tensions, friction between Asian newcomers and natives, intergenerational conflicts and a nagging identity crisis afflict the community.

And Asian Americans say that they do not feel fully vested in America's social, corporate and political life. They often are made to feel like foreigners, no matter how long their families have been here.[2]

All over America, Asian Americans are in pursuit of the pearl. Yet can it be said that any have found it? Could it be that they are spending their lives chasing after a counterfeit? Two Mercedes in the garage and three children at MIT are not what Jesus had in mind when he told that tale about the pearl of great price. He was referring to something called God's kingdom, not so much a place as it is a realized way of living in synchrony with a present and active God.[3] Scripture tells us that God's kingdom will not fully arrive until Christ returns to earth. Until then, God's kingdom is partly here whenever and wherever two or more are gathered in Christ's name.[4] Whenever we love God and love the person in front of us. Whenever we risk uttering truth in love. Whenever any of us console the sick and the dying. Whenever we dare to fight for the oppressed and embrace the overlooked. To be and bring the Good News that Jesus, God's only Son, is our salvation and the world's singular hope.

The pursuit of this level of meaningfulness can begin only when one has come to the sober realization that getting into Harvard does not compare to getting in on what God is doing. Once you wake up to this eternal truth, Madison Avenue, Wall Street, and Hollywood cease to define what that exquisite pearl is. More and more you want what Jesus wants. That becomes your prize, your pearl. Compared with God's kingdom, the American dream looks like cheap costume jewelry. It was Jesus who told his eager followers,

> If anyone would come after me, he must deny himself and take up his cross and follow me. For whoever wants to save his life will lose it, but whoever loses his life for me will find it. What good will it be for a man

if he gains the whole world, yet forfeits his soul? Or what can a man give in exchange for his soul? For the Son of Man is going to come in his Father's glory with his angels, and then he will reward each person according to what he has done. I tell you the truth, some who are standing here will not taste death before they see the Son of Man coming in his kingdom.[5]

Asians may come to this country with dreams of building their own kingdoms on earth. Like the anonymous merchant in Christ's parable, they and their offspring are determined to possess what they believe to be the pearl of great price. Whatever generation they might be, we who are Christians must be prepared to show them that the jewel is Jesus and his sacred kingdom. To do that for the Americanized Asian Americans, I believe we are going to need special kinds of churches.

THE INEVITABLE FLOW OF THE GENERATIONS

It was 1995. I was the speaker for a group of Korean American pastors gathered at a picturesque retreat site in Chesapeake Bay, Maryland. I had spent the first three plenary sessions trying to help them understand the marvelous applicability of M. Scott Peck's version of James Fowler's stages of faith development,[6] a key concept in our Evergreen-LA approach to reaching unconvinced Americanized Asian Americans. I could sense that many of these faithful pastors were having trouble connecting with the relevance of this paradigm. Finally, during a question-and-answer session, one of them said, "Dr. Fong, I am having a hard time applying this to our youth and young adults. They are not as Americanized as yours." That's when it hit me. "Most of you are '1.5' generation; born in Korea and reared here. My parents are what you would call '2.0,' born and reared in America. Your children are the same generation as my parents, even though my parents are in their seventies! That makes me the same generation as your yet-unborn grandchildren! No wonder we're having trouble connecting. My teaching you is like hearing from your children's children, even though I am almost the same age as you. I would say that we have a serious generation gap here."

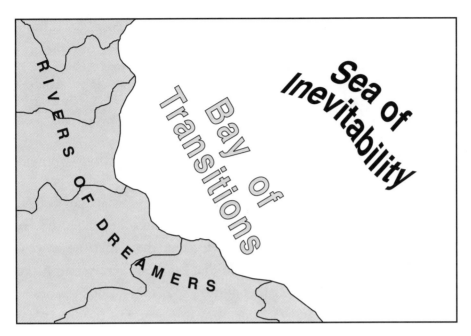

Figure 2.1
River > Bay > Sea Model

My saying that resulted in many raised eyebrows and slowly nod-
ding heads. Here I was, practically the same age, yet two generations
ahead as far as immigration history went. These pastors were the
same generation as my grandparents, yet their respective arrivals on
these shores were separated by at least forty years, not long in terms
of time but worlds apart nevertheless. Was there any way that I could
paint a better picture of this multigenerational progression that had
suddenly become so apparent to me?

That's when I turned around, toward the expansive picture windows that had been behind me while I lectured. As I gazed upon the
scene beyond the panes, I suddenly beheld a perfect model of what I
was trying to explain. "Look here. Do you see the various rivers that
are flowing? They are like the different streams of immigrants from
Asia that have come to America at distinct times. No matter when
they started flowing, each river is moving certainly toward the bay. In
the bay, the waters of each river begin to mix. But the water does not
stay in the bay; instead, it continues to flow out toward the horizon,
toward the deepest part of the sea. Because of our different immigration timetables, most of you still live and work in the 'river,' while

people like me who have acculturated further are already out there in the ocean. We are all 'fish,' but we require different kinds of water in order to live. One is certainly not better than another, but we are clearly at different places in our acculturation and accommodation."

Ever since that day, I have been fleshing out this flow of generations model. It is a simple model, so it does not answer every question, nor does it pretend to do that. And it is merely a model of the complex reality of the acculturation process. Still, it has proven quite useful to enable Asian Americans from the many different generational classifications to envision where everything seems to be heading. I share it because I hope this model will help current and future ministry leaders appreciate how explicitly ministering to Americanized Asian Americans is as valid as ministering to immigrants and their families.

With every large-scale influx of immigrants to this country, Asian or otherwise, it is as if rivers of dreamers began to flow across the land and toward the sea. This has always been one of the core elements to the story of America: Dreamers leave behind their native lands to come and make a better life for themselves and their offspring. But unlike the European immigrants, immigrants from Asia take much longer to blend in. L. Ling-chi Wang, a historian at the University of California Berkeley, put it this way:

> On the one hand, we have been successful in high tech, in education, science and several other fields. But on the other hand, we remain a minority in the eyes of the majority, and America continues to view Asian Americans not as an integral part of its identity, society, and culture. That's where the uniqueness of Asian Americans really is.[7]

My grandparents were part of that huge wave of immigrants from southern China who arrived not too long after the turn of the twentieth century. My paternal grandfather, Fong Him, who died when my father was only nine years old, stepped onto the rickety wooden dock at Angel Island as a raw-boned, penniless adolescent. He had come to Gold Mountain to make his fortune and then go back to his village in southern China. Even more so than many of today's naive Asian newcomers, he came here without realizing the impact his decision would have on each future generation. If he could have grasped the far-reaching consequences of his decision to come to America, would he still have made the trip? If he knew beforehand how much this quest was going to cost, would he still have paid the price?

Do you think he anticipated that his oldest son (my father) would someday wear an American uniform and go to war against the Nazis? Do you think he could have known that of the four grandchildren from that son, none would speak a word of Cantonese, and one would marry a Japanese American, another a Guamanian/Filipino, and another an Irish blend from the deep South? Do you think he would have cared that half of his eight great-grandchildren would be of Chinese extraction while the other half would be either Korean, an alloy of Chinese, or half black and half white? I never got a chance to meet this patriarch of our family; I never got to pose these questions. But judging from the responses that I get from recent first-generation immigrants, my guess is that when my grandfather came here, changes like these were not part of his dream for a better life for his family.

As each wave of Asian immigrants established a place of permanence in this country, it was like starting the flow of a river toward the sea. One river might be labeled Korean, another Taiwanese, another Filipino. Initially, most of them probably knew that coming here would transform them and their progeny, but my guess is that most of these courageous pioneers underestimated the power of the invisible forces of acculturation. As their children have begun to attend American schools, watch television, make friends, participate in life as Americans, the unseen forces of acculturation are constantly at work, pulling each succeeding generation further and further away from their roots and making them more and more American and less and less Asian.

THE FLOW OF GENERATIONS MODEL

In our model, acculturation is much like gravity. As each river gets established, the forces of acculturation (like gravity) take hold and make each river of dreamers flow toward the Bay of Transitions and out toward the Sea of Inevitability. As more of the pioneers wake up to the fact of the power of this gravity, they become understandably alarmed and try to erect structures to resist this ongoing exodus of their offspring.

Oftentimes it seems that Asian churches in America are supposed to function like dams, stopping the flow of the generations in its tracks, creating cultural and genetic reservoirs where future generations can languish and thrive. However, in almost every case, this proves to be a serious miscalculation of the drawing power of this force.

Their offspring, much more part of the mainstream of American life, will grow restless and frustrated in these reservoirs; eventually many of them will find ways around the dams, to the chagrin of the pioneers. These escapees may initially find solace in the Bay of Transitions, places like college campuses or various social groupings where the flows from various rivers of Asian immigration mingle and mix. Some groups, like the Chinese and Japanese, having longer histories in America, come together more readily. However, as other Asian groups become more settled, we are seeing the introduction of, for example, Vietnamese, Korean, and Filipino members into the Bay of Transitions. This is a transitory stage, though. The forces of acculturation are constantly drawing people away from the rivers that spawned them. There is always movement out toward the yet-uncharted depths of the Sea of Inevitability, places where one's cultural distinctiveness is now only one part of the dynamic of creating emerging new multi-Asian and/or multi-ethnic confluences.

Let's stay with our rivers>bay>sea model but employ it another way to appreciate why each succeeding generation of Asian Americans will not stay in or come to the reservoirs. Let's use the analogy of water conditions.

Rivers brim with fresh water. A bay is a mixture of fresh water and salt water, while the sea is salt water. In real life, rivers can support only freshwater fish, like bass. If you throw a bass in the ocean, even though it's in water, it will die. The same will happen if you throw the majority of ocean fish into a river. There are a few, like salmon, that can exist in both places.

Since the rivers represent the streams of Asian immigrants, it makes sense to equate fresh water with those who are the first to call America home. Let's call them *imported bass*. These imported bass are much more comfortable in their native languages and cultural settings. They view the world from an immigrant's perspective, as freshwater fish.

The second generations are more akin to *salmon*. They are born in fresh water, but as they mature, they move downstream into the Bay of Transitions and eventually out to the Sea of Inevitability. (I am tempted to say that salmon always return to the rivers to spawn, but I won't!) They are truly adaptable creatures, minimally bilingual and bicultural and able to function in both freshwater and saltwater conditions.

Their children, however, usually turn out to be saltwater denizens, in spite of their parents' best efforts to indoctrinate Asian culture into them. They are like cod, as are all the succeeding generations to intensifying degrees, knowing nothing but the expanse of the sea. *Acculturated cod* usually speak only English (although many now in California are fluent in Spanish) and view the world through Americanized lenses. This does not mean that acculturated cod never have any curiosity about their freshwater beginnings. However, it is the rare acculturated cod that can truly thrive in freshwater settings.

Therein lies the problem with the ongoing efforts of the vast majority of Asian churches in America. Since most of them were planted by imported bass to reach other imported bass, they are essentially freshwater river churches. As such, they call an imported bass to be their pastor, and he or she naturally helps to perpetuate a freshwater environment. They are only doing what anyone would do: create an environment in which they themselves can survive and thrive.

Naturally, most imported bass would like each succeeding generation to be freshwater fish like them. Knowing that their decision to move to America makes this extremely difficult, they hope to use their churches like dams, creating a reservoir of their beloved culture and customs for their offspring. However, the gravitational forces of acculturation regularly thwart their hopes of establishing freshwater havens for salmon and acculturated cod. Salmon may stay because they still can identify with much of the ethnic culture and/or do not feel as comfortable in non-Asian churches. Sooner or later, however, most of the acculturated cod leave because they cannot thrive in fresh water. They must find conditions that are more suited to their makeup.

"We'll create a separate pond over here for you and fill it with salt-water!" exclaim the concerned imported bass church leaders. "We'll find a salmon or cod to pastor you, and then we can all stay together. We didn't come all this way and make so many sacrifices only to see our extended family spread all over the map. Please, stay. We don't want you to leave us."

Blinded by their love for their families and influenced by the family-centered teachings of Confucius, the imported bass cannot fathom that their efforts are insufficient. So long as the overall environment is fresh water and the leadership is fundamentally imported bass, the prevailing culture will never be salty enough to satisfy the needs of acculturated cod. And if they cannot keep their own offspring from leaving, how can they expect the unchurched and unconvinced saltwater fish to come?

As millions of Asian Americans continue to pursue what they believe to be the priceless pearl along the inevitable flow of the generations, churches are needed all along the flow of acculturation that can provide the right conditions for each of the three types of fish. And with the bulk of the efforts going toward immigrants and their children, if we are going to reach significant numbers of Americanized Asian Americans, we must be prepared to sell everything.

EVERGREEN-LA'S EXAMPLE

Evergreen Baptist Church of LA has sold everything at least twice in its long history in order to be more effective in reaching more acculturated Asian Americans. Planted in 1925 in East Los Angeles, its original mission was to evangelize the burgeoning number of Japanese immigrants in the community. Without a doubt, the original church was designed to be a freshwater church for imported bass. The first few pastors were imported from Japan, and everything was done in Japanese.

Twenty-five years later, the church found itself in a difficult spot, one that should be familiar to established freshwater Asian churches in this country. A sizable gap had opened up between the older pioneers and the next generation of young adults. Evergreen had followed the typical growth pattern of ethnic American churches: start with everything being done in the native tongue, and as the numbers of young people increased, add English translation to the worship service; then move to an English service in concert with a language one. It became obvious to the leaders that their latest effort to stem the exodus of young families and youth was a bust.

So, after much prayer and deliberation, the membership voted to split the congregation into two separate churches. The Japanese-speaking members, most of whom were the parents of those who stayed, moved across the street and became the Japanese Baptist Church of Los Angeles. The others remained at the original site and began to develop something never seen before: an English-only Japanese American ministry.

Unbeknownst to them, this decision would later prove to be the key to evangelizing the future generations. Nearly every positive development toward becoming a cutting-edge, multi-Asian/multi-ethnic ministry can be traced back to this postwar decision. Because the first generation's leaders were willing to launch their offspring as a separate work, because they were all willing to sell everything in order to keep pursuing the kingdom of God, countless Americanized Asian Americans have been saved and blessed.

Making that decision may have cost the Japanese-speaking pioneers their church. For a variety of reasons, it has struggled to survive over the past twenty years while their English-only offspring's church has flourished. To their eternal credit, as difficult as it has been for them, they still believe it was the right decision. As Jesus said, pursuing the pearl of greatest worth can be costly.

From 1980 through 1995, God blessed the ministry of Evergreen-LA tremendously. With English as the only language and with a third-generation Japanese American senior pastor (Rev. Cory Ishida) and a third-generation Chinese American senior associate pastor (me), Evergreen-LA became a prototype of a Japanese/Chinese American saltwater church. The congregation kept growing, the church relocated to the suburbs further east, and the programs proliferated. However, by 1995 it was becoming apparent that a kind of malaise had settled on the church. Attendance had slipped to fewer than a thousand, and a good number of people were becoming disenchanted. Most significantly, though both of us were still committed to reaching more unconvinced Americanized Asian Americans, the senior pastor and I began to realize that the Lord was taking us in different directions in our search for God's pearl.

And so, in 1996 the membership was asked to make another painful decision to strategically hive the congregation into two amicable but separate churches. Hardly anyone was in favor of this initially, but after a year of reflection and dialogue, almost everyone was ready to take a giant step of faith if, once again, this was what the Lord wanted.

Since March 1997, Rev. Ishida has led the sizeable portion that left. Calling itself the Evergreen Baptist Church of San Gabriel Valley, it continues to reach out to English-speaking Americanized Asian Americans and those who identify with this emerging subculture. Ishida's plan is to accomplish this mission by becoming a church of more than one thousand that will operate from a still-to-be-built family-centered campus and by aggressively planting other Evergreens with predominantly homegrown pastors.

At the same time, I have been leading Evergreen-LA to become something I never used to think was preferable or possible: a multi-Asian/multi-ethnic, multisocioeconomic, multigenerational[8] congregation. Most intriguing to me is the broad spectrum of generations of Asian Americans we have. I used to think that having too many imported bass would always make the church become more of a freshwater ministry and we would lose our appeal to our primary target group, acculturated cod. This is not the case. In what at first appears to be a glaring contradiction to the river>bay>sea model, Asian immigrants are intermingling splendidly with second-, third-, and fourth-generation Asian Americans, not to mention the swelling numbers of white Americans, African Americans, and Latino Americans. How can this be? Didn't the model propose that freshwater fish and saltwater fish require separate and distinct environments?

This is teaching me that while acculturated cod may not be able to adapt, some imported bass can and will. Because our pastoral leadership is all Americanized, whether Asian American or not, and because everything is still conducted only in English, we remain part of the Sea of Inevitability. Some first-generation Asian Americans, because of their youth or their strong desire to become more a part of mainstream Asian America, eagerly adapt to these foreign conditions that our paradigm presents. A combination of prevalent saltwater conditions, adaptable imported bass, and the wondrous grace of God have allowed us to begin to explore another part of the heretofore-unexplored depths of the Sea of Inevitability.

Those who are committed to perfecting Americanized Asian American ministry are typically afraid that moving toward being multi-ethnic is a threat to this process of contextualization. While this is a possibility, I would argue that attempting to forge an intimate bond among disparate partners would accelerate the process of redeeming more Asian elements of the faith. For example, before I married my wife, I did not think that I was that Chinese. If I had married a Chinese American woman, we would be so similar that many of our Chinese cultural peculiarities would remain invisible to us. By marrying someone different from myself — a Japanese American from Hawaii — I quickly discovered that we did not see the world through exactly the same kind of eyes. Having a wide variety of Asian Americans and non-Asian Americans together brings about the same kind of undeniable chaos that provides ample opportunities for everyone to learn and grow. Besides, what other way will Asian American churches embrace the increasing numbers of ethnically mixed couples and families? In many respects, moving in this direction is probably God's way of fighting the onset of cultural myopia that is so prevalent in much more homogeneous congregations. It provides more evidence of the coming of Christ's kingdom in our midst.

Two years after the strategic hive, by the grace of our Lord, both churches are growing and going strong. We see ourselves as living proof of God's faithfulness when churches are willing to sell everything in order to keep pursuing the pearl along the inevitable flow of the generations.

THINGS TO THINK ABOUT

1. If you came here from another country, what were you hoping to find that you could not find in the place you left? If your predecessors immigrated to America, what was the priceless pearl that they came seeking? Did they or you ever find it?

2. What do you think about the flow of generations model outlined in this chapter? How much more apparent is it to you now why no single church can reach all the generations of Asians in America?

3. Think back over the history of Evergreen Baptist Church of LA and when the decisions to split the church amicably occurred. Now sketch out a timeline for your church, indicating on it where in the flow of generations you are. How long before your church will be faced with the same kind of difficult decision to split off an English-only church?

4. Are you surprised at the multi-Asian/multi-ethnic and multigenerational nature of Evergreen-LA? What do you think are the critical factors that are producing this generationally and ethnically complex congregation? Would this ever happen at your church in the foreseeable future? Would it ever become a necessity?

Chapter Three

EMERGENCE OF
A MERGING MINORITY

In every assimilation, there is a mutiny against history but there is also
a destiny, which is to redefine history. What it means to be American in
spirit, in blood is something far more borrowed and commingled than
anything previous generations ever knew. Alongside the pain of migra-
tion, then, and the possibility, there is this truth: America is white no
longer, and it will never be white again.   — ERIC LIU[1]

THE CHANGING FACE OF AMERICA

When the census is taken in 2060, there is every reason to believe
that white Americans will be a minority group in this country. Before
that day arrives, the presumption that the typical United States citizen is someone who traces his or her roots to Europe will be a thing
of the past. The neighborhoods and communities that make up this
nation will be so ethnically diverse that most of the myths and self-
concepts that this country has cherished will have to be discarded or
expanded. "Once America was a microcosm of European nationalities.
Today America is a microcosm of the world."[2]

A Majority of Minorities

Currently one American in four defines himself or herself as Latino
or nonwhite. Experts project that the Latino American population will
have grown an estimated 21 percent, the Asian American presence
about 22 percent, black Americans up to 12 percent, and white Americans just barely more than 2 percent by the end of the twentieth

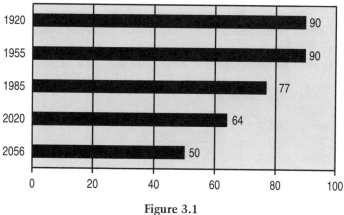

Figure 3.1
Whites: A Future Minority

century. By 2020 the number of Latino or nonwhite Americans will have more than doubled to nearly 115 million, whereas the population of white citizens will probably not increase. Even more startling (or disturbing, depending on one's bias) is the prediction that by 2056, the average resident, as defined by the census statistics, will trace his or her ancestry to Africa, Asia, the Latino world, the Pacific Islands, or Arabia, in other words, almost anywhere but Europe (fig. 3.1).[3] For those living in two of the nation's biggest states, the evidence of this shift is already occurring. On January 8, 1999, for example, it was reported that in the previous year, Jose beat out perennial favorites like John, James, Michael, Robert, and David as the most popular name for baby boys in California and Texas.[4] As we used to shout out when we were children, "Ready or not, here we come!"

The reason for this increasing displacement of white Americans as the majority group is simple: the other groups are growing at a faster rate (fig. 3.2). During the decade of the 1980s, of the four major ethnic categories, white Americans averaged an increase of less than 5 percent.

Compare this with the Asians/Others category, which, even though it has fewer people, increased more than 55 percent during this same period. Simple mathematics, then, provides the basis for the prediction that this group, in combination with Latino Americans and African Americans, will inevitably outnumber the white Americans. In a little more than fifty years, there will be no clear majority group in this country.

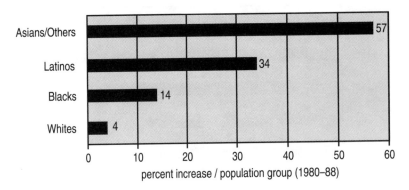

Figure 3.2
Other Groups Are Growing Faster
Source: *Time*, April 9, 1990

Behind this vast disparity in growth rates are the combined effect of birth rates and the frequency of immigration (fig. 3.3). If the natural increase of any population group is understood to be the number of births minus the number of deaths, then white Americans have barely been able to sustain a natural increase of 5 people per every 1,000. In contrast to this, black Americans have a natural increase of almost three times this rate, with Latinos and Asians/Others experiencing a biological growth rate that is four times higher than that of white Americans.

The other major factor is the current rate of immigration. During the same aforementioned time period, the net number of non-Latino

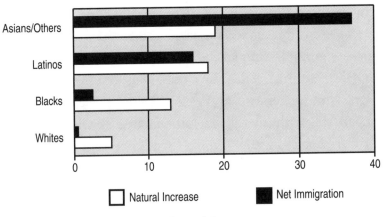

Figure 3.3
Higher Birth Rates and Immigration
Source: *Time*, April 9, 1990

Europeans who immigrated to the United States was almost negligible. African Americans also had a very low rate of immigration, but even with that, it was still almost three times that of white Americans. But the group that outstripped all others was the Asians/Others, with a net immigration rate that was forty times higher than that of white Americans. The net immigration rates, taken in conjunction with the rates of natural increase, are the reasons the nonwhite segment of America is growing faster.

What was once thought to be the great melting pot is more like a pluralistic stew pot that is rapidly filling with an increasing variety of savory ingredients. The all-American stew is being made now with curry, sushi, fish sauce, rice, chitterlings, and corn tortillas, not just meat and potatoes. It remains to be seen whether the traditionalists will take to this new and exotic concoction as standard fare. Regardless of whether they do or not, there is no doubt that this stew will never be made the same way again. For "the new world is here. It is now. And it is irreversibly the America to come."[5]

Still Coming to America

No one really knows when the first Asians set foot on American soil. There are those historians who believe that some daring Asian explorers arrived before Columbus. And there are records of some Chinese seamen being in the United States seaports of Boston and Philadelphia in the late 1700s. But since the 1850s, when the first Asian fortune-seekers from China came to California, the wave of Asian immigrants has never stopped. This has held fast even in the face of untold hardships, devastating setbacks, persistent racism, rampant injustice, and long seasons of anti-Asian immigration policies. After almost a century and a half of immigration, the Asians are coming in even greater numbers to America.

Since that day when those first Chinese migrants arrived in what was then a very foreign land, the cluster of Asian immigrants has slowly but steadily been increasing in its heterogeneity. This has especially been true since the late 1960s. In 1980 the census bureau identified and counted seventeen Asian American groups and nine

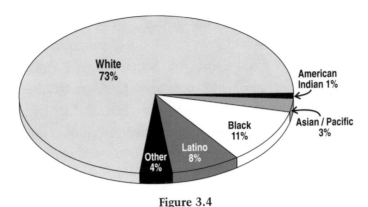

Figure 3.4
1990 U.S. Population

Source: "Suddenly, Asian-Americans Are a Marketer's Dream,"
Business Week, June 17, 1991, 54

groups of Pacific Islanders. As was evidenced dramatically in the previous section (see fig. 3.2), Asian Americans represent the fastest growing ethnic minority group in the United States (figs. 3.5 and 3.6). Even as quickly as the Latino American population is growing, there have been periods when the Asian American population has grown faster. During the 1970s, the Latino population increased by 38 percent, compared with 143 percent for the Asian population.

Ronald Takaki, professor of Ethnic Studies at the University of California Berkeley, describes this profound upsurge in the numbers of Asians in America:

> The target of immigration exclusion laws in the nineteenth and early twentieth centuries, Asians have recently been coming again to America. The Immigration Act of 1965 reopened the gates to immigrants from Asia, allowing a quota of 20,000 immigrants for each country and also the entry of family members on a nonquota basis. Currently half of all immigrants entering annually are Asian. The recent growth of the Asian American population has been dramatic: in 1960, there were only 877,934 Asians in the United States, representing a mere one half of one percent of the country's population. Twenty-five years later, they numbered over five million, or 2.1 percent of the population, an increase of 577 percent (compared to 34 percent for the general population). They included 1,079,000 Chinese, 1,052,000 Filipinos, 766,000 Japanese, 634,000 Vietnamese, 542,000 Koreans, 526,000 Asian Indians, 70,000 Laotians, 10,000 Mien, 60,000 Hmong, 161,000 Cambodians, and 169,000 other Asians. By the year 2000, Asian Americans are projected to represent 4 percent of the total U.S. population.[6]

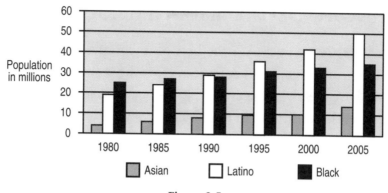

Figure 3.5
Minority Population Growth

Source: U.S. Census Bureau

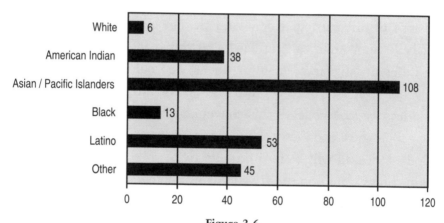

Figure 3.6
Percent Change: 1980–90

Source: "Suddenly, Asian-Americans Are a Marketer's Dream,"
Business Week, June 17, 1991, 54

Population experts originally predicted that when the results of the 2000 census are tallied, the number of Asian Americans would turn out to be some 8,000,000. As of 1998, there are 9,600,000. Pundits predict that by 2010, their current proportion of 4 percent of the total United States population will double. This is a group to be reckoned with, not only sociologically and demographically but also spiritually. There are increasing missionary opportunities across the street from many of us.

TRYING TO DEFINE "ASIAN AMERICAN"

Before we set off armed with the best of intentions to reach the millions of unconvinced Asian Americans for Christ, we must be certain that we have clearly delineated which group of Asian Americans we believe God has called us to reach. That distinction can make all the difference in the world.

One Label, Two Meanings

The 1990 census revealed that there has been an explosion in the variety and numbers of Asian Pacific Americans. An examination of the figures in table 1 (see the Appendix) gives a sense of the daunting dimensions of this particular demographic. Yet how often do you hear the label "Asian American" utilized as if this incredibly diverse group with different languages, customs, foods, and cultures were one big, happy, homogeneous family? Nothing could be further from the truth, and unless we look beneath this convenient label, our efforts to bring these people the Good News about the forgiveness of sins and new life in God's kingdom will be far from effective.

As if things were not already confusing enough, these days the terminology has been expanded to include those of Polynesian extraction. So instead of just having to untangle what is meant by "Asian American," quite often one is saddled with the latest all-encompassing label, "Asian and Pacific Americans." Except for the fact that most have brown eyes, black hair, and nonwhite skin, what do Asians have in common with people from Hawaii, Samoa, Tonga, Guam, and the Fiji Islands? While the political advantages of expanding the boundaries of one's interest group are obvious, it only serves to confuse the issue as far as missions is concerned. So, for evangelistic reasons, when we employ the term "Asian American," we are not including those Pacific Islanders if they cannot or do not identify with being Asian Americans. This is not meant to be a slight; rather, it is to clarify the specific group that we feel God is calling us to reach with the gospel.

By extracting the nine identified Pacific Islander groups, we have now narrowed our focus to the remaining seventeen groups of Asians in America. This is far from being a homogeneous unit. More sifting needs to be done. For our purposes, there are two basic ways to go about this.

One approach would separate all the distinctive Asian ethnic groups from one another. This would logically then produce seventeen different groups consisting of the Chinese, Filipino, Japanese, Asian Indian, Kampuchean, Pakistani, Laotian, and so on. Upon further examination, though, it would soon be discovered that each of these distinct groups has many subgroups within it. Some are based on regional differences that have been brought over or that are operational here, others on dissimilar dialects, while still others may have intricate caste-type systems in place. Eventually you would arrive at a number of homogeneous groups that would be much larger than the original seventeen.

This approach, though tedious, is valuable. There is no question that it should be utilized in any efforts made to bring the pearl of great price — Jesus and his kingdom — to each generation of Asian Americans. To their credit, many whom God has called to this much-needed missionary endeavor in America follow this practice. They take the time to learn the specific dialects and cultures of a particular Asian American group. Some, though not nearly enough, even attempt to look for signs of God's presence that the Lord has already placed in these cultures. Their goal is to incarnate God's Word, to clothe the Good News in the culture of a unique group of God's children.

All of these things are noteworthy and necessary. But as good as it is, this approach creates a tremendous blind spot in the vision of those same concerned people. As they go about trying to separate out all the obvious homogeneous groups, the assumption is made that each of the seventeen major Asian ethnic groups is distinct from the others and will always want to remain that way. There are even those who will go so far as to claim that the immigrants (Nuclear Ethnics or imported bass) and each succeeding generation, though all from the same ethnic roots, are discrete groups that need to be evangelized with suitable methods. This point of view, while not very popular with those born overseas, is gaining wider acceptance among those born in America. But there is still that troublesome blind spot. The only way you are able to see this blind spot is if you take a second and simple approach to sifting through the myriad distinctions of Asian Americans.

Admittedly, this second approach is not perfect either; it leaves many questions that the first method deals with better. However, the pure value of this alternative is that it eliminates the blind spot that the first one creates. As long as you understand that, it is worth the risk. The second strategy involves assuming that when people speak of Asian Americans, they are using the same label to refer to two dissimilar groups of Asians.

This one label–two meanings element has been the cause of much confusion. Most people are thinking of it as a generic term for Asians who live in America. Further probing will usually reveal that what they really mean when they talk about Asian American ministry is ministry that is focused on one of the seventeen identified groups of Asians or a related subgroup of one of them. For example, let us say that the American Baptists decide to convene a conference with the theme "Asian American Ministries in the Twenty-first Century." Although the term "Asian American" would figure prominently in the literature and presentations, the vast majority of resource people and conferees would assume that this was all about furthering the separate efforts to reach the Chinese, Korean, Southeast Asians, and so on. Such usage of the term is often an obstacle to understanding what people mean when they talk about ministry to Asian Americans.

For there are others, albeit a minority, who are operating with a second definition of this term. When they say "Asian Americans" they are not using this taxonomy as a collective way of describing still-separate groups. Instead, they are referring to the growth of a circle of Asians from a variety of different cultural strains who identify with one another. In other words, when they say "Asian American," they mean an emerging, merging minority. By referring to themselves as such, they are identifying with an emerging new subgroup that is invisible to those assuming that the members of each Asian ethnic group will never mix, marry, or merge.

To believe that is to expose one's ignorance about the effect America has on all of its inhabitants.

The Asian American Model

In the last chapter of *Asian Americans: Emerging Minorities*, Harry Kitano and Roger Daniels present a model for classifying Asian Americans into four different groups. This model should help us better understand who it is that we have been trying to define. In the study of the many adaptive patterns exhibited by Asians in America, two variables come up repeatedly. The sorting process is based on two variables, assimilation and ethnic identity:

> The *assimilation variable*...includes integration into the schools, the work place, the social groupings, as well as identification with the majority and marital assimilation. The *ethnic identity* dimension is essentially a pluralistic adaptation, focusing on the retention of ethnic ways.[7]

The model itself is straightforward and can be found in figure 3.7.

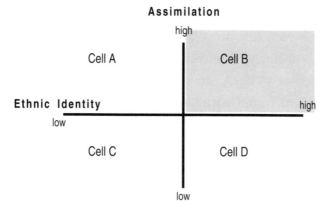

Figure 3.7
Assimilation and Ethnic Identity Model

Source: Harry H. L. Kitano and Roger Daniels, *Asian Americans: Emerging Minorities*
(Englewood Cliffs, N.J.: Prentice-Hall, 1988), 191

There are four types of Asian Americans associated with this model, with each type being represented by a corresponding cell. What follows is a brief description of each of these. For more detailed descriptions, consult chapter 13 in Kitano and Daniels's book.

Cell A: High Assimilation, Low Ethnic Identity.[8] The Cell A Asian American is high in assimilation and low in ethnic identity. Therefore, the person is more American than Asian. Recalling the diagram in figure 1.1 (p. 10), the Cell A Asian American would be equivalent to the Alienated Ethnic. It is not uncommon for many members of the second generation to be born here and also Asian Americans who grow up cut off from American Asian communities to fall into this category. Most of this type would tend to marry non-Asians, especially the females (see fig. 3.9, p. 46). The Asian American slang term "banana" (i.e., yellow on the outside, white on the inside) would be appropriately applied to the Cell A Asian American. It is possible that the specialized ministry that we are in the process of defining would affect some people from this category, but the likelihood is not very great. The vast majority of Cell A Asian Americans would feel as out of place in a large gathering of Asians as the average white person often does. In the parlance of our river>bay>sea model (see chap. 2), they would not only be considered acculturated cod but also denizens of the deepest parts of the Sea of Inevitability.

Cell B: High Assimilation, High Ethnic Identity. The Cell B Asian American is often just as assimilated as is the Cell A type. The major difference between the two types is that the Cell B person retains a strong Asian identity. This person is truly bicultural, able to move smoothly between the Asian and American cultures. This type of Asian American would correlate with the Marginal Ethnic listed in figure 1.1. The Cell B Asian American is interested in keeping his or her ethnic heritage alive and is usually knowledgeable about it. At the same time, a Cell B Asian American clearly identifies with being from America. Once again, calling upon the nomenclature of the water and fish model, Cell B Asian Americans would be akin to acculturated cod. However, unlike their Cell A saltwater cousins, Cell B Asian Americans would choose to live in the part of the Sea of Inevitability that lies closer to the Bay of Transitions. Because of this, some Cell D Asian Americans (imported bass) are finding it is much easier to blend in with this more acculturated group. This kind of Asian American is exactly the type that this study is attempting to address, Americanized Asian American (AAA).

Cell C: Low Assimilation, Low Ethnic Identity. The Cell C Asian American is estranged, disenchanted, and disillusioned. This person has failed to find a place in either of the two primary cultures. Not many Asian Americans fall into this category. The group we are defining would not contain many Cell C Asian Americans, for these wretched souls do not feel any affinity to just such a group. There is no corresponding label in figure 1.1 and no equivalent label from the river>bay>sea model.

Cell D: Low Assimilation, High Ethnic Identity. This cell is made up of most of the newly arrived immigrants and any Asian Americans who identify more closely with their Asian community than with the American one. The former would match up with the Nuclear Ethnic label and the latter with the Fellow Traveler Ethnic label in figure 1.1. Those in this category who were born in the United States may have learned to function in the wider society, but they choose to spend most of their time within their ethnic community. Intermarriage is highly unlikely, for the Cell D Asian American is more ethnic than American. Although this also is not the type of person we are trying to reach, some of these freshwater imported bass, to our delight and surprise, are ready and willing to join a school of acculturated cod and become important members of Americanized Asian American and multi-Asian/multi-ethnic churches.

This model supplied by Kitano and Daniels, while it is not perfect, helps us to sharpen our focus for ministering to Asian Americans. Exceptions aside, Cell B Asian Americans are the ones we want to reach.

THE AMBIVALENT AMERICANS

With the exception of Native Americans, this is a nation of immigrants. Those who left their homelands in the belief that life in America held greater promise for them and their progeny people it. The earliest migrants came on ships, sailing across the two great oceans that embrace this country's eastern and western flanks. More recently, they have flown in on giant jets,[9] arriving much less worse for wear then their predecessors did, but in possession of the same dreams as before: dreams of freedom, of prosperity, of opportunities, of happiness. In the entire world, only America is so identified with such hopes and dreams as these — all because this is a country that owes its existence and success to the pluck and vision of immigrants.

Since that time when people first began arriving on America's

shores, living in this uncommon new land has had a profound effect
on its inhabitants. Away from oppressive ruling forces and centuries
of tradition, new Americans discover that they can begin to carve out
new identities and lives for themselves. But guilt and fear oftentimes
accompany that freedom. There is guilt over shedding the layers of
one's ethnicity and culture, and there is a concomitant fear that ab-
sorption into American culture is to lose one's true identity. Is having
the pearl of the American dream worth such a high price?

American Asian immigrants share this ambivalence toward their
adopted homeland. On the one hand, they have come to the Mountain
of Gold *(Gam Saan)*[10] to make money and provide better opportunities
for their children and grandchildren.[11] America is supposed to be the
place where, if you work long and hard enough and make the requi-
site sacrifices, you can improve your living standards and boost your
children up a rung or two on the socioeconomic ladder.

Many Asian Americans have worked hard to make this American
dream come true. For many, higher education has provided a pathway
for many of them to take to the top. As a result, 33 percent of Asians
and Pacific Islanders are college graduates (the national average is 16
percent).[12] Twenty-five percent of the undergraduates at Stanford and
Wellesley are Asian Americans. The numbers are virtually identical
at Harvard, Northwestern, and the University of Pennsylvania. Home
to nearly 40 percent of all Asian Americans, California is experiencing another kind of gold rush these days as its vaunted University of
California system is inundated with eager Asian American students.
Most of the undergraduates at University of California Irvine (University of Chinese Immigrants) are Asian Americans, and they constitute
the largest racial group among undergraduates at UCLA (University
of Caucasians Lost Among Asians), University of California Riverside
and Berkeley. Stanley N. Katz, a historian at Princeton, is not alone
in predicting that these Asian American students may become the
next minority group to profoundly shape American intellectual life. He
said, "Some, maybe most of the very best students, are Asians. These
kids strike me as the Jews of the end of the century."[13]

In 1979, the Asian and Pacific Islander median family income was
$22,700 as compared with the national median of $19,000. Though

they lagged behind the total population in home ownership in 1980 (52 percent of them either owned or were buying homes compared with a median of 64 percent), those who did owned residences with a much higher median value ($83,000) than did all homeowners ($47,200). Some of this disparity is due to the fact that most Asian and Pacific Islanders live in the West and in urban areas where homes cost more.[14]

Of course, there are still many Asian and Pacific Islanders who have not "made it" and who challenge the notion that, as a group, they are the model minority (see fig. 3.8). What is more, many of those who have become quite successful as far as finances, education, and professions are concerned wonder if the accompanying loss of ethnic pride, language, and culture has been worth it. This explains the periodic feelings of ambivalence toward being bona fide Americans.

This ambivalence is not restricted to Asian Americans. Every immigrant, ethnic American population has struggled with the same issues. The big difference here, though, is that nonwhites do not have as real an option of blending into the all-American, Norman Rockwell–type picture. "White Americans are accustomed to thinking of themselves as the very picture of their nation."[15] And as another writer put it aptly:

> Asians in general are still strangers in the Western paradise, and they are keenly aware of their status....
>
> Paradise has turned out to be less than perfect and more than a little disconcerting. What was it they set out to find, and why is it yet to be found? Even as their numbers and their influence expand, Asian Americans are pondering those very questions.[16]

Thus, Asian Americans in particular feel tension from several different directions. I think that this is what it often feels like for many of the first generation. There is the aforementioned desire to make the most out of being in this land of opportunity. So we work hard and sacrifice for our children's benefit. But in order to make it here, we feel we must become more like the dominant culture in order to fit into the larger societal scheme of things, to be accepted as equals. With mixed feelings, we see this happening naturally as we encourage our children to compete on the level playing field of school and the professions.

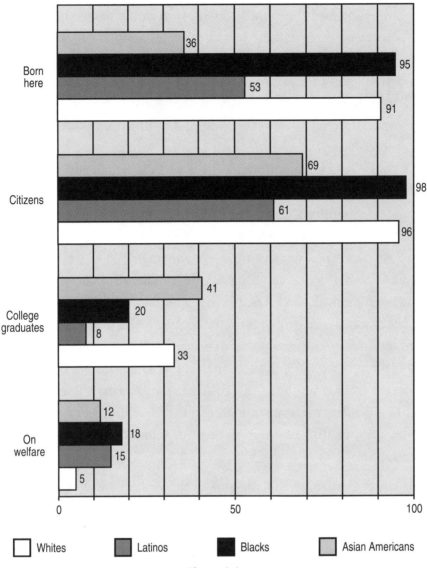

Figure 3.8
1997 California Population Profile

Source: 1990 census, Current Population Surveys, 1994–97,
and U.S. immigration data

Yet there is also some residual pride in our ethnic heritage that many of us do not want to lose. We are uncomfortable with the prospect of becoming a banana. But we also know that in many social and business situations, our almond-shaped eyes and nonwhite complexions will keep us from being fully accepted as Americans, so why try? However, to live mainly within our Asian community's cliques causes us to be criticized for not trying to blend into the larger American scene. Sometimes it feels as if we cannot win for losing.

What does it mean to be an American when you are of Asian descent? Some have given up; some have given in; others have decided to try out life in a newly emerging Asian American subculture.

COMMON LANGUAGE, COMMON DIRECTION

The generations that emanate from the immigrants sooner or later become culturally and racially diluted. It happened to the English, the Irish, the Swedish, and the Jews. And there is no reason for it not to happen to the Asians. Being one of the Asian groups that has been here the longest, the Chinese began to experience this more than forty years ago when

> in the mid-1950s, about half of the Chinese American population was native born, and this segment of the population, reinforced by elite emigres from Nationalist China, was becoming increasingly middle class, disassociating itself from the concerns of the American Chinatowns and striving for acculturation, if not assimilation, into American society.[17]

There still are the significant factors of having nonwhite skin and a non-European pedigree, definitely liabilities, or assets, depending on your bias. But even with those, the drawing power of the American culture is relentless. To those who welcome it, it can seem as innocuous and essential as gravity. However, those who fear it might liken it to a racial and cultural black hole that, given enough time and proximity, will swallow entire foreign systems, leaving behind nothing of what used to be.

While the pull of American culture is irresistible, it does not always need to be feared. The Americanization of each succeeding generation is a part of the package that the original migrants bought into when they made the fateful decision to emigrate to this country. They may argue that this ramification was never explained to them beforehand, but their choosing to remain and to rear their families here was a tacit approval of the whole process. They may not approve of their grandchildren's different values and physical features, but those young people had no part in the decision to uproot and settle in America. That was their predecessors' prerogative. But one thing is certain: those grandchildren are not going to move back to the old country. And why should they? For them, this has been and will always be home.

That is the natural attitude of a growing number of Asian Americans. Most of these are younger than fifty years old because they represent the third, fourth or even fifth generations that have grown up in the United States. Unlike other Asian Americans, they all speak English fluently without any trace of an Asian accent because this was the primary, if not sole, language spoken at home. Some have learned to speak the language of their ancestors, but this has taken place in a classroom, not in their families. In every sense of the word, English is their native language.

These Asian Americans, while affirming their ethnic roots, identify the United States as their homeland. They are Americans, and they have never felt like anything else. Intellectually, they realize that their roots lie buried in a patch of Asian soil far across the Pacific Ocean, but at a visceral level, they feel that they are from wherever they were born or grew up, be it Los Angeles, Phoenix, or Boston. This is in contrast to their more immigrant-oriented brethren who, when queried, would be much more likely to identify themselves as, say, Korean or Filipino than American.

Even with a more American mindset, these Asian Americans often find themselves living at the intersection of two different worlds. In the world of the larger American society, they know that they can move about more comfortably and garner wider acceptance due to their more westernized upbringings. In a church setting, there are many who would feel more at home in a white congregation than in an Asian one that was dominated by immigrant attitudes. Or they might feel equally uncomfortable in both. But being Cell B Marginal Ethnics, they still have ties to their Asian roots, ties that they have no desire to sever. In fact, many of the core traditional values of their Asian culture continue to influence their decisions.

This aspect is often denied, but upon further investigation, it usually is a case of them not being in touch with how Asian they still are, in spite of all of their Western ways. For instance, although they may be more open than their parents, they do not divulge as many details about their home situations as their non-Asian co-workers are wont to do. The Asian value of discretion is at work. Or some non-Japanese person may ask a Sansei (third-generation Japanese American) for a favor, such as borrowing his pickup truck for the weekend, and he may find himself quietly resenting the person for making such a direct request and thereby obligating him to comply. This is an example of the combination of two Japanese values, not obligating others and being as indirect as possible so as not to risk offending the other person. Evidence of such enduring Asian influences abounds. So even though the more Americanized Asians may gravitate away from those who are more immigrant-centered, they are still bicultural people.

A survey taken in 1985 of third- to sixth-generation Japanese American college students in Southern California supported this observation. Even though the respondents were several generations removed from Japan, they still valued hard work, a solid education, strong family and community ties, and perseverance. These were the identical values embraced by their first- and second-generation forebears. And in spite of their innate abilities to mingle and mix, many of the Japanese American students in the study reported that they still preferred hanging out with other Asian Americans and they still belonged to Asian American organizations. At the same time, the majority believed in the validity of interracial dating and marriage. "Therefore, there appears to be a continuity between the Japanese generations on certain values, but the belief in interracial marriage adds to the possible acceleration of assimilation as the future of the Sansei [third generation] and subsequent generations."[18]

One sure sign of the move away from an immigrant outlook is the increasing number of marriages to those outside of one's own ethnic enclave. As children who come from English-speaking homes attend integrated schools, they naturally begin to form friendships with those of other races. When the time to start dating arrives, the next natural step in the progression is to seek someone from his or her pool of friends. So if the friends' pool is interracial, there is a great likelihood of interracial dating occurring. The next natural step is interracial marriages. This is even more pronounced if minority children are reared in isolation from their ethnic communities for, outside of their families, they are rarely confronted with the fact of their ethnicity. These children usually grow up to feel more comfortable in white settings than Asian ones. They fit in the category of Cell A or Alienated Ethnics (see fig. 1.1) and are most likely to marry someone who is not Asian.

This trend toward marrying outside one's racial group seems to be a strong indicator of the degree to which a minority group is acculturating. For every group of people, the choice of a lifelong mate is a serious commitment. Both parties and their families must feel good about the combination of backgrounds, families, and values if the marriage is going to be a sound one. Thus, the rate of intermarriages is a much better indicator of acculturation than is, say, membership in a multiracial church or club. It is one thing to socialize across color and culture lines and another thing altogether to merge families and bloodlines.

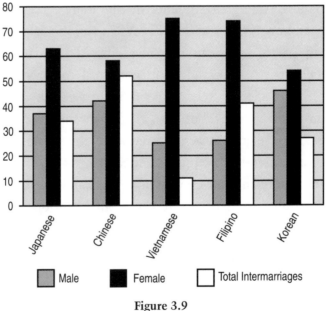

Figure 3.9
Mixed Marriages

Source: Los Angeles County Marriage License Bureau

As you can see from the graph in figure 3.9, this tendency to marry outside of one's ethnic group has already taken root in three Asian groups. At least four generalizations can be made from this graphic:

- The Japanese marry out more often than do the Chinese, Korean, Filipino, and Vietnamese (they marry out more often than any other group in this country).

- The length of time an Asian group has been here is directly correlated to the incidence of intermarriage.

- Other factors, such as how a group has been culturally programmed to deal with changes or adaptation, may also play a significant role in the incidence of intermarriages.[19]

- The females consistently marry out at a higher rate than do males. Worth noting in this regard is the extremely high rate of intermarriages for Korean women, even though overall Koreans as a group registered the least number of intermarriages in that period. Since it has been estimated that between only 5 and 10 percent of these intermarriages are between Asian groups, the vast majority of such marriages, at least in Los Angeles, are interracial.[20] When the discrepancy between genders becomes so pronounced, at what point do the group's males begin to feel threatened?

These statistics are quite disturbing to many older Asian Americans. They can still recall the sting of anti-Asian sentiments and blatant acts of discrimination. They worry about the clashing of cultures and the loss of their ethnic heritages. And they fret about whether part-Asian children will ever be fully accepted, even in our increasingly pluralistic society. But with each passing generation of Asian Americans, there is an ever-increasing probability of intermarriages occurring, for such is the awesome drawing power of America's culture.

Calling upon Donald McGavran's eight key characteristics of a definable homogeneous unit,[21] let's briefly see how Cell B Asian Americans measure up.

Unique self-image. Americanized Asian Americans see themselves as being Americans with distant roots in Asia. With high degrees of assimilation and ethnic identity, Cell B Asian Americans clearly possess a self-image that is different from that of most Americans in general and Asian Americans who fall into the other three quadrants on the Kitano and Daniels grid.

Marriage customs. Americanized Asian Americans exhibit a pronounced proclivity for marrying outside their own ethnic enclave. And even if they married within it, they are not averse to their children marrying outside of it. There is also a much greater degree of egalitarianism within marriages than is customary among more traditional American Asians.

Elite or power structure. Given the elevated percentages of their academic achievements and/or their greater ability to climb corporate ladders, Americanized Asian Americans are establishing themselves as key leaders in charting the courses for academia, technology, politics, entertainment, and finance. Additionally, they form a substantial middle and upper middle class.

Land-ownership rights (neighborhoods). With the convergence of factors such as education, wealth, and professionalism, a good number of Americanized Asian Americans enjoy, at minimum, middle-class status and are no longer excluded from purchasing homes in what used to be white enclaves. They are free to own whatever they can afford. This separates them from their Asian American brethren who for various reasons cannot yet take advantage of this privilege.

Sex mores. Unfortunately, unlike the earlier generations, many of the Cell B Asian Americans have adopted the looser morals of American society. Living together outside of marriage, engaging in premarital sex, getting divorced, or accepting homosexuality no longer carries many stigmas for them. They may not be as liberal about these things as are Cell A Asian Americans, but they are definitely not as conservative as are Cell C immigrants. In any case, this shift in sex mores is further evidence that they are a definable subgroup.

People consciousness. As we have discussed and will explore more in chapter 4, a new identity was birthed in the late 1960s and is still taking shape. This identity blurs some of the sharp lines that typically divide the Chinese, the Korean, the Japanese, the Filipino, the Vietnamese, and the Indian from each other. In its place there is a collective sense of being Asian Americans, what we are calling Americanized Asian Americans. At this stage, one is just as likely to refer to herself or himself as Asian American as Vietnamese.

Where people live. When the opportunities are there, many Cell B Asian Americans choose to live outside of Asian ethnic ghettos (e.g., Chinatown or Koreatown) but where there are pronounced numbers of other Cell B Asian Americans and proximity to Asian foods, markets, and cultural or religious venues.

Language. Speaking English is the norm. And if there is any accent, it's more likely to be from Texas than Taiwan.

Those who match these characteristics are members of the hidden group, Cell B Asian Americans, that we are targeting for ministry and evangelism. Anyone who feels called to this work must acknowledge their existence and affirm their subculture. In chapter 4, we will turn our attention to what appears to be the center of this new subculture, namely, the Japanese American culture.

THINGS TO THINK ABOUT

1. How obvious is the growth of the broader American Asian population in your area? What are the demographers predicting in regard to American Asian influx for your area over the next ten years?

2. Look through your local phone book and list all the American Asian ministries, separating them by ethnic identities and, if applicable, language and/or dialect. How many of these ministries cater primarily to Nuclear and Fellow Traveler Asian Americans? How many are deliberately positioning themselves to minister to marginal, Cell B, Americanized Asian Americans? Even if it is part of their vision to reach AAAs, based on what you've learned so far, how likely is it that they will succeed?

3. Where are you in the acculturation process? Using Kitano and Daniels's grid, select the cell that comes closest to identifying you. Before sharing your conclusion, ask a colleague what cell he or she thinks you occupy. How accurate is your self-assessment? If you happen to see yourself as a Cell B Asian American, how well do you fit in with the typical American Asian ministry in your area? What are your options?

4. How comfortable and confident are you about inviting unconvinced Cell B Asian Americans to attend your church's worship service? If you had a blank sheet of paper and could design a ministry that would be attractive to both Christian and unconvinced AAAs, how would it look? Would it be radically different from what you have now? How much of the status quo would you retain and why?

5. Are you picking up signs of a newly emerging, merging group of marginalized Asian Americans? Where is this happening? How much access do you have to this emerging community? Where is its pulse, and what is its impression of the typical American Asian church?

Chapter Four

JAPANESE AMERICANS – VANGUARD OF AN EMERGING SUBCULTURE

We need to be more accepting of the differences within our own ethnic group. Some Japanese Americans don't look Japanese American at all.
— BILL WATANABE[1]

By now you are supposed to be convinced that a more American-ized Asian American not only exists but also exists in large enough numbers to merit intentional ministry approaches. Yet there still may be iconoclasts who claim that "there is no such thing as an 'Asian American.' "[2] The thinking here must be that this is a convenient collective term, a conceptual aid to discussing perpetually divergent Asian groups, rather than a description of a fresh, homogeneous group. But such thinking is off the mark, for a more generic type of Asian American exists in ever-increasing numbers. And the Japanese Americans are living proof of this, leading the way in defining this new culture for the rest of us.

EXCEPTIONAL BEGINNINGS

While every American Asian group can lay claim to a unique history since coming to these shores, the Japanese seem to possess one of the more exceptional examples. As one historian recently put it, "The history of Japanese Americans is a story of tragedy and triumph. Few people came to America more predisposed and determined to be good Americans. Few met such repeated rebuffs and barriers including bar-riers of mass internment camps or more completely triumphed over it all."[3] As we now draw from some of the critical aspects of their past and present, it will become only too apparent why they have fallen into the role of vanguard for a newly emerging culture for Americanized Asian Americans.

Unique Immigration Patterns

Among Asian Americans, the Japanese have the second longest history of being in the United States. One generation after the Chinese began arriving during the Gold Rush of the 1850s, the Japanese started to migrate in significant numbers to the then independent kingdom of Hawaii as indentured laborers. Even though the conditions were extreme and the pay was meager, these pioneers from Japan had come to a tropical land where the majority of the people were Asian. Although the white minority controlled just about everything, by themselves the Japanese made up 43 percent of the islands' population, and they soon learned how to organize their community to see that their basic needs were met.

Following the United States' annexation of Hawaii in 1898, many Japanese moved from Hawaii to the West Coast. Those in California found that they were once again the largest Asian group, but this time they made up only 2 percent of the population. Discrimination against them was rampant, and the immigrants, mainly young men, were forced to form Japanese American communities in order to create work and have housing. By 1900 there were 25,000 Japanese living on the West Coast. Over the next twenty years, their numbers swelled to more than 110,000, with two-thirds of them settled in California.

In 1870, after their own two decades of immigration, the Chinese had increased their numbers to 60,000, with 80 percent of these in California. At first glance, the immigration patterns of these two groups seem to parallel each other, but there are some singular differences to go along with the similarities.

Most of the immigrants in both of these groups were men of peasant stock who were forced to work at menial, low-paying jobs. The Chinese worked on the railroads, in the mines, and in the fields, and their Japanese counterparts also worked in agriculture and railroad maintenance.

As far as differences go, the Chinese came from the same district (Toishan) in South China (Kwantung), whereas the Japanese hailed from rural areas from different prefectures of Japan and what was then called the Ryuku Islands (Okinawa). Of much greater significance for our purposes are several distinctions.

The Chinese were leaving a backward nation that was becoming even more backward; the Japanese were leaving a modernizing nation that was beginning to garner respect from the Western nations and in which public education had been in effect for some time, making most of their emigrants literate. In fact, some of them could even read and write in English. It is noteworthy that the emigration from Japan to America came at a pivotal time in Japan's history. In 1868, flush from the overthrow of the ruling Tokugawan shoguns, the nation of Japan was establishing not only a new government but a new set of corporate values and aspirations.

Christened the Meiji Restoration, this era ushered in a period when Japan was fascinated with the West. Without the stifling isolation demanded by the shoguns, Japanese people began to receive regular reports about the amazing opportunities available in the West. Inspired, pioneers left Japan for the distant shores of America. When they arrived, they brought those Meiji-era values with them, which endured here long after Japan itself had moved on to other ones.

Those pioneers from Japan, in contrast to their Chinese counterparts, came with several key advantages to adapting more readily to their new homeland. The new Japanese government had introduced the study of English in its secondary schools in 1876 and had allowed the establishment of Christian churches and schools. Meiji-era public leaders and intellectuals were effusive in the praise for almost all things American. As historian Thomas Sowell pointed out, "Unlike other nations, Japan did not send America its tired, its poor, its huddled masses. The Japanese were perhaps unique among immigrants to America in the extent to which they were a highly selected sample of their homeland population.... The rising role of Japan on the world scene made it easy for them to maintain their pride in being

Asian American Milestones

1848: First Chinese immigrants arrive in San Francisco. They provide essential labor for the Gold Rush and later are instrumental in building the transcontinental railroad, completed in 1869.

1870: Naturalization Act excludes Chinese from citizenship and prohibits wives of Chinese laborers from entering the United States.

1871: In Los Angeles's Chinatown, the first of many anti-Chinese riots breaks out. A mob hangs fifteen Chinese and shoots four others to death.

1910: Naturalization Act of 1870 is expanded to exclude all Asians from citizenship.

1913: The California Alien Land Act, aimed at Japanese farmers, bars anyone ineligible for United States citizenship from purchasing land. The California Supreme Court rules the act unconstitutional in 1952.

1922: Under the United States Cable Act, any woman marrying an immigrant ineligible for naturalization will lose her citizenship.

1942: After Japan's attack on Pearl Harbor, a presidential order forces internment of more than 120,000 people of Japanese ancestry.

1943: Public response to China as a World War II ally prompts Congress to repeal ban on Chinese immigration and naturalization.

1946: Filipinos and Asian Indians become eligible for naturalization. Japanese immigrants follow in 1952.

1948: The United States government passes an act allowing former Japanese American internees to file claims against the government for financial losses.

1956: Dalip Singh Saund, of Asian Indian descent, is elected to Congress from a district in the Imperial Valley of California and serves three terms.

Japanese, while following American ideals that were already part of the culture in Meiji Japan."[4] The Japanese were therefore eager and better equipped to adapt to the many challenges presented by their new environment.

Coming from a country with very little political clout, the Chinese were essentially on their own. They were subsequently on the receiving end of inordinate amounts of discrimination. The ultimate act of

1957: *The New Adventures of Charlie Chan*, the first show featuring an Asian American character in a title role, comes to television for thirty-nine episodes. Irish American actor J. Carrol Nash plays the role of Chan, based on real-life police detective Chang Apana.

1959: Hiram Fong of Hawaii becomes first Asian American elected to the Senate and is followed by fellow Hawaiian Daniel Inouye in 1962.

1965: Immigration and Naturalization Act of 1965 abolishes national origin quotas and substitutes hemispheric quotas, allowing many more Asians to immigrate to the United States.

1968: Asian American students join blacks and Latinos in protesting lack of ethnic studies at San Francisco State. Other protests follow at University of California Berkeley and elsewhere. Acting San Francisco State President S. I. Hayakawa is later elected to the Senate.

1975: A wave of Southeast Asian immigration is touched off at the end of the Vietnam war.

1980: The census shows the Asian/Pacific American population at 3.5 million, or 1.5 percent of the total population.

1982: Amid controversy, Vietnam Veterans Memorial designed by architect and sculptor Maya Lin is dedicated in Washington, D.C.

1988: Congress passes a bill publicly apologizing for internment of Japanese Americans and authorizing payment of $20,000 to each eligible former internee.

1993: Connie Chung of CBS becomes the first Asian American to co-anchor a television network news show.

1996: Gary Locke is elected governor of Washington State, the first Asian American to head a mainland state.

1997: A dozen Asian Americans become enmeshed in widening scandal arising from fund raising during the 1996 presidential election.

Source: "Reaching Critical Mass," *Los Angeles Times* series, July 12, 1998.

overt racism against them occurred in 1882, when the United States government adopted the Chinese Exclusion Act, which barred immigration of Chinese laborers for ten years. The Chinese government's protests fell on deaf ears. After being renewed in 1892, the Exclusion Act was then made permanent in 1902. A Chinese songwriter captured the essence of his compatriots' frustrations when he penned these trenchant lyrics:

My family is poor and suffers from shortages of firewood and rice.
So I borrowed money to come to the Golden Mountains.
But it is difficult to escape from the interrogation of the immigration
   officer.
And I was sent to the Island like a prisoner.
Arriving here, I sighed deeply in a dark room.
When a country is weak, others often treat it with contempt.
She is like a domesticated animal passively awaiting destruction.[5]

Japanese immigration did not begin in earnest until after the passage of this anti-Chinese legislation. The Japanese government, fully aware of it, made certain that the United States government did not pass similar legislation aimed at its emigrants. Their efforts allowed the Japanese to soon outnumber their Chinese predecessors.

Because of their government's incessant pressure, the Japanese enjoyed a much less restrictive immigration than did the Chinese. In 1890, eight years after the Chinese Exclusion Act, there were only 2,039 Japanese on the mainland. But by 1910 they outnumbered the Chinese 72,257 to 71,531. Two decades later, the Japanese population had nearly doubled to 138,834. Meanwhile, the Chinese population had scarcely grown.[6]

The Japanese government was not able to prevail against the forces of racism and sinophobic politicians indefinitely. However, they did manage to keep the window of immigration open for their people until 1924, giving them twenty years that the Chinese did not have.

During this time, another significant change occurred: the immigration pattern of the Japanese changed from a male-dominated one to one that was dominated by females. With this balancing of the sexes, they were able to establish a native-born, citizen generation of Japanese, the Nisei [second generation], who by 1940 would greatly outnumber their parents.

This was in stark contrast to the Chinese situation, in which there was a heavily unbalanced sex ratio in their communities. In 1890 there were twenty-seven males for every female. Although subsequent census records indicate that this ratio declined steadily (though by 1930 it was still four to one), there still was the problem of a tremendous age gap between the sexes. In 1920, the median age for Chinese males was forty-two years; it was only nineteen years for the females.

Add to this other factors (e.g., a culture that was traditionally extremely chauvinistic, the extreme degree of cultural differentiation between Chinese and most Americans), and one can begin to understand why acculturation took relatively long for Chinese Americans as a community. As Sowell remarked,

> Perhaps the greatest tragedy of the early Chinese immigrants was that a people so dedicated to the family were denied the possibility of having families in America. . . . This meant that the cultural assimilation of the groups as a whole was retarded. The virtual absence of an American-born second generation not only statistically left most of the Chinese population foreign born until about 1940, but it also meant that the absorption of the English language and American customs via the school was delayed and that the usual role of second-generation children in helping their parents become acculturated was aborted.[7]

Without the wherewithal to build their communities on the foundation of marriages and families, the Chinese experienced a serious decline in numbers for almost fifty years. It was not until the 1950s that they began to return to the population levels they had enjoyed in the 1880s.[8]

Since this was not the experience of the Japanese, they saw only a small dip in their numbers in the 1930s. Even more impressive was the fact that by 1940, almost two-thirds of them were native-born American citizens. The Chinese enjoyed a fifty-year head start on the Japanese, and yet by 1940 the latter had acculturated to a much greater degree than had the former. The Japanese were already showing signs of being the vanguard in the Asian American acculturation process.

Concentrated in Camps

Ask most Americans born before 1950 what significant event happened on December 7, 1941, and they may echo the words of then President Franklin D. Roosevelt and tell you that was "the day that will live in infamy," referring to Japan's nefarious bombing raid on Pearl Harbor, Hawaii. This act led the United States to declare war on Japan and to join forces with the Allies against the Axis forces that were already wreaking havoc in Europe. But ask them the importance of February 19, 1942, and you will probably get a blank stare in return. This difference in date recognition is both ironic and sad, for here is another date that will live in infamy, at least in the memories of Americans of Japanese heritage.

On that fateful date, President Roosevelt issued Executive Order 9066, which, as a matter of "military necessity," empowered the army to evacuate "any or all persons" from as yet unspecified "military areas." This later turned out to mean the state of California, a good portion of Washington and Oregon, and part of Arizona. And to their horror and disbelief, Japanese Americans quickly learned that "any or all persons" meant them and no one else.

In the hysterical aftermath of the unexpected attack on Pearl Harbor, feelings against all people of Japanese ancestry in America were ugly. Unscrupulous people who had the most to gain if the Japanese "yellow peril" were removed from the West Coast economy capitalized on this opportunity to eliminate their hated competition. Fanning the flames of people's fear with warnings of imminent invasion by the Japanese, they convinced the necessary powers to act. With little advance notice, those living in the affected areas were rounded up and summarily herded off like traitors or prisoners of war, first to assembly centers close by and then to one of ten remote relocation centers that were situated at "safe" distances from the West Coast. Denied due process and forced to exist in barren compounds surrounded by barbed wire and guard towers, the Japanese Americans would never be the same.[9]

> This wartime exile and incarceration...was and remains the central event of Japanese-American history. It makes that history unique, setting off the Japanese-American experience from that of not just other ethnic groups from Asia but from all other immigrant ethnic groups.[10]

Many were psychologically destroyed and financially ruined by this dark chapter in America's history. Yet there was an unforeseen outcome of this forced evacuation: "the wartime evacuation affected the acculturation of the Japanese, especially the Nisei. New exposure, new opportunities, the dissolution of old institutions and structures, and life away from the ghetto hastened change."[11] In a bizarre twist, this acceleration of the Nisei's acculturation was a direct result of the concentrating of nearly 90 percent of the Japanese living in America

(Hawaii was not yet a state) in those ten camps. The impact of that experience was both painful and profitable.

The ghettos and "Jap towns" on the West Coast were eliminated. This has never happened to any other Asian group in America on such a large scale. Having to establish new communities quickly and from scratch, the incarcerated Japanese Americans chose to abandon many of the old social structures in favor of new ones.

Due to camp policies that required positions of responsibility to be filled by American citizens, the Nisei were thrust into the stations of power and influence while they were still quite young. This effectively moved the Issei out of their central roles in the community, influencing the structure of the Japanese family and allowing the Nisei to act without the Issei. Due to the closed environment, Nisei were able to occupy positions in the camp structure that would normally be reserved for dominant group members in the outside world. Into the resulting vacuums that the camps created, the Nisei teenagers became the high school heroes and class officers. Here, Nisei could also pursue careers that would normally be off limits to them, for since they were only competing against each other, race was no longer an issue for employment. In this enforced homogeneous world, racial prejudice aimed at Japanese had virtually disappeared, allowing the Nisei to experience a more complete participation in "society."

The evacuation had a telling effect on the family structure. All meals were served in noisy mess halls and eating soon ceased to be a family affair. The mothers ate with their young children, the fathers ate with the other men, and the older children dined with their peers. This eventually resulted in the loosening of the social controls normally present in the family. Japanese husbands and fathers were also forced to redefine their traditional roles. In many cases their wives and children were working and earning the same wages as they were. No longer were they the major breadwinners of the family. The outcome was a general loss of self-esteem on the man's part and a gain in independence on the part of the wife and children. In general, this led to the destruction of established family patterns of behavior. Dependence on the government, something almost unheard of before among the Japanese, also assumed a major role in the camp.[12]

Even though the critical decisions were still made by whites and they were being confined against their wishes, the Japanese Americans got their first taste of what it was like to be in an American small community. They learned to organize as blocks, to perform community services, and to take responsibility for the direction of their community. Years later this type of experience gave them the confidence and inspiration to tackle the problems of not only the Japanese-American community but also the larger society as a whole. Prominent Japanese American statesmen like Spark Matsunaga, Daniel Inouye, and Robert Matsui are examples of those who have taken their civic pride and responsibility beyond the ethnic circle and entered into the realm of national policy making.

As the war began to wind down, the camps were only half as full as they were in the beginning. Thousands of the inhabitants had either received permission to attend a college or take a job in the East, or they were busy helping to defeat their country's enemies in the European or the Pacific theaters. Those who found themselves living in cities where there had been no Japanese communities before the war were exposed to a much broader slice of American life. They also presented positive new images of Japanese Americans to challenge the post–Pearl Harbor stereotypes of white Americans. As for those who served in the military, they too returned home after having had their horizons stretched. Their much-celebrated heroics in the field of battle also forced many white Americans to see them for who they were: their fellow American citizens. As one observer remembered, "[Then] Interior Secretary Harold L. Ickes wrote in 1945 that the outstanding record of the units was 'the most important single factor in creating in this country a more understanding attitude toward people of Japanese descent. The goal for which they strove, acceptance for their families and themselves as loyal Americans, is being achieved.' "[13]

Having been unlawfully imprisoned by their own country, which was at war with their homeland, caused the Japanese to engage in much soul-searching during World War II. Were they Japanese or American? Those with the closest ties to Japan had great difficulty with this question of both nationality and ethnicity. For most of the

Nisei, this experience served to solidify their full identity as loyal American citizens.

The question of ethnicity had to be dealt with differently in light of what had transpired. Before being forced to leave their homes and businesses, many of the Japanese, especially the Nisei, might have fancied themselves to be "American" through and through. But they had been removed from society to these forsaken camps simply because of their Japanese ancestry. They had to face up to the fact that they might never be seen as anything more than hyphenated Americans. Over time, they not only came to accept this, they took a renewed pride in their ethnic heritage as "Buddhaheads."

When the war was finally over, the Japanese Americans had to put their shattered lives back together. Some five thousand decided that they had had enough of this country and either emigrated or repatriated to Japan. But many others had already decided that America was their country, good or bad. They still faced hardships and lingering persecution, but they had found a new strength and forged a new identity in those concentration camps. They were proud of their Japanese community and equally committed to participating in the wider American scene. They had gone through a terrible trial together and they had survived. The future only seemed to be full of promise for them now.

A RELUCTANT LEADER

Let's say that, after studying the above section, you approach a Japanese American Sansei at the office and ask, "So, how does it feel to be the trendsetters for the establishing of a more generic Asian American culture?" She would probably stare at you as if you had lost your mind. Most Japanese Americans are too humble to think that they are leading the way for other Asian Americans, even if they are. And if you asked a similar question of a Japanese American Sansei Christian, he would no doubt give you that cross-eyed look, too. Most Japanese American churches that I know are, like other local churches, caught up in managing their own corporate life. Most are wondering how to chart a fruitful future for both the English speakers and the Japanese speakers, most of whom are business families that will be returning in a few years to Japan. Many are struggling to survive. Is it any wonder that Japanese American Christians are reluctant to lead the way in establishing vibrant ministries for Americanized Asian American people? Reluctant or not, it will become quite clear that God has cast them in this role.

Dwindling Numbers

If the size of their population is important to them, the future does not seem bright for Japanese Americans. The simple fact is that their numbers are dwindling. After surging past the Chinese in the first half of the nineteenth century, they have not been able to keep up with the growth of the other American Asian groups. The 1990 census tallied 7.3 million Asian Pacific Americans (table 1 in the Appendix). The largest groups ranked by size were Chinese (1,645,472), Filipino (1,406,770), Japanese (847,562), Asian Indian (815,447), Korean (798,849), and Vietnamese (614,547). Japanese Americans made up 20 percent of the total Asian American population in 1980 but only 11.7 percent in 1990. A glance at the projections for the year 2000 (fig. 4.1) will show that they are expected to drop from third to sixth place, a projected decrease of nearly 12 percent. Table 2 (in the Appendix), which compares how much each of the five largest groups grew from 1980 to 1990, provides another snapshot of the ongoing free fall of the Japanese American segment.

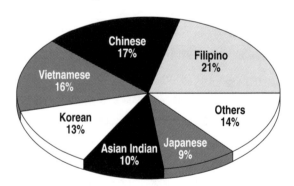

Figure 4.1
Projected Percentages of Asian Americans by 2000

Source: Robert W. Gardner, Bryant Robey, and Peter C. Smith, "Asian Americans: Growth, Changes, and Diversity," *Population Bulletin* 40, no. 4 (October 1985): 37, table 16; in Kitano and Daniels, *Asian Americans: Emerging Minorities* (Englewood Cliffs, N.J.: Prentice-Hall, 1989), 161

Further food for thought is the fact that in the 1970 census the Japanese ranked first, and there were very few Vietnamese and Koreans living here. These numbers reflect the increased immigration rates of every listed group except one: the Japanese. The Japanese who come from Japan for the most part are businesspersons who have no plans to make America their new permanent residence. They stay long enough to finish their business and then return to Japan. And of course, there are the tourists, who are here on holiday, not to stay. There are few true immigrants coming from Japan these days.

Take a look at the graph in figure 4.2, paying particular attention to the third bar in each column. This is a picture of the percentage of each listed group's population that has come to the United States since 1970. Since that year, the Koreans and Vietnamese have swelled their ranks through a massive and continuous exodus of migrants. In stark contrast is the percentage of immigrants during that same period for the Japanese: 14 percent. The only group with lower immigration figures is the Hawaiians.

What this does not mean is that Japanese Americans are a dying people or that they should have the government classify them as an

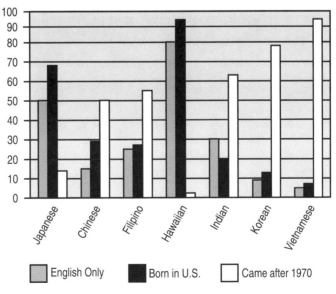

Figure 4.2
Which Groups Would Blend Best?

Source: "Pacific Rim Profiles," Los Angeles United Way,
November 1985, 80, 103, 146–60

endangered species. (They are not the Asian American equivalent of the snail darter or spotted owl!) Lest we forget, there were more than 700,000 of them in 1980, and there should be close to 1,000,000 Japanese Americans in 2000. Their numbers can be said to be shrinking only when they are looked at in concert with the figures from the other groups. This is the perspective that is significant for our purposes, because it highlights that their growth in the future will be primarily linked to births of increasingly Marginal Ethnics rather than to a continuous influx of Nuclear Ethnics.

Further perusal of figure 4.2 will reveal that Japanese Americans are second only to the Hawaiians when it comes to the portions of their group who only speak English and who are native-born Americans — key characteristics of acculturated cod or Americanized Asian Americans. None of the other Asian groups comes close to challenging the Japanese Americans in this regard.[14] This is another reason why they are acculturating at a faster rate than the rest and why some feel that they are leading the way toward establishing a more generic Asian American homogeneous unit. They may be the most Americanized Asian American group in this country. As their numbers are not being replenished by jetloads of immigrants, they do not have the luxury of ignoring this inevitable process. To survive, they must adapt to their situation. And since they come from an island culture, they should already be quite familiar with this requirement for survival.

Highest Intermarriage Rates

With Japanese Americans intermarrying at the rate of 50 percent in cities and 70 percent in rural areas, Japanese Americans often look white, Latino, or black. For almost two decades, studies show, families with one Japanese parent have exceeded the number of families with two Japanese parents.[15]

The rate of intermarriages is one of the strongest indicators of how far a minority group has assimilated into the majority culture (see chap. 3). Marrying someone from the dominant group is a sign that some of the previous stigma between both groups has diminished,

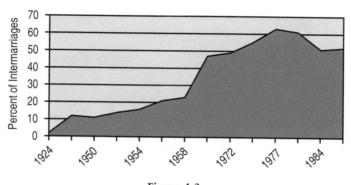

Figure 4.3
Intermarriages of Japanese Americans
Source: Los Angeles County Marriage License Bureau

meaning that the members of the minority group enjoy more acceptance and are being gradually absorbed by the majority. A halfway step
is when members of one minority group begin cross-marrying with
members of another minority group who share some of their values
and background. Japanese Americans lead the way statistically in both
categories.

Figure 4.3 shows the direction of marriages by Japanese Americans in Los Angeles County from 1924 to 1989. Until the watershed
case of *Perez v. Lippold* (1948), interracial marriages were illegal in
California. There was a steady gradual annual increase in the rate.
Then the 1970s witnessed a dramatic upsurge in intermarriages. During that period, at least every other Japanese American was marrying
outside of his or her race. There was an apparent dropoff during the
first half of the 1980s; it is not clear yet if this signaled the beginning of a trend toward a decreasing rate. We should note that the
1989 figure, though lower than the peak in 1979, was still 52 percent. That means that every other Japanese American was choosing
to intermarry.

There must be some correlation between the fact that Japanese
Americans continue to have the highest rate of intermarriages of any
minority group and the fact that they are acculturating faster than
the rest (fig. 4.4). When a Japanese American selects a marriage partner who is not Japanese, this is not only a move toward merging
by the bride and the groom; this also constitutes a merging of extended families. There may be some resistance from either or both

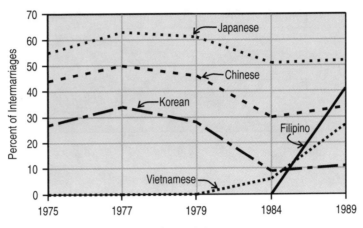

Figure 4.4
Intermarriage Trends of Asian Americans,
Los Angeles County, 1975–89

Source: Los Angeles County Marriage License Bureau
No data were collected prior to 1989 for Filipinos and prior to 1984 for Vietnamese.

sides when the couple first announces their intentions, but this usually begins to dissipate once the marriage is begun. Then the arrival of grandchildren is a significant event in the merging process, for in welcoming these interracial (*hapa*, a Hawaiian word for half) children into their families, they are affirming the acculturation process even further.

With their rate of intermarriage having been elevated for such a long time, the odds are that every Japanese American couple has at least one or two *hapas* in their extended families. As a group, they seem to be able to handle this better than do other Asian Americans. This may stem back to their cultural ability to make the most of a situation. In fact, this *shi-kataganai* (It can't be helped) cultural attitude can also help to explain why they have been so quick to carve out their own niche in American society — one that is attracting more and more marginal Asian Americans.

A Magnet for Other Marginals

These factors from the unique history of the Japanese in the United States validate the contention that the Japanese Americans, in the process of forming a new subculture for their increasingly marginalized selves, have inadvertently been propagating a culture that is attracting non-Japanese Cell B Asian Americans. As these other marginalized Asian Americans search for symbols of a new identity, they have been gravitating toward the subculture that the Sansei (third generation) have developed for themselves. To many of these, being Asian American in some ways means being Sansei.

But in many ways, the Japanese Americans have been the oblivious leaders of this Asian American movement to merge. This is most true of the Sansei, who, though they are much more acculturated than are the two generations that preceded them, admit to struggling with their identity more than the other two do. They want to know: Are they Japanese Americans or Americans of Japanese ancestry?

John W. Conner, a professor of anthropology at California State University, Sacramento, has done extensive research on the Japanese Americans. Sacramento has a sizeable Japanese American community with a high percentage of the Sansei attending its many colleges. From his campus vantage point, Conner has observed many of the young Sansei trying to establish a new identity. Some object to the term "Oriental Americans," preferring to be called Asian Americans. The former perpetuates the negative stereotype of the shy, submissive, and docile Oriental, whereas the latter connotes an Asian who is not afraid of being assertive.

Conner believes there to be some truth in this assertion. His findings have shown that the Sansei retain some of the core Japanese characteristics, while in other ways they more closely resemble the white group than do their parents or grandparents. When the Sansei express a concern for retaining their ethnic heritage, they seem to want to perpetuate more of the symbolic, artistic, or aesthetic aspects of it rather than the psychological or behavioral components of it.

Their preparation to succeed and their openness to acculturation, Conner believes, mean that the Sansei will continue to be further incorporated into the mainstream of American society. It also does not hurt that those Japanese Americans who have gone before them have already established a reputation for hard work, perseverance, diligence, and dependability. Thus, he concludes, that in a very real sense "far from being excluded from full participation in American society, the Sansei may find that they will be in a process of continually reassessing their ethnicity and periodically redefining the elements that are essential in maintaining a distinct ethnic identity."[16]

Conner's prediction underscores the contention made at the opening of this section. For he agrees that the Sansei are involved in an ongoing process of establishing an Asian American identity that is simultaneously ethnic and American. We are just broadening his perspective on the Sansei to include other Cell B Asian Americans. In their efforts to define a new Asian American identity for themselves, the Sansei inadvertently have been creating an identity to which other marginal Asian Americans can relate as well. Without intending to, they have created a subculture that is attracting others who are seeking an Asian American identity to call their own. The quest for identity will always be meaningful to those Americans whose skin color is something other than white. Stressing this, Conner goes on to say that

> acculturation is by no means a unilateral process. By this is meant that the preservation of an ethnic identity is functionally adaptive for a highly visible racial minority, especially for the Japanese Americans who have become victims of two contrasting stereotypes. On the one hand they were once the victim of severe racial prejudice, which has continued... on the other, they have also been praised as a "model minority" and congratulated on the speed, success, and thoroughness of their acculturation.
>
> ...both stereotypes are erroneous. Despite the advancements, even the Sansei do not as yet feel completely comfortable or "at home" in the larger American society. There is, therefore, an adaptive need for what might be called a periodic retreat into ethnicity to escape the stresses of encounters with the larger society.... The ingredients of this ethnic identity are more likely than not to be composed of unrelated and imperfectly understood bits and pieces of the older culture. Thus, many Sansei have already put together an "Asian American" identity that would almost certainly mystify their grandparents.[17]

This desire for a "periodic retreat into ethnicity" will probably exist so long as white skin is held up as a major prerequisite to being fully accepted as an American. Many minorities may not be consciously aware of the daily stress they undergo by trying to fit into the popular portrait of America. But it is there nevertheless, and the comfortable feeling they get when they are around "their kind of people" supports this idea. Cell B Asian Americans are looking for just such a group to which they can relate and belong. Who might these other Cell B Asian Americans be? Is it possible that this bicultural magnet that the Sansei have made for themselves would draw every English-speaking, Americanized person of another Asian background? Or is it more likely that, for the time being, only a select few of the other Asian groups would be naturally attracted to it? To answer these questions, let us examine some pertinent data.

Take another look at figure 4.2. Compare the percentages of each Asian group that speak only English, are native-born citizens, and arrived in the United States since 1970. Let us begin by testing the assumption that having high scores in the first two areas and a low score in the third would be a central part of the profile of a highly acculturated group that would tend to gravitate toward a Japanese Sansei brand of Asian American culture.

The Asian American group with the highest percentage of people in the first two categories and the lowest in the third are the Hawaiians. The Japanese Americans, as significant as their scores are, finish a distant second to them. The influence of Hawaiian culture on the emerging Asian American one is just shy of that of the Sansei's. Many non-Pacific Islander Asian Americans relate quite positively to Hawaiian Americans or at least to their culture. This is probably due to the fact that Hawaiian culture projects popular and positive images for its largely Asian population, especially the Chinese, Japanese, and Polynesians. In Hawaii there is definitely a sense that it is better to be an Asian or a Polynesian than a *haole* (white). Where else in the United States is this true? It is not surprising then that the emerging Asian American minority is fond of embracing Hawaiian euphemisms and symbols in addition to Sansei ones.

But this does not mean that Hawaiian Americans are one of the groups merging into the Japanese American subculture. On the whole, they tend to be rather insular, especially when it comes to mingling and merging with Asian Americans on the mainland. One possible reason is that Pacific Islanders and Asians do not naturally consider each other to be cut from the same bolt of cloth; one is from silk, the other from tapa. Harry H. L. Kitano and Roger Daniels believe that being lumped with Asians with roots in the Far East has been detrimental for the Hawaiians. This is because "the backgrounds are vastly different and place the islanders at a disadvantage when competing for federal funds and other forms of assistance."[18]

Hawaiians and Japanese Americans, although they both have an elevated percentage of highly acculturated people, are not intermarrying in any significant numbers. This is true even in Hawaii, where members of both groups grow up next to each other. If the people are not marrying each other, then the groups are not merging, despite other appearances to the contrary.

The same can be said for Filipino and Indian Americans. Although they have the third and fourth highest percentages of people who can only speak English and the fourth and fifth highest of those who were born here, they too are not intermarrying with Japanese Americans to any great degree. Once again, the fact that the backgrounds of both these groups are more dissimilar to the Japanese culture might also explain why there has not been much merging in America thus far.[19]

At the same time, there are signs that some of the Filipino Americans are showing interest in joining with the Japanese Americans. At Evergreen Baptist Church of Los Angeles, which began in 1925 as a mission to Japanese immigrants living in Boyle Heights but is now a burgeoning ministry to a multi-Asian / multi-ethnic, English-speaking congregation, there has been a slow but steady influx of Filipino Americans since 1990. Some come as one-half of an interracial marriage. Still others come who are single because they say they enjoy the worship services, which seem comfortably Asian American without being overtly Filipino.

It would appear that the three factors — English only, born in the United States, arrived since 1970 — are not reliable predictors of the blending potential of each Asian American group. Held up against things like intermarriage rates and observations of social groupings, those factors prove not to be that helpful. This is not to say that they are not useful for measuring the degree of a group's acculturation.

As the number of people who can speak only English and who were born here expands and as the number of new immigrants diminishes, the group as a whole will be moving from being Cell D (Low Assimilation, High Ethnic Identity) to Cell B Asian Americans (High Assimilation, High Ethnic Identity). But as far as predicting the merging aspect of acculturation, it would appear that other factors are more significant.

What would these other factors be? If the members of another Asian ethnic group are intermarrying and intermingling with Japanese Americans in increasing numbers, it can be said that a significant portion of that group is being attracted to the Sansei-based subculture. According to this indicator, Chinese and Korean Americans are the Asians merging with the Japanese Americans in the greatest numbers, with the Chinese ranking higher then the Koreans.

The growth in the number of intermarriages among these three groups can be traced to the social groupings that occur in school. In high schools where there are large numbers of Cell B Japanese, Chinese, and Korean Americans, the student organization they usually all identify with is the Asian Student Union or the Asian Club.[20] Although their parents or grandparents might still harbor ill feelings toward the other groups, the young people do not always carry the same prejudices. With each succeeding generation, there are more young people who see others with the same black hair, brown eyes, and similar cultural values as fellow Asian Americans. Many of them go on to college, where they join Asian American fraternal organizations, social cliques, or Christian organizations (e.g., Asian American Christian Fellowship, sponsored by the Japanese Evangelical Missionary Society). The next natural step is to date those within one's social circle, leading to more marriages among these three Asian ethnic groups.

When I wrote my doctoral dissertation in 1990, even though Koreans and Vietnamese had the highest percentage of new immigrants, the Koreans were included in the preceding triumvirate and the Vietnamese were not. This was partly based on observations of Korean American young people intermingling more with Chinese and Japanese American young people than were their Vietnamese American counterparts (see fig. 3.10 and note how many Korean American females are intermarrying). But it was also because of the stark contrast between these two immigrant groups.

The pullout of the United States from Vietnam in 1975 began the second wave of immigration from that country. Having left a nation with a derelict economy that had been ravaged by decades of war, the Vietnamese arrive more as refugees, with very few skills and finances. Even those who were educated and who held prestigious positions in Vietnam were forced to take more menial jobs here. Many of the adults, with a longing to return one day to Vietnam, were not in favor of wide-scale Americanization. However, following the typical pattern (the flow of generations model), the younger refugees began adapting much more quickly to American life, excited about the opportunities in this country. In 1989 there still seemed to be some resistance from the already established Chinese and Japanese Americans to view them as ethnic peers. And as was shown in figure 4.4, little intermarriage was occurring in this group prior to 1984. But the figures since then indicate that that pattern has been changing dramatically.

The Koreans who have come since the passage of the Immigration and Naturalization Act of 1965 are part of the third wave of Korean immigrants to this country. They are among the fastest-growing ethnic groups in this country. According to Kitano and Daniels,

> the growth is almost entirely due to immigration; thus, this population is primarily a two-generation group, that is, immigrants and their children. However, unlike the early Chinese, Japanese, and Filipinos, who came largely as individuals, Korean immigrants often arrived in family groups.... As a consequence, intergenerational differences in terms of acculturation, identity, language facility, and coming to grips with the dominant culture have an immediacy that was delayed for the older Asian groups.... For the Koreans, generational terms often have not been meaningful.[21]

Until 1997 the nation of Korea was in a much better position in the world than was Vietnam. Its migrants were leaving a country that had already established its position as a world-class industrial giant. Thus, like the early Japanese pioneers, they arrived in America with a positive self-concept, much more so than the Vietnamese did. This was a significant factor in their rapid acculturation to a new life in

America. Add to this their greater ability to secure higher-paying jobs here, and it was apparent that the Korean Americans were on a much faster track to merge into the Asian American subculture than were the Vietnamese. (The serious economic crisis of 1997 that devastated South Korea continues in 1999. Repercussions on outlook, cultural self-esteem, and so on are very real.) Thus, another gauge of a group's merging potential is how quickly its members can attain the coveted middle-class status that is already enjoyed by many of the Cell B Chinese and Japanese Americans.

Factors such as openness to intermarrying, comparable academic aspirations and career paths, and a fluency in English all have proven to be helpful in predicting either future amalgamations or explaining present ones. Our experience at Evergreen-LA since 1997, when surprising numbers of Taiwanese, Thai, Vietnamese, Indonesian, Filipino, and Burmese Americans began to join us, further substantiates the hypothesis that other Asian American people, as they continue to acculturate, will be attracted to what were once historically Japanese American churches or ministries. For now, much of what is understood as Asian American is traceable to Sansei Japanese American culture. However, I predict that even this is ever evolving. Increasing numbers of other Asian Americans will continue to enter the mix. Ministries that were once Korean-only or Chinese-only will enthusiastically embrace other Asian Americans. The added impact of incoming *hapa*, Latino, black, and white Americans will become a much stronger factor than it is today for some Asian American churches. And sometimes, some first-generation imported bass may surprise some of us Cell B Asian Americans by showing up with deep sea diving suits on. Thus, the answer to the question "What is Asian American?" will continue to change as the constituency of various blends of Asian Americans keeps expanding.

Japanese Americans, whether they realize this or not, are leading the way toward the future for Asian America. They are living proof that this new blend of Asian and other people is emerging daily and requires our special attention now. These are the people who need to experience the true and priceless pearl that is Jesus and God's kingdom. How to do that?

THINGS TO THINK ABOUT

1. How well do you identify with the label "Americanized Asian American"? Have you experienced any of this coming together or merging? If so, how and where?

2. How have intermarriage rates influenced your family? Extended family? Circle of friends? Families in your church? How do you feel about the high rates of Asian American intermarriages?

3. What is your response to the author's assertion that there is an emerging, merging new Asian American subculture and that the Japanese Americans, especially the Sansei, are unwittingly leading the way?

4. If this theory is valid, what might be some of the critical implications for Japanese American Christian churches and ministries and other American mono-Asian Christian churches that feel God is calling them to reach their more Americanized generations for Christ?

*Chapter
Five*

COLORING OUTSIDE THE LINES

The Church has a choice: to die as a result of its resistance to change or
to die in order to live.   — MIKE REGELE[1]

METHODS THAT MATCH PEOPLE

For as long as there have been Christians with a zeal to bring the
good news of salvation to unreached peoples in sundry parts of
the world, there have been different ideas as to how to tackle this
evangelistic task.

There are those who would argue that since faith is a gift from
the Almighty (e.g., Romans 1:17), methods are relatively meaningless.
After all, even the best methods can be seen as a form of manipulation. And if the Lord is not already moving in a person's life, causing
him or her to become more aware of God's presence and of one's sin-
fulness, methods will not move that person to make a confession of
faith and a commitment to Christ. No, it is ultimately the mysterious
orchestrations of the Holy Spirit that prepare an individual, or even a
tribe, to respond affirmatively to the invitation to embark on a new
and fruitful life in Jesus Christ.

Others would agree that our sovereign God is somehow behind the
conditions of people's hearts as far as the gospel is concerned, but even
so, they still maintain that certain approaches to delivering that good
news are more effective than others. From something as obvious as
providing translations of the Bible in a people's native language to
something as intricate as identifying the clues to salvation that God
has already placed in a culture, the efforts we make to initiate people

into life in God's kingdom can take many different forms. What is important is for all involved to see how often the Lord works in concert with creative, insightful, and inspired attempts to ignite the sparks of faith that the Spirit of God has already placed in people's hearts.

God can and does work without the involvement of fervent and faithful Christians, churches, and agencies. But God seems to prefer combining the Spirit's inner workings with our best efforts. As Paul wrote to the believers in Rome, " 'Everyone who calls on the name of the Lord will be saved.' How, then, can they call on the one they have not believed in? And how can they believe in the one of whom they have not heard? And how can they hear without someone preaching to them? And how can they preach unless they are sent? As it is written, 'How beautiful are the feet of those who bring good news!' " (Romans 10:13–15).

If we are blessed with the awesome responsibility to deliver God's message of salvation, we must be sure that our methods are faithful to the Scriptures and at the same time are geared to our intended audiences. This will require our remaining open to the Lord's course corrections and to new ways that God wants us to retell God's story. As always, the results are the Lord's responsibility, but if it is true that the fields are waiting to be harvested and if we are employing anointed methods, then more often than not we should hope to see more and more people committing their lives to Christ.

If this does not occur, the problem is most likely ours and not God's. The Lord has already scattered the seeds of faith in fertile hearts. These people in our target group are poised to receive the gospel, with eyes to see and ears to hear. The difficulty may be with the incarnation that we are presenting, that is, the Word of God has not been wrapped in the symbols and flesh of the people. We need to have methods that match the people.

Paul's Experiment with Radical Matching

Anyone the least bit familiar with him knows that the apostle Paul was not afraid to color outside the lines, that is to try new or different ways to introduce Jesus Christ to an unconvinced people. He was able to see that the well-intentioned methods of the Jewish Christians in Jerusalem were not appropriate for Gentile evangelism. He sensed that Gentile hearts were open; they were not open to becoming Jewish in the process of accepting Christ.

With radical insight, Paul perceived that the Gentiles needed to be confronted with a Gentile Savior, not a Jewish Messiah. This must have been threatening to many of the fundamental Jewish believers: How could anyone accept their Messiah without fully accepting his Judaism too? This skepticism continued for some time after Paul and Barnabas had succeeded in planting churches among the Gentiles throughout Asia Minor.

This all came to a head when some members from the Jerusalem church with more fundamentalist tendencies (i.e., the Judaizers) made a special trip to the church in Antioch. They demanded that these Gentile believers convert to Judaism, for they were still operating with their Pharisaical mindset. They said, "Unless you are circumcised, according to the custom taught by Moses, you cannot be saved" (Acts 15:1). Luke records that this assertion of theirs resulted in an intense challenge from the likes of Paul and Barnabas (Acts 15:2). In the end, they agreed to take their dispute before the council in Jerusalem, where Paul successfully argued for the legitimacy of his non-Jewish approach to the Christian faith.[2]

Paul could see that a different approach was crucial to extending the hand of grace and truth to the Gentiles. It did not matter to him that the Jewish traditionalists could not fully fathom his reasons for making such a radical departure from what worked for them in Palestine. He was in Asia Minor, working among a different people, and he saw the need to incarnate Christ in the trappings of their culture. Having grown up among them, he was a bicultural Jew, a distinct advantage when it came to doing missions in a cross-cultural context. Maybe he did not use such fancy terminology, but he instinctively saw there was a need to match his methods to the people he was trying to reach.

What mattered most to him was that more of God's prodigal children would return home to be with their heavenly Father. To see this end accomplished, he would learn how to become, in a sense, a Christian chameleon, adapting himself and his approach — but not the essential message — to fit his audience. He declared this to the believers in Corinth:

> Though I am free and belong to no man, I make myself a slave to everyone, to win as many as possible. To the Jews I became like a Jew, to win the Jews. To those under the law I became like one under the law (though I myself am not under the law), so as to win those under the law. To those not having the law I became like one not having the law (though I am not free from God's law but am under Christ's law), so as to win those not having the law. To the weak I became weak, to win the weak. I have become all things to all men so that by all possible means I might save some. I do all this for the sake of the gospel, that I may share in its blessings. (1 Corinthians 9:19–23)

These are the words of a person who was convinced that the call is not to serve any particular method but to make sure that all methods serve the ends of the gospel. And this is from the pen of the same man who wrote that, although this may involve different people utilizing disparate evangelistic methods, "only God . . . makes things grow" (1 Corinthians 3:5–7). So Paul too believed that God was the ultimate source of spiritual life, but he also knew the value of matching methods to people. And he saw firsthand how effective this creative approach could be.

What the apostle had put his finger on was the same a priori assumption behind everything presented in this study thus far, namely, that people naturally approach having faith in God through the unique matrix of their cultures. By culture is meant "the customary beliefs, social forms, and material traits of a racial, religious, or social group."[3] Many of us are just waking up to what Paul had come to realize about the critical role culture plays in shaping missionary endeavors.

Father Vincent J. Donovan is one of those who have come to appreciate anew the precociousness of Paul. Laboring for seventeen years among the Masai in East Africa, he too came to believe that culture is all encompassing and all-important in the history of salvation.[4] In rethinking that original order that sent missionaries all over the world, Donovan began to take exception to the modern translation of the Greek word *ethne*. Christ is quoted as directing all Christians to preach the gospel to all the nations *(panta ta ethne)*, yet Donovan

doubts that the biblical writers knew of nations in the modern political sense of the word (e.g., the nations of Germany and America). It
would make more sense that ethne

> would refer more to ethnic, cultural groups, the natural building blocks
> of the human race. While the political nation of the United States might
> have very little to do with salvation as such, the Masai culture or a
> Hindu culture or the cultures that make up America might have very
> much to do with salvation.
>
> It is surely here in the midst of the cultures of the world . . . that the
> ordinary way of salvation must lie. . . . Or else it is a very strange God
> that we have.
>
> . . . God enables a people, any people, to reach salvation through their
> culture and tribal, racial customs and traditions. . . .
>
> . . . In those customs lay their possibility of salvation. . . .
>
> An evangelist, a missionary must respect the culture of a people, not
> destroy it. The incarnation of the gospel, the flesh and blood, which
> must grow on the gospel, is up to the people of a culture. . . .
>
> The gospel is, after all, not a philosophy or set of doctrines or laws.
> That is what a culture is. The gospel is essentially a history, at whose
> center is the God-man born in Bethlehem, risen near Golgotha.[5]

Donovan is convinced that God has embedded clues to salvation
in every culture of the world. By listening to the stories of a particular
people group, by learning what they already have come to believe about
God, the world, and themselves, he believes that those clues can be
unearthed and connected to the essential message of the gospel. In
this way, the people of that culture will naturally start to recognize the
truth of God in their midst. This is the same idea behind missionary-
author Don Richardson's well-known book, *Peace Child*. In applying
this belief to his work among the Masai, Donovan capitalized on the
cultural clues he uncovered, and he eventually was witness to entire
tribes turning their lives over to Christ.

This approach to evangelism is both arduous and time-consuming.
You must immerse yourself in the culture, embracing these people the
way Christ would, until you know what makes them tick. It is also
stretching, for if you want to uncover the faith clues in a culture, you
must often move beyond your own conversion experience and be prepared to see how God is moving in radically different ways in another
culture. How you came to Christ may have little relevance to how they
will come to Christ. At the least, if you hail from the same culture, you

must delve beneath the cliche-ridden explanations of your conversion to trace the cultural roots of it.

It is always easier to color inside the lines, to find a method that works and then use it for whatever group we are trying to reach. But church history has shown that one size does not fit all and that we must continually strive to find methods that are appropriate for every group of people. Like Paul, we must be prepared to move beyond whatever our comfort zones are so that, by all possible means, some might be saved. Therefore if we are going to reach marginal Asian Americans for Christ, we must design methods to match their emerging new culture. Even if it means coming up with some different approaches. Even if it means at times being misunderstood and criticized by uninformed Christian brothers and sisters.

Paradigms and Paradigm Shifting

How familiar are you with the concept of paradigm shifting? Even if the word *paradigm* is not an unfamiliar term for you, let's have business writer John Huey spell it out for us:

> A paradigm — in its business connotation — is simply the conventional wisdom about how things have always been done and must continue to be done. A paradigm shifter is someone who throws out the rules of the game and institutes radical, not incremental, change — a leader who foments revolution, not evolution. Typically, paradigm shifters come from outside, or on the fringes of, existing organizations or industries.[6]

The following words represent subsets of the paradigm concept, arranged on a continuum ranging from malleable to formidable. As you examine them, consider how each implies boundaries, rules, and regulations that would be necessary for reaching one's goals.

> Theory
> Model
> Methodology
> Principles
> Standards
> Protocol
> Routines
> Assumptions
> Conventions

Patterns
Habits
Common Sense
Conventional Wisdom
Traditions
Cultures
Mindset
Values[7]

A paradigm shift, then, is a radical retooling of how we behave and what we believe. When a paradigm shifts, just about everything that we know up to that point is replaced by a new and vivid perception of ourselves, even of the world around us. To ignore the paradigm shift for whatever reason is to no longer be a significant player in the new game. For when a shift happens, everything goes back to zero. It does not matter that you or your group used to call the shots or were once a force to be reckoned with. You have become a sad relic, suited for a place in a museum, not a place in people's futures.

Our world has been dramatically transformed by paradigm shifters, people who were able to see beyond the status quo, to imagine new ways of thinking and living: Christopher Columbus, Marie Curie, Albert Einstein, Susan B. Anthony, Martin Luther. Modern-day paradigm shifters are responsible for bringing us fast food eateries (Ray Kroc of McDonald's), twenty-four-hour television news (Ted Turner of Cable News Network), overnight package delivery (Fred Smith of Federal Express), and desktop computers (Steve Jobs of Apple Computers). People who refused to believe that there was no way to improve on something were the ones who dreamed up most of the conveniences that we take for granted. Because of this inquisitive and restless mindset, they were able to envision fresh, relevant models that were waiting to be discovered while their peers were blinded by the stubborn belief in their own paradigms. As Thomas Paine once aptly put it, "a long habit of not thinking a thing wrong gives it the superficial appearance of being right."

Do you know that our knowledge base doubles every seven years? That means that even if you are an expert in a particular discipline, in seven years you will know only half of what you need to know if you have not kept up. If we Christians are going to rise to the challenge of taking an unchanging gospel to an ever-changing world, we must dare to be paradigm shifters. Jesus was the ultimate paradigm shifter, redefining once and for all what the pearl of great value is. As the first missionary to the Gentiles, the apostle Paul too was a paradigm shifter, boldly reinterpreting physical circumcision and giving full status to Gentile believers. If we are serious about building fruitful ministries in the yet uncharted waters of the Sea of Inevitability, we must be willing to pay attention to our present surroundings. We must be prepared to become ministry paradigm shifters.

The word *paradigm* has been in common usage for some time. In the 1960s, then MIT professor Thomas Kuhn published a widely read book entitled *The Structure of Scientific Revolutions*. As Huey writes: "Kuhn used paradigm to describe archetypal scientific constructs such as Newton's laws of physics that define the way other scientists come to look at the world. Like a virus, the word spread far beyond science and came to mean any dominant idea."[8] Anne Wilson Schaef and Diane Fassel summed up his work:

> For Kuhn, a paradigm is a scientific theory, and it is more. A paradigm is a belief and explanation of observed phenomena that a specific community of people shares. It is what they believe about the way things are. A paradigm is both content (ideas) and process (method). A paradigm is a superstructure that is a way of explaining what has been observed.[9]

If paradigms are grids that we place on life in order that it seems to make sense to us, then Christianity is a paradigm. While it might be offensive to classify our sacred belief in Christ in this manner, objectively, someone who was without bias could argue that a religious person is anyone who has made a decision to believe in a particular spiritual paradigm. Thus, whether one believed in Jesus or Buddha or Krishna or no one, that belief in a system of thinking would then color one's experiences. A Christian might firmly believe something was a miracle while an atheist would believe just as resolutely that it was pure coincidence.

Paradigms are not limited to the realm of religions. Societies as a whole are subject to a priori ways of interpreting reality. However, as in every other facet of life, even societal paradigms can shift dramatically. When they do, everything in that society goes back to zero. No one can claim to be an expert anymore. Everyone must learn anew how to thrive in a new environment. American philosopher Eric Hoffer astutely noted that "in times of change, learners inherit the earth, while the learned find themselves beautifully equipped to deal with a world that no longer exists." If any of us hope to make any headway in reaching unconvinced Americanized Asian Americans for Christ, we must begin by coming to grips with a major societal paradigm shift that was born in the turmoil of the 1960s.

A Primer on Postmodernism

Civilization has experienced essentially three broad paradigms. The first is called premodernity, the second, modernity, and the current one, postmodernity. We must learn to adapt our ministry methods to this third one if we hope to reach the growing numbers of unconvinced Americanized Asian Americans.

During most of human history, people held what is called a premodern paradigm. They did not place a high degree of confidence in things like reason or knowledge because they lived during the centuries when supernaturalism and superstition held sway. In the absence of scientific thinking and tools, people turned to shamans, witch doctors, medicine men, and priests for explanations about life and the world. If a loved one fell ill, they were told that this was the result of a curse, a demon, or a pigeon staring cross-eyed at them. They had no way of knowing about the microscopic world of germs and bacteria. And their region's religious beliefs or superstitions dictated what people believed. In those days, anyone foolish enough to challenge the prevailing beliefs, to try and shift the dominant paradigm, would be branded a heretic and either excommunicated or executed. Still, we must remember that God sovereignly chose to send Jesus to earth during this premodern paradigm. In fact, the first sixteen hundred years of the church's history were couched in this epoch of spiritualism and mysticism. Even though there were church excesses and atrocities during this span, the Lord still managed to move Christ's body forward. The premodern era was thus not a God-forsaken one.

But the beginning of the end of that time was launched when people like Copernicus and Galileo began to redefine what we understood about the earth in relationship to the sun. It was during the seventeenth century that the paradigm began to shift. Inventions like the telescope and the emergence of the hard sciences (mathematics, physics, chemistry, biology, botany, etc.) ushered in a newfound optimism: If there were fundamental laws governing life in the universe, then no one would be subject any longer to the whims of the religious institutions. The emergence of science and the Age of Enlightenment, followed by the Renaissance, caused people to believe that one day there would be bomb-proof truth. People became enthralled and entranced with this paradigm shift into what is known today as modernity. Things could be explained reasonably, without the need for any shaping by a monk, a priest, the pope, or the Bible.

Obviously, this came as a threat to the religious powers that were. In the beginning of the shift to modernity in Europe, the church tried to use its considerable powers to threaten and censure the budding thinkers and scientists. They assumed that modernity was a God-forsaken paradigm, that since God began relating to them in premodern times, that the former was the only paradigm that God would bless. They were wrong. And eventually the church began to redefine faith in Christ as a rational pursuit, verified by fulfilled prophecies and apologetic arguments. Over the next three hundred or so years, the church talked more about systematic theology than supernatural miracles, repositioning itself in alignment with the paradigm shift to modernity.

Many believers today are oblivious to this evolutionary aspect of their faith. Surrounded by the fruits of the modern era, they assume that this highly rational approach to Christianity is not only the only way to be. They also assume that this scientific approach to matters of faith is traceable all the way back through Jesus and the patriarchs. They routinely study Scriptures through their literal, modernistic lenses, assuming that the authors of the Bible utilized the modern paradigm. Additionally, they consider the dawning of postmodernism a serious threat to the veracity and vitality of the church. In arming themselves against this latest paradigm shift, they are dooming themselves to be irrelevant relics in the days to come.

Modernism was supposed to be our salvation. Scientists and inventors were the new priestly caste, and science was the global religion. All of that new knowledge was supposed to make the world a safer and better place to live. But since the 1960s, people began to question whether this was ever going to happen. No cure for cancer had been found. Atoms had been split, but bombs became the by-product rather than pollution-free transportation. With dramatic increases in the speed of travel and communications, people also came to be aware of the vast complexity of this planet, of the myriad competing systems of thought. Thus, in the second half of the twentieth century, another societal paradigm shift occurred, introducing the era of postmodernism.

Coinciding with the eruption of the information age in the last quarter of the twentieth century, postmodernism's emergence was the inevitable reaction to modernism. Just as the prophets of modernity eventually exposed the ignorance of the priests of premodernity, the prophets of postmodernism are intensifying their scrutiny of the arrogance of all of modernity's priests. They pointedly ask, "How can you claim that truth is absolute when it is always filtered by the subjectivity of each purveyor? The 'facts' of history merely represent the biases of each historian. The 'deep knowledge' that science claims to possess merely points to greater and greater mysteries, not verities. And as for those who insist that their religion is true because their sacred writings say so, they must now concede that no one can come to that conclusion without first choosing to ignore the doubts that are always there. If something is good for you, fine. Just don't tell me that it has to be good for me, too." While postmodernism has ushered in unsettling values such as hypertolerance, relativism, and anti-institutionalism, it is also forcing us to reexamine the nature of grace, truth, and what Christ intends for the church.

Like each of the major societal paradigms, postmodernism is far from being perfect or Christ-centered. And, like either of its predecessors, an unexamined postmodernism also runs the risk of doing great

damage to society and the church. However, an increasing number of
us Christians believe that, if God's Spirit has thrived in the midst
of the ignorance of premodernity and the arrogance of modernity,
the Holy Spirit will also indwell the uncertainty of these postmodern
times. Far from being a God-forsaken threat to the foundations of the
Christian faith, postmodernism's challenges are God's way of calling the modernistic church to reclaim some of the essentials it has
lost. What are those challenges, and how might they cleanse and
strengthen the church? As we examine what it is going to take to reach
the twenty-first-century unconvinced Americanized Asian Americans,
you will appreciate why we must embrace this latest paradigm shift.

UNCONVINCED AMERICANIZED ASIAN AMERICANS IN THE TWENTY-FIRST CENTURY

Jesus promised that when we know the truth, truth will set us free.
From a Christian perspective, there is no greater truth than this: "For
God so loved the world that he gave his one and only Son, that whoever believes in him shall not perish but have eternal life. For God did
not send his Son into the world to condemn the world, but to save the
world through him. Whoever believes in him is not condemned, but
whoever does not believe stands condemned already because he has
not believed in the name of God's one and only Son" (John 3:16–18).
If we are going to reach the overwhelming numbers of postmodern
pagans in the first half of the twenty-first century with this eternal
truth, we must face another hard truth in the face of tremendous
resistance. Plenty of people are still clinging to the pillars of modernity, even though they are now riddled with fissures. In fact, it seems
that most evangelical Christians belong to conservative churches and
support conservative media outlets and politicians in order to protect
their modernistic versions of the faith and society. Nevertheless, I believe that Jesus is challenging a significant number of us to risk our
reputations and lay down our expertise so that we might pioneer ministries that can thrive within the new boundaries of postmodernism.
Without people today who are willing to step out in the radical spirit

of the apostle Paul, we should not think that we will reach twenty-first-century unconvinced Americanized Asian Americans with the Good News.

Would you recognize a twenty-first-century unconvinced Americanized Asian American if you met one? And if you did, would you be prepared to be and share the gospel with him or her that appealed to a postmodern mindset? Contrary to the modernistic evangelistic training that many of us received, we must not seem to be know-it-alls. Postmodern people are suspicious of people who think they have all the answers, especially if they are not willing first to understand what the questions are asking. It does not substantiate our arguments or positions by quoting numerous Bible passages to them, for many of them do not believe that the Bible is authoritative. Throwing more Scripture at them is only going to make matters worse.

The first truth a postmodern person responds to is you: who you are in relationship to him or her. Not too long ago, you could tell someone, "Look, you may think I'm arrogant or dogmatic. But that doesn't change the fact that the things I'm telling you are the truth, especially since I've recited Scripture to you. So you might want to write me off, but you still have to deal with the truth of my message." These days, however, a truly postmodern-wired person would respond, "If I think you're arrogant and obnoxious, then nothing you say has any validity to me. How could these things be true if you are that way? If you are an example of what happens when someone believes in Jesus, then that's the last thing I would want." This is a prime example of how God might be using the shift to postmodernism to reconnect the messenger with the message. Postmodern people need to encounter the Word become flesh in our flesh. They need to meet Jesus, not so much in what we describe to them but who we are in relationship to them. If they cannot deny that we have been a true person to them, then and only then will they give any credence to what we have to say.

It was Paul who said, "Be wise in the way you act toward outsiders; make the most of every opportunity. Let your conversation be always full of grace, seasoned with salt, so that you may know how to answer everyone" (Colossians 4:5–6). Chances are, you are not going to get to know any twenty-first-century unconvinced Americanized Asian

Americans by spending all your time with Christians or by trying to direct and control all of your conversations with them when you meet them. Seek them out where they are comfortable and where you are probably uneasy. Take a sincere interest in getting to know them and why they believe what they believe. And when it comes to answering them, admit you are biased and that you do not have all the answers.

Remember what matters most is that you are a true person, not someone who claims to know the truth. That means undergoing a rigorous self-examination prior to and during your encounters. When was the last time you questioned why it is you believe what you believe about God and life? If someone made a convincing case to you about the greater truth of his or her beliefs, would you be willing to change your beliefs? How can we expect these things of a twenty-first-century unconvinced Americanized Asian American if we are not willing to apply the same expectations to ourselves? They are not so concerned about the specific answers to these questions. What matters to them is that we are willing to pose them to ourselves, not just aim these questions at them. Five main areas define the typical twenty-first-century unconvinced AAA.

Culturally Concerned

"Christianity is for whites. How can I embrace Jesus if it means rejecting my own family, culture, and ancestral connections? And if you're right, why would I want to spend eternity with a bunch of white people I don't even know or care about? If there is a hell, I'd rather spend eternity there with people that I love. Christianity is only for Asian Americans who have deep self-hatred or who don't want to examine the core of their identity."

Before you try to respond to any of those piercing questions, ask yourself: How cut off am I from my ethnic and cultural identity? Do I have any cognitive dissonance where my Christian thinking separates me from all my nonbelieving and dead relatives? To what degree am I aware that my wholehearted embrace of Christianity might be a deliberate move on my part to quell my own self-hatred as an American of Asian ancestry?

When he was twenty years old, Edward Iwata borrowed fifteen hundred dollars from a friend and secretly underwent plastic surgery in order to look like a white person. As the surgeon was making suggestions about making changes to his face, he remembers what ultimately moved him to go through with the irreversible procedure.

> Why not? I had thought. Didn't I want to distance myself from the faceless, Asian masses? I hated the pale image in the mirror. I hated the slurs hurled at me that I couldn't shut out. I hated being a gook. A Nip. It's a taboo subject, but true. Many people of color have, at some point in their youths, imagined themselves as Caucasian, the Nordic or Western European ideal. Hop Sing meets Rock Hudson. Michael Jackson magically transformed into Robert Redford. For myself, an eye and nose job would bring me the gift of acceptance. The flick of a scalpel would buy me respect.[10]

Asian American self-hatred does not usually express itself through cosmetic surgery. Nevertheless, that same self-hatred subconsciously moves many of us to perform psychic surgery on ourselves as we strive for greater acceptance by the mainstream Euro-based culture in America. Oftentimes, in our efforts not to be different, so Asian, we do not see how our running away from who we are still dictates many of our attitudes and choices. Eric Liu, born to Chinese immigrants, helps us appreciate the surgical precision of self-inflicted psychic surgery.

> But I had already resolved not to be active in any Asians-only group. I thought then: I would never *choose* to be so pigeonholed.
>
> This allergic sensitivity to "pigeonholing" is one of the unhappy hallmarks of the banana mentality. What does the banana fear? That is, what did *I* fear? The possibility of being mistaken for someone more Chinese. The possibility of being known only, or even primarily, for being Asian. The possibility of being written off by whites as a self-segregating ethnic clumper. These were the threats — unseen and, frankly, unsubstantiated — that I felt I should keep at bay.
>
> I didn't avoid making Asian friends in college or working with Asian classmates; I simply never went out of my way to do so. This distinction seemed important — it marked, to my mind, the difference between self-hate and self-respect. That the two should have been so proximate in the first place never struck me as odd, or telling. Nor did it ever occur to me that the reasons I gave myself for disassociating with Asians as a group — that I didn't want to be part of a clique, that I didn't what to be absorbed and lose my individuality — were the very developments that marked my own assimilation. I didn't need that crutch . . . that crutch of

racial affinity. What's more, I was vaguely insulted by the presumption that I might.

...I resented the faintly sneering way that some whites regarded Asians as an undifferentiated mass. But whose sneer, really, did I resent more than my own?[11]

While it is probably true that most Asian Americans today are struggling with various degrees of self-loathing, it has been my experience thus far that many postmodern twenty-first-century AAAs have confronted this self-hatred by coming to celebrate their cultural and ethnic ties. Although they may not deliberately practice these things every day of their existence, they have found great meaning and worth in affirming this essential part of their identities. They probably took some courses in Asian American history in college. They are the ones most likely to be found working or volunteering in the Asian American community. Even though they could blend in quite readily to the predominant culture, they often choose to be outspoken advocates and activists on behalf of their fellow yellow brothers and sisters.

Evangelical Asian American Christians by and large are conspicuously absent from these arenas. We are more apt to be found serving the downtrodden in Mexico rather than in Little Saigon. As a group, we are rarely seen at political rallies or heard speaking out against injustices. This only serves to validate the contention of many twenty-first-century unconvinced AAAs that we are not only trying to run away from our roots but also trying to replace them with a grafted-on identity: American evangelicalism.

The 1970s saw a marked increase of Asian Americans on college campuses. As enrollment of Asian Americans tripled, there was a concomitant swelling of Asian Americans who participated in evangelical campus ministries such as Campus Crusade for Christ, InterVarsity Christian Fellowship, Navigators, and the Asian American Christian Fellowship. Nearly thirty years later, that trend has intensified. On some campuses, whether or not the chapters are set up to be Asian-specific, the vast majority of attendees are Asian Americans. For example, in 1999 the avowedly multi-ethnic IVCF chapter at University of California Berkeley had three hundred students involved, with 90 percent of these being Asian Americans. Could some of this be attributed to the aforementioned move to find a new identity in evangelicalism? In an essay written for UCLA's *Amerasia Journal* in 1996, Stanford professor Rudy Busto came to the following conclusions:

> Taking the theological call for Christians to be apart from the world (e.g., 1 John 2:15), or more generally, "chosen" one step further, it may be helpful to think about Asian American evangelicals as part of a larger Christian "people" or "incipient ethnicity." Conceptualizing evangelical Christianity as "ethnicity" may account for the curious disappearance of Asianness in the discourse and practices of Bible study groups organized, paradoxically, by and for specific Asian groups. Evangelicalism as a common religious ideology and culture shared by a diversity of students in large parachurch organizations seems to function like ethnicity in supporting and protecting otherwise stigmatized brothers and sisters from outside political tempests and negative stereotypes. In addition, Asian Americans benefit where evangelicalism overlaps and coincides with dominant American culture rendering them less foreign.[12]

Busto clearly asserted that he was not arguing that evangelicalism operates as a new or an alternative ethnicity for Asian American students. However, he made the suggestion that it might be doing this to provoke discussion. He warned that the parent parachurch organizations should take care not to add to these students' self-hatred by assuming that a multi-ethnic community has formed when in fact many of these students have come to escape a hated part of themselves. This is a perfect example of how some of us must retrain ourselves to think if we are going to be taken seriously by twenty-first-century unconvinced AAAs. For this purpose, what matters most is not that we come to some grand conclusion about the question of whether many Asian Americans become Christians to run away from their self-loathing. Rather, unconvinced people who are culturally concerned need to hear that Asian American Christians are also exploring issues tied to their particular culture and ethnicity.

Each of us, if we have not done this already, needs to explore our roots, to delve into our heritages. We need to struggle with what can and should be redeemed and what deserves to be jettisoned. The next time someone asks us why believing in Jesus doesn't make us feel cut off from our ancestors we must be comfortable giving a paradoxical answer. We must display enough honesty and humility to say, "You know, having grown up in a Christian family and having gone to church my whole life, that was simply never an issue for me. But given how you grew up surrounded by Asian culture and religion, I am starting to appreciate why that would be problematic for you. Hearing your pain raises new questions in my own heart and mind; I realize once more that I don't have it all figured out. I probably never will. Yet I still cling to my belief that Jesus is the only way."

Not long ago, an unconvinced Japanese American woman in her late fifties completed our ten-week course for seekers (QUEST; see chap. 6). She promised me that, though she was not a Christian, she would attend an investigative Bible study later that year. Before she could fulfill this vow to me, she came alongside her elderly mother, who was dying of cancer. That experience soured her interest in Christianity. "Ken, those last months at my mother's bedside, with my sister, were like a gift. She got to give us her blessing; we got to thank her for her many sacrifices on behalf of the family. I'll always cherish my memories of those times. But if I understand you correctly, my saying yes to Jesus is like simultaneously saying 'Go to hell' to the people that I love the most, some of whom are already dead. Bringing my mother's ashes back to the family plot in Japan also served to reinforce my Japanese identity for my daughter and myself. Because of all this, I am no longer coming to that Bible study. I don't want to ruin the wonderful memories of my mother's last months with us. Her dying peacefully is an enduring memory that I frankly don't want to jeopardize by embracing Christian doctrines that say she is lost to me forever."

Hypercritical of the Church

Surfing the Internet these days often underscores how harshly critical many secular people are of organized religion of any stripe. Here's a sample of what's on the World Wide Web for all to read:

> Y'all are nuts.
> You can call god George, or Ming, or Jose, or Pete, or cow, or Mork or anything else you want to. It really doesn't matter. God is quite simply god. God doesn't even need a name. It's humans who need a name for god.

All religions are wrong. They all descend from a system of belief and ritual and myth that evolved into another. Religion is the invention of humankind. God had nothing to do with religion. Humans invented religion, god simply is.

The problem with religion is that followers spend their life studying and propagandizing their religion. Much better to spend one's life pondering and pursuing god and the mysteries of life and the universe on a personal level rather than to continue to attempt finding meaning in dogma and doctrine.

There's the deity and there's the dogma. One has nothing to do with the other. A fact regularly dismissed in all these religion-related newsgroups.

Contrary to what you may believe, you won't know what happens next until you're dead. All else is speculation. I don't care what you believe, think or have been raised/told/forced to "know," you don't know jack until you get there.

Going on endlessly about one form of belief or another does nothing for humankind. Give your time and money to charity and good works. Something useful might actually happen and something good get done.

Have a nice night.   —Anonymous

Do you know anyone who shares this opinion of Christians and the church? I do. Since 1991, I've been going with a handful of members to a drug rehabilitation program for Asian Americans and others. Each month, we talk with this rough-looking bunch about how God's grace is an essential part of their ongoing recovery. Sometimes we do an inductive Bible study, and sometimes I take them through a relevant Christian book. Things between the staff and us are wonderful now, but it did not start out that way. They initially were suspicious of our motives, thinking probably that we were there to assuage our consciences for a while, then move on to something else. This attitude began to change as they monitored our early sessions and discovered that we were not there to push our agenda down people's throats but to partner in the unending battle to end substance abuse in our community.

Around the second year of our involvement, they invited me to accompany them to a national conference in Washington, D.C., on substance abuse issues in Asian/Pacific families. Talk about feeling like a fish out of water! There I was, out of my element, mingling with people who seemed to epitomize twenty-first-century unconvinced

Americanized Asian Americans. As soon as they spied the "Rev." in front of my name, they began to hammer me with criticisms about the Asian American evangelical church's turning a blind eye to the drug problems in our communities. "How can you people sit there, studying your Bibles and patting each other on the back, when drugs are ruining lives and destroying the fabric of our society? What good is a religion that teaches its people to bury their heads in the sand?" I soon realized that the best way to respond to these challenges was to confess that they had us dead to rights. Our complacency and self-absorption all these years were, in our terms, sin. We had been absent from the communities that spawned us. Now some of us were waking up to the need to join hands with others and make a difference beyond the walls of our churches. "Why else would I have come to this conference?" In a matter of seconds, the anger was wiped off their faces. They had heard a confession, not a lame excuse. And they could not deny that I was there with them.

"Dear children, let us not love with words or tongue but with actions and in truth" (1 John 3:18). Those words from John's pen are ones we especially need to take to heart. How are we, as churches, demonstrating Jesus' love with actions and in truth? Those who are activists in the various Asian American arenas, fighting against injustice and speaking out for the oppressed, are not impressed hearing of the quality of our church school program or that so many hundred people come to worship each week. They want to know how or if we are giving back to the community, not lavishing blessings on ourselves. I believe that Jesus wants to know the same things about us, too.

Since 1997, Evergreen Baptist Church of Los Angeles has continued to establish ministries that aim to serve the overlooked around us. We have forged a partnership with the local crisis pregnancy center, offering a support group and a supportive church family for single, unwed mothers who live in the vicinity. We have joined hands with Derek Perkins and the Harambee Family Center in one of the poorest, most crime-infested parts of our valley. We have launched an ongoing ministry to the divorced and widowed. We are involved in ministering to the dying at a local AIDS hospice. Lord willing, we hope to establish our own nonprofit community service center sometime in the future to further reach out to our neighbors with the love of Jesus. We are also serious about becoming more of a multi-Asian, multi-ethnic, multisocioeconomic, multigenerational church. Are we moving in this direction to make a good impression on those who are hypercritical of the church? No. We are doing this because Christ's love compels us. Slowly but surely, some of our worst critics are becoming some of our staunchest allies!

Totally Tolerant

"Christians are the most intolerant people on the planet. You're against gays. You're against a pregnant woman's right to choose. You're against affirmative action. You're against women in leadership. And you're against any other form of belief other than your own. You can't seem to live and let live, can you? There is no way that I would trade in my accepting spirit for such intolerance."

The Bible tells us that Jesus came to us from the Father, full of grace and truth (John 1:14). So what happened? Why is it that evangelical Christians in general stand accused of being graceless? One of the things that apparently has happened is our emphasis on truth first, rather than grace. As many American Asian churches recoil from the shift into postmodernism, the instinctive move is push truth more than grace. After all, if the message from outside the church is that there is no such thing as absolute truth, there is nothing more crucial than us asserting the truth of God's Word. As societal norms and standards continue to disappear under a giant cloud of supertolerance, the church should make clear how it still operates by a higher set of norms and standards. However, just as grace without truth promotes licentiousness, truth without grace promotes legalism. A healthy helping of God's grace can be like that spoonful of sugar that helps the medicine go down easier.

Even so, this characteristic of so many twenty-first-century unconvinced AAAs is begging to be confronted. Quite often, those who condemn Christians for being so intolerant of others smugly believe themselves to be superior moral beings due to their high degree of tolerance. I never tire of pointing out to them that no one should get credit for being tolerant of people who share their own beliefs and values. In fact, tolerance is in play only when we are faced with those whose beliefs and values are repugnant to us. Thus, if they deem themselves to be so tolerant, why is it that they cannot tolerate some of us Christians? Making them face their glaring inconsistency will not necessarily cause them to open their hearts to Jesus. However, I think it's important for them to admit that they are not as tolerant as they claim. The difference between them and us is that Christ calls us to be graciously intolerant. In other words, no gloating allowed.

Radically Relativistic

"There are no absolutes. Everything is relative. One truth is just as good as another."

This characteristic of twenty-first-century unconvinced Americanized Asian Americans also comes with a built-in logical inconsistency, one that they often fail to see on their own. Do you know what it is? Go back and read their belief statement. Now do you get it? It is not possible that there are no absolutes and that everything is relative, because that statement itself is making an absolute claim. If one truth is as good as another, then why should anyone believe in that very statement? As gently as possible, I point out to them that if what they believe is absolutely true, they would never be able to state it. For nothing is supposed to be absolutely true, not even the belief that everything is relative!

That being said, in light of the postmodern shift that has taken place, we must be willing to die to our obsession with the bomb-proof certainty of truth. Christian futurist Mike Regele spelled it out when he wrote:

> The side of the church that has tied its future to absolutism will continue to paint itself, and those who follow it, into a corner. . . . In a world in which the field of knowledge doubles every eighteen months, the potential for a new info-bomb to reorder our basic assumptions — our paradigm of reality — is great and to be expected. A rigid commitment to an unassailable worldview, such as is typically the case in more conservative circles, increasingly runs the risk of shattering all faith — needlessly. We believe that the future lies in abandoning

modernist foundationalism and adopting an epistemological position based on the principle of unsurpassability — and in learning to live with relative confidence and a certain level of faithful agnosticism.

[This] is not the same as wishy-washy relativism.... Rather, it is the best form of certainty we can expect in a universe that we increasingly recognize is infinitely more complex than would have been thought in earlier times. If we expect people of intellectual integrity to find a place in the community of faith, we must pursue this course. Without this position, the schism between science and faith will grow ever wider, and many people of faith will fall into the widening gap.[13]

With so many twenty-first-century unconvinced AAAs having science backgrounds, we would do well to heed Regele's counsel. Are you ready to be faithfully agnostic?

Primarily Pluralistic

"The world is filled with spiritual options. All paths lead to God."

Not too long ago, a person could live and die in this country without ever crossing paths with a Buddhist or a Muslim. Nowadays, the person in the carrel next to you is wearing a turban, and some of your children's best friends are Buddhist or Hindu. Now that people are befriending persons from other religious backgrounds, it has become much more difficult to dismiss their non-Christian faiths out of hand. You know these adherents to be real people with similar values and aspirations for their loved ones and the world. Thus, it should come as no surprise that many Americans today, including our twenty-first-century unconvinced Americanized Asian Americans, hold to a pluralistic view of the world's religions, one that flies in the face of Jesus' claim that no one gets to the Father except through him (John 14:6).

For most of my Christian life, I used to be skilled at picking apart somebody else's religion. Not that my successful efforts ever resulted in any instant conversions. But what mattered to me was that Christianity always came out on top. Then, several years ago, I happened to be in a small group with a fellow who had a master's degree in Zen Buddhism and a doctoral degree in clinical psychology. That didn't faze me. I proceeded to tell the group what Buddhists believe. That's when he politely interrupted me. "Buddhists don't all believe the same things. There are several schools of Buddhism. I'm so tired of Christians talking as if they know what we believe when they don't. Where did you get this information? Have you read our sacred documents? I've read the entire Bible and Barth's *Church Dogmatics* in order to understand your religion." I had nowhere to hide, so I confessed to him that I was not aware that there were various schools of Buddhism. I also admitted that I had never read a Buddhist text; my information came from a little Christian paperback, written years before, that criticized the other major religions in the world. Then I said to him, "Okay, I'm all ears. Please teach me why Zen Buddhism has proved to be so meaningful for you." As of this writing, he still practices Zen, and I am still a born-again believer. But we have become good friends in the process of learning from each other.

I doubt that any of us researched all the religions before settling on Christianity. I know that I did not. I was brought to the local Chinese American Baptist church while I was still a toddler. So when I am confronted with people from other faiths these days, I tell them that I cannot say that I became a Christian because, after testing all religions, I was convinced that this was the only possible way to find peace, purpose, and salvation. And frankly, I am not interested in doing that research now because I am truly settled and satisfied with my faith in Christ. As far as all paths leading to God, I must first contend that all stories are not equally valid. If, for example, there were a religion that taught that all children born on Tuesdays must be sacrificed to appease their gods, I do not think that many of us, Christian or otherwise, would merely smile and say, "Whatever you believe is fine with me." To say that all stories are the same is not to listen closely to what each story is saying. Christianity does not teach exactly the same things as does Islam or Buddhism. If they all were the same, they would all be one big religion. Pluralism disrespects the unique histories and teachings of the world's religions.

After having said that, I would then admit that, given my lack of experience with all religions and given my finite mind and Christian bias, I do not know for certain how God is going to treat devout people of other faiths. I believe that Jesus is the only way to God, but I also trust Jesus to know the score when it comes to other religions, and I trust him to make the right call. Here again is where Regele's call to faithful agnosticism comes into play. While this may not be strong enough for some of you, all I can say is that taking this approach has resulted in a greater openness to knowing more about Jesus. As my Zen Buddhist friend said to me, "This is the first time a Christian ever asked me to teach him something about Buddhism. What kind of Christianity allows you to ask me about my faith?" I replied, "The kind that is centered in Jesus."

Obviously, the preceding characteristics are not unique to twenty-first-century unconvinced Americanized Asian Americans. Most of them apply to a good number from the baby boom generation and describe most of the Gen-Xers. All this tells us is that, in reaching out to twenty-first-century unconvinced AAAs, we also have the potential to reach many others who need to be convinced that knowing Jesus has not stripped us of our humanity.

THINGS TO THINK ABOUT

1. How clearly do you see evidence of the paradigm shift from modernism to postmodernism? In society? In school? In yourself?

2. Given the description of twenty-first-century unconvinced Americanized Asian Americans, do you still believe that your current ministry or church can successfully reach them without learning to embrace what is healthy about postmodernism? Explain.

3. Where can you find twenty-first-century unconvinced AAAs in your vicinity? How willing are you to become a part of their world first? How comfortable do you think you will be dialoguing with them about spiritual things or the validity of your church?

4. When Paul risked shifting the paradigm in order to reach Gentiles, he came under fire from the traditionalists. If you venture down this road of radical matching, what kind of criticisms do you think will be aimed at you? How will you deal with them?

*Chapter
Six*

A SHARED PURSUIT
OF THE PEARL

The idea of an "evangelistic program" would not even have made sense to the New Testament Christians. "Evangelism" was the gospel message simply overflowing from their adventure with Christ and each other. They were announcing the kingdom of God as they were in the midst of living in it.
— KEITH MILLER[1]

A THEOLOGY OF EVANGELISM

Establishing significant relationships and engaging in meaningful dialogue should be part of everything that we do in the name of Christ. Otherwise, we will end up treating unconvinced people as souls to win rather than fellow seekers of food for the soul. The area of evangelism is no exception to this principle.

Before revealing what an informed approach to evangelism to unconvinced Americanized Asian Americans might look like, we must define the theology behind the approach, since evangelism itself is such a crucial element of proliferating Asian American ministries.

There is a rising consensus among Christian leaders that evangelism must become a top priority for the modern church. Much concern has been expressed over the drastic reduction in the number of people in the world who take Christianity seriously. Many of the churches in Europe are lifeless and insipid. The media delight in focusing on the church's rogues and feuds instead of on its saints and how it is saving and salvaging lives. In the United States, the majority of citizens identify themselves as Christians, yet closer inspection reveals these so-called believers to be more akin to assenters. In summarizing a recent poll conducted by his organization, George Gallup Jr., stated some of his conclusions:

> We boast Christianity as our faith, but many of us have not bothered to learn the basic biblical facts of this religion. Many of us dutifully attend church, but this act appears to have made us no less likely than our unchurched brethren to engage in unethical behavior.
>
> We say we are Christians, but sometimes we do not show much love toward those who do not share our particular religious perspective. We say we rejoice in the good news that Jesus brought, but we are often strangely reluctant to share the gospel with others. In a typical day the average person stays in front of the TV set nearly 25 times longer than in prayer.[2]

Faced with such a banal brand of spiritual commitment, Christian leaders from all points on the theological spectrum have been showing a renewed interest in evangelism.

Whether or not this ongoing zeal for evangelism is rooted in a rejuvenated commitment to the Great Commission's mandate or the fear of seeing one's favorite denomination or church go the way of the dodo bird is not pertinent to our purposes. What is of concern is that so many of the resulting programs and practices, in my opinion, are not grounded in a clear theology of evangelism. The primary focus is on running evangelistic programs before there is much understanding of what evangelism is. There has been an explosion of programs and procedures without a clear theology of evangelism to inform them.

In his seminal work entitled *The Logic of Evangelism*, William J. Abraham goes through a lengthy process to generate just such a theology. Those interested in his treatment of this subject should read the book. For our purposes we will outline his resulting theology of evangelism.

Abraham believes the Bible teaches that evangelism is intimately related to an eschatology that is grounded in a vision of the present and coming kingdom of God. He writes that

> eschatology is a vision of the coming of the kingdom of God that was initiated in Jesus of Nazareth, was experienced and cherished by the community that arose after his death and resurrection, and is now within the grasp of those who will repent and receive the gift of the Holy Spirit; yet it remains to come in all its glory and fullness. If this vision

is correct then there is good news for the world; there is indeed a gospel worth sharing. Moreover, evangelism is an activity of the followers of Jesus that should be rooted and grounded in this dynamic, mysterious, numinous reality of the rule of God in history.... Evangelism is at the very least a continuation of vital elements in the work of the early apostles, prophets, and martyrs who found themselves dramatically caught up in the reign of God in the world.[3]

So whatever evangelism is, it must be rooted in a belief in the continuing rule of God. Based on this conviction, Abraham maintains that evangelism should be construed as

that set of intentional activities which is governed by the goal of initiating people into the kingdom of God for the first time.... To initiate someone into the kingdom of God is to admit that person into the eschatological rule of God through appropriate instruction, experiences, rites, and forms.[4]

This concept of evangelism as "initiating someone into the kingdom of God" is valuable if only for the fact that it incorporates the three prevalent understandings of evangelism and their subsidiaries.

Converting people to Christianity. This is popularly known as "winning souls." After being presented with the facts of the gospel, the unbeliever is prompted to ask Jesus to be his or her Lord and Savior and to invite the Holy Spirit to dwell in his or her heart. The belief is that so long as the person has made a confession of faith, he or she is saved, completely forgiven of sin and destined to go to heaven after death. Whether that person ever becomes a regular worshiper or displays the evidence of a life under Christ's lordship is secondary, if not optional.

Witnessing to nonbelievers about their need for Christ. What is stressed is the one-to-one sharing of one's testimony with an unbeliever. This is related to the definition of evangelism that emphasizes proclaiming the gospel to nonbelievers through Christian tracts and Scripture verses. The hope is to convict people of sin and a need for forgiveness, but success is not measured in numbers of conversions. Rather, it is a matter of proclaiming the gospel to as many nonbelievers as possible. Once they have heard it, they are then accountable to God.

This second major definition, though also emphasizing verbal sharing of one's faith, places more of an emphasis on describing one's personal experiences with faith in Christ than on Christian doctrine. Here again, the attitude is that those who have heard the personal testimonies of Christians have been evangelized.

Another variation is to broaden the concept of witness to embrace anything done to bear witness. Instead of the verbal sharing of one's faith, acts of compassion are stressed. This definition is popular with Christians who feel called to be more direct in changing society. Consistent with the other witness definitions, proponents of this definition also believe that those who have been given food, shelter, justice, and so forth have been evangelized.

Transforming nonbelievers into faithful followers of Jesus Christ. Reacting in large part to the first definition's apparent lack of concern for the maturing of new believers' faith, some have argued that the essence of evangelism is found in teaching converts to be faithful followers of Christ. To fail to nurture and train these babes in the Lord is to be responsible for countless people who are spiritually stillborn. The belief is that someone has not been evangelized until he or she has been discipled to the point where he or she can lead another person to Christ and then do the discipling.[5]

Though each of these concepts derives from a belief in the reign of God and as such has validity, each fails to capture the larger dimensions of life lived in that kingdom due to focusing only on individual aspects of it. The concept of evangelism being that set of activities that initiates someone into that kingdom is much more inclusive. "To be initiated into the rule of God is to encounter a transcendent reality that has entered history and to find oneself drawn up into the ultimate purposes of God for history and creation."[6]

Responsible application of this theological concept should result in believers who personally embrace their faith in the triune God, the gathered fellowship of believers, the historical Christian propositions about themselves and God, a particular moral vision based on the two greatest commandments (Matthew 22:37–40), the spiritual gifts and capacities given to them for acts of ministry and service, and the primary spiritual disciplines that are necessary for them to keep their faith in Christ alive until the end. As Abraham concluded:

> In all, initiation involves a complex web of reality that is at once corporate, cognitive, moral, experiential, operational, and disciplinary. Initiation into the kingdom of God is not only one of these; nor is it all of these strung together as a mere human enterprise driven simply by earthly passion and planning; it is all of these set and bounded within the dramatic action of God that is manifest in Christ and fueled by the Holy Spirit.[7]

Therefore, when we state that our goal is to enable more unconvinced AAAs to become Christians, what we have in mind is far more expansive than leading them in the Sinner's Prayer and leaving it at that. Instead, we hope to initiate them into the lifelong pursuit of the pearl of great price.

GRADUAL EVANGELISM

An engaging Bible study would be to reread the Synoptic Gospels, tracing the gradual process of initiation that the Twelve experienced as they followed Jesus. Contrary to the instant-conversion spin that Western-cultured people like to put on their testimonies, the disciples continued to grope for more faith the entire time they were with Jesus.

While it is true that they had accepted Jesus' invitation to become fishers of people, the record shows that the disciples did not become experts overnight. Being born again did not mean that they became instantly mature in their faith; they literally experienced a new beginning. They had to start growing up all over again, this time into a new life with Jesus as their Lord and Savior. It was a gradual process.

The recapturing of this integral fact of the Twelve's spiritual development provides ample validation for our approach to evangelizing today's increasing numbers of unconvinced AAAs. In general, unconvinced AAAs have retained the fairly ubiquitous Asian value of taking a long time to make important decisions. Any decision that will have long-term consequences for you and your family needs to be made soberly and wisely. So when it comes time to buy a new car or refrigerator, the head of the clan starts doing research months before the anticipated purchase date. He or she studies the consumer magazines, reading the reviews of competing products. Once the choice has been narrowed down to just a few, the responsible family member then may interview his or her relatives and friends to get their opinions, especially if they have purchased that same item recently. Are they happy with it? Would they buy it again, knowing what they do now? Finally, she or he looks for the store that will sell this quality item at the lowest price. (Admittedly, this last element may be more important to some than others.) Even if some in that family do not agree with the final decision, at least they cannot accuse that clan leader of being irresponsible, since she or he went through such a thorough process of deliberation.

If unconvinced AAAs take a long time to make important decisions, it must seem to them that we Christians are contradicting ourselves when we say things like, "Becoming a Christian is the most important commitment you will ever make — it may even end up costing you your life! Now take ten minutes to go through this little pamphlet with me, and then I want to lead you in a prayer of confession and commitment."

This approach is entirely too confrontational for many people with Asian backgrounds, especially the Japanese. Many times, unconvinced AAAs will secretly resent the person posing such a direct challenge to them, for in most Asian cultures, direct confrontation is avoided at all costs because of the inherent risk of unnecessarily obligating someone and/or causing another to lose face. Those are grave social errors. Even worse, to any thoughtful person, unconvinced AAA or not, what we are saying is that this commitment must not be that critical if it can be made without serious deliberation.

This high-pressure approach to witnessing is not only culturally offensive to unconvinced AAAs but flies in the face of Christ's own instructions to count the cost carefully before following him (Luke 14:25–33). Everyone who enters into this new endeavor should plan on completing it, being able to echo Paul's own words as he neared the end of his earthly life: "For I am already being poured out like a drink offering, and the time has come for my departure. I have fought the good fight, I have finished the race, I have kept the faith. Now there is in store for me the crown of righteousness, which the Lord, the righteous Judge, will award to me on that day — and not only to me, but also to all who have longed for his appearing" (2 Timothy 4:6–8).

Is the choice to start this fight, enter this race, and embrace this faith merely an initiation into a lifelong process of initiations, a continuous attempt to recover the wholeness and oneness that God originally created for us all in the garden? If it is, then at least two obvious ramifications emanate from this perspective.

First, we must admit to ourselves and to those we are trying to reach that what Christ is asking of us is not easy. I have spoken to myriad unconvinced AAAs who are mystified and somewhat intimidated by the apparent doubt-free faith that so many Christians profess to have acquired so quickly and easily. How can it be so simple to make such a revolutionary switch? How does one go from not believing in an invisible God to believing unequivocally in mere minutes? Obviously, it cannot be that quick or simple. But that is the predominant impression we give. And it is the wrong one.

At Evergreen Baptist Church of Los Angeles, God has been teaching us to present faith for what it really is: a risky venture, going out on a limb and not on fact. Come to think of it, it is something that fits much more naturally with postmodernism than with modernity. In appreciation of this, we have been trying to emulate the refreshing attitude of Frederick Buechner, who provides us with this fresh perspective on faith and doubts:

> Faith is better understood as a verb than as a noun, as a process than as a possession. It is on-again-off-again rather than once-and-for-all. Faith is not being sure where you're going but going anyway. A journey without maps. Tillich said that doubt isn't the opposite of faith; it is an element of faith.
>
> Whether your faith is that there is a God or that there is not a God, if you don't have any doubts you are either kidding yourself or asleep. Doubts are the ants in the pants of faith. They keep it awake and moving.[8]

With this in mind, our evangelism program is not a program per se but an informed approach that guides many different aspects of our ministry. Leading the way in promoting our church's "Love God, Love

People" mission motto, each of our four ministry councils is constantly striving to make the church community more inviting and embracing. We want the unconvinced and the overlooked to feel that this is a place where all are welcome and everyone is encouraged to wrestle with spiritual matters.

There have been some highly effective changes made in the areas of preaching and worship, but these will be elaborated on in the next two chapters. Christians of different ages and at various stages in their faith development usually share their stories during the services at least once each month. They are instructed to spend the bulk of their seven minutes revealing how the Lord has become more real to them lately without making it all sound unduly simplified or pain-free. In this way, unconvinced AAAs and the rest of us are exposed to the incarnation at work in different individuals, none of whom are claiming that believing in God has won them all the raises and solved all their problems. We hope that more unconvinced Americanized Asian Americans began to appreciate that these are ordinary people pursuing an extraordinary God.

For a change, these are more likely to be people to whom they can relate — people who have surrendered to Christ but who admit to having a long way to go yet. Putting one's faith in Christ is portrayed as being inherently paradoxical: easy but not simple. As one writer so aptly put it:

> Dying to self is not a thing we do once and for all. There may be an initial dying when God first shows these things, but ever after, it will be a constant dying, for only so can the Lord Jesus be revealed constantly through us. All day long the choice will be before us in a thousand ways.[9]

If unconvinced AAAs feel overwhelmed by the prospect of making such a critical commitment based fundamentally on faith, we let them know that that is how they should feel, for faith involves risk. Yet we all — convicted and unconvinced together — must still make commitments based on faith.

Everyone is afraid of making mistakes. No one wants to get hurt, and yet millions still choose to get married each year, in spite of the divorce rates being what they are. Why? Because there will always be people who correctly surmise that they will miss out on the potential for growth and joy if they fail to make certain critical commitments. And what is true for marriage is also true for the marriage to Christ. Those willing to take that scary step of commitment are embarking on a new path of growth and change. It takes enough faith to make that initial commitment to open the way to a beautiful new relationship.

The second ramification stemming from this approach to evangelism as initiation is that we should be more generous in our attitude toward others who are seeking for the truth but who have yet to make a confession of faith. Somehow, using only "Christian" and "non-Christian" to describe everyone now feels not only limiting but also arrogant at times. How would we like it if our Hindu or Buddhist friends started referring to us all the time as "non-Hindus" or "non-believers" because we do not happen to share their beliefs? Yet we do it all the time without a second thought. To many postmodern unconvinced people, we Christians have the annoying habit of reclassifying everyone else in the world according to our particular convictions. That is why Evergreen-LA has taken to referring in print to people who do not share our faith in Jesus as the unconvinced. This is much less disparaging and puts the onus on the shoulders of those of us who perhaps need to be more convincing examples of followers of Jesus!

It is far too common for us to be perceived as Pharisees, confidently categorizing everyone in the world into two groups, those in the kingdom of God and those outside it. Yet so many of the people that the self-righteous Pharisees judged to be "out" were closer to the kingdom than they were.

Jesus was not fooled. He allowed those who were truly seeking him to draw near to him, regardless of their appearance or reputations. He treated them as children of God. As for the Pharisees, he let them know what he thought of their "holier-than-most" attitude when he called them whitewashed tombs (Matthew 23:27–28). Obviously, they were making some grave errors in their assessment of the spirituality of people outside of their tight religious circle of friends.

Bounded Sets, Centered Set

We are much too quick to write off those who are surreptitiously seeking spiritual truths. One of the best ways to illustrate this is found in figure 6.1.[10] Our all-too-common tendency to be overly exclusive is represented by the collection of circles on the left. Each of the circles is called a bounded set and represents a different Christian coterie, be it a local church, a denomination, a sect, or a parachurch organization. Each bounded set insists that "certain minimal essentials provide a clear boundary between those who are on the inside and those who are on the outside. . . . Within a bounded set there is no room for growth and change."[11]

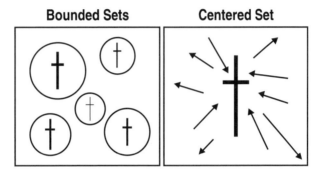

Figure 6.1
Bounded Sets versus Centered Set

Let us say that Person A wants to join Bounded Set X. Within a relatively short time, it becomes clear to Person A that she must not wear lipstick, not speak in tongues, read only the King James Version of the Bible, and submit to all men in order to join Bounded Set X. This is not to her liking, so Person A decides to check out another group of Christians called Bounded Set Z. She discovers that this bounded set is much more liberal than the other, so she decides to stay, glad that she has finally found a bounded set that is "doing what the Bible says."

In this example, the members of both bounded sets have established their boundaries based on their personal and corporate convictions. Given this, it is only natural to exclude those who fall outside of a group's particular boundaries. The obvious drawback of this system is that people are far too easily convinced that their bounded set is the most genuinely Christian one, while all the rest are seen as suspect.

In our example, all of this sorting involved people who were already card-carrying Christians. If Christians already have the habit of excluding other Christians, it takes no imagination to see how unconvinced people who are sincerely searching out spiritual matters would be left out. This is where the other system of categorization shown in figure 6.1 proves to be of inestimable value.

This alternative set puts its emphasis on its center instead of the boundaries. Thus, although it has parameters, it is referred to as the centered set. As in the bounded sets, Christ is also placed in the center. But the difference is that the most important criterion is a person's orientation to Jesus. The question now being asked is whether someone is moving toward Jesus or away from him. The arrows depict this.

While this alternative way of understanding people is not without its own flaws,[12] its primary value is that "it takes the focus away from the boundaries and relocates it in the relation between the [seeker] and center; and it allows plenty of room for movement and growth."[13]

We have discovered that it is not only helpful but also accurate to refer to newcomers who are not professing Christians as "people on their way to God." Most of them would not be making the effort to come to the weekly services, classes, or studies if they were not in search of spiritual truth. Taking more of the centered-set approach, we have experimented since 1982 with meeting seekers where they are.

Centered-Set Approaches to Evangelism

In the early 1980s I attempted to design a course that would appeal to unconvinced persons wanting to know more about how Christianity works. Calling it "Nuts and Bolts," I made sure that it was held during the church school hour so that it would be convenient for those already coming to one of the worship services. It ran for ten weeks and addressed such topics as "How Do You Explain Miracles?" "What About Creation and Evolution?" "Is It Wrong to Be Rich?" "Does Prayer Change Anything?" and "Where in the World Are Heaven and Hell?" These topics were selected because they were some of the most frequently asked questions. And they tended to deal with subjects that many of us Christians try to gloss over too quickly.

We promoted the course with a catchy brochure and encouraged our members to invite their curious family members and friends to attend. Since the enrollment in adult church school had been seriously depressed for the past four or five years, we figured that 35 to 50 students would be a generous projection. I will never forget that first day of class, when almost 120 people showed up! Many of these were members who had always wanted to raise these questions, but at least 20 percent were people on their way to God.

During the several years that we offered "Nuts and Bolts," approximately 250 people took this annual class, with an increasing proportion of the students being unconvinced AAAs who were looking for a way to believe in the God of the Bible. We appreciate the "Nuts and Bolts" class for what it proved to be: a forerunner of more refinements to the gradual initiation process of evangelism, allowing people the time and breathing room to explore different aspects of the Christian faith. Although no statistics were kept, the general sense is that this class played an important part in helping many curious, unconvinced AAAs eventually confirm their faith in Christ. There were always those who were not quite there yet, but we affirmed for them that this did not mean that they were nowhere. We encouraged them to stay focused on Jesus and to keep coming to church, doubts and all. We could still seek him together.

Although "Nuts and Bolts" dealt with some arresting questions, given its large-group format, it was not the place to investigate some of the more rudimentary elements of the Christian faith. For that reason a cadre of us then designed an experience called BASICS that was launched in January 1991. Since we still believed that unconvinced AAAs require opportunities to give serious consideration to the sundry aspects of Christianity, this course was designed to expose them to a variety of those.

The BASICS trainers teamed up each for one quarter each year to guide a class of no more than fifty students in a ten-week study of M. Scott Peck's little-known book, *What Return Can I Make? Dimensions of the Christian Experience*. It was felt that Peck's material would be the perfect catalyst for a group wanting to examine the process of coming to faith in Christ. Peck's having experienced this as a

reflective adult made his writings seem so appropriate for meeting unconvinced AAAs where they were. He brought a refreshing openness
and sensitivity to some of the basic issues of faith. For example, in
describing what it was like to warm up to the notion of believing in
Jesus, Peck — a noted psychiatrist — initially feared that he might be
going insane. How else might someone in his profession describe the
subjective sensation of having more and more intimate conversations
with Jesus? Why wouldn't he find it quite disturbing to hear himself
tell others that he now had a relationship with a man who had been
dead for twenty centuries? He wrote: "I wondered if I was not losing
my mind."[14]

How many times have you heard of discovering faith in Christ de-
scribed as the fear of going insane? That may sound quite odd or
ominous to someone raised in the modernistic Christian church, but
to those who were not and especially to those with a postmodern
mindset, this has a certain ring of authenticity to it. We believed that
people on their way to God, especially unconvinced AAAs, would be
able to relate quite well with someone who maintained that,

> while there is only one Lord, each of us must approach Him and be
> approached by Him through the context of our own utterly unique
> individual limitations, gifts, and experience.
>
> ...It was the contemplation of my unique experience over the years
> which led me to conclude for myself that Christian doctrine was not a
> collection of imagined fables and wishful thinking, but the most pen-
> etratingly accurate approach I know to the way things really are. Ever
> so gradually and against virtually all of my intellectual instincts, I came
> through reflection on the particular happenings of my life to personally
> discover the incredibly wonderful Judeo-Christian God of Presence — a
> God who is actively present, every minute, in the here and now — a
> very active, living, and suffering God, who personally loves me and all
> His creatures. And — as if that were not enough — even more slowly it
> began to dawn on me that this marvelous God was indeed inextricably
> interwoven with the human Jesus.[15]

Each member of the class was given Peck's materials to read as
homework, along with journaling materials and appropriate Bible
verses already printed out for them. Everyone would congregate once
a week at the church, where the BASICS trainers enabled the class

members to share their reflections in set small groups. The areas that we addressed were conversion, grace, Jesus, guilt, faith, worship, communion, wisdom, the Holy Spirit, sacrifice, vulnerability, and, in response to all that God has already given us, what return we can make to God (hence the book's title).

The BASICS course, based solely on Peck's book, reinforced an earlier hunch, that is, that many churched Christians were aching to delve deeper into the philosophical underpinnings of their faith and were able companions to the unconvinced on this search. Quite often, as educated, life-weary adults, they were longing to upgrade their theological software from the second-grade church school version they had secretly outgrown. Bringing those two groups of seekers together often created a marvelous synergy, fueled by their shared earnestness and honesty. God seemed to create a close-knit community out of strangers each time we gathered in our shared pursuit of the pearl of great value.

By 1993 BASICS had evolved. Still driven by the vision to create a nonconfrontational, grace-based, centered-set evangelistic community, we retooled what was BASICS and renamed it QUEST. Keeping the ten-week format, we compiled a workbook filled with provocative excerpts from an eclectic assortment of Christian sources, such as R. C. Sproul, Anthony Campolo, Daniel Taylor, M. Scott Peck, and Mike Yaconelli. Billed as "ten weeks that will change the way you see God forever," QUEST continues as of this writing to be what author George Barna called Socratic evangelism. It is not a Bible study, but Scripture is used. It is not a course on apologetics, and it is not where someone with questions is going to find all the answers. Rather, QUEST is good conversation, a guided tour of not only the philosophical elements of faith in Jesus but also of how the Christian life is lived.

More than anything, QUEST teaches everyone, both Christian and unconvinced, how Jesus often quietly shows up whenever those few gathered have mutual respect and love for one another. God's Spirit has captured so many hearts during those ten weeks of tender-hearted and open-minded discussions because people experience a semblance of Jesus' unconditional love and acceptance. Many of the graduates now regularly attend church; a good number have been baptized, while some now serve as QUEST facilitators. Because they were able to experience firsthand what God's love for them feels like through others, most of those who were once unconvinced are now committed Christians.

While it remains to be seen how effective this gentle process of initiation and exploration will be, what you should remember is that all this grew out of the awareness that God is already at work in many peoples' lives, long before they ever profess faith in Christ. The key the Lord has taught us is that everyone deserves to be treated with dignity. "Everybody has worth to God, and from their God-given worth comes their dignity.... The failure to give dignity to those whom the gospel addresses will cut us off from society and lay waste our proclamation."[16]

Too many programs or approaches do not afford the unconvinced much dignity, because they do not allow them enough room to let a relationship with Christ emerge gradually and naturally. In many such cases, a person is invited to attend an evangelistic service or is guided through a gospel tract, only to be challenged to make an immediate commitment to Christ. That is like being asked out on a blind date, only to have your date make a proposal of marriage by the evening's end. You may be open to marrying the person some day, but if you are like most people, you require more time before you are ready to make that kind of long-term commitment.

That is why we at Evergreen-LA refer to what we have been doing as gradual evangelism. We feel that there is no need to pressure unconvinced AAAs into choosing to believe in Christ. That is something between the Lord and them. We are here, rather like spiritual go-betweens, trying to arrange dates between two parties that we think would be great together. In some cases, it is like love at first sight, while in others the bond of love comes only after many fights and frustrating moments. Whatever the case may be, we want to be there for them, adding the wisdom that can come only from having been through this ourselves. This commitment is not only for the courtship but also for the strengthening and deepening of the commitment after it has been made.

In this sense, evangelism and discipleship for unconvinced AAAs are almost indistinguishable from one another in our gradual approach to kingdom initiation. Like the Twelve who went before them, these people at some point are already disciples: ignorant, yes; fallible, yes; rebellious, yes; but nevertheless pursuers of Jesus long before their faith has matured. So another way to describe this approach to evangelism is to say that it is the discipling of people on their way to God.

Even as we have seen a positive response to this approach, we also know that methods, no matter how inspired or culturally informed, are not magic. Only the Lord knows why some people are ready for a committed relationship with God and others are not. As sad as it is, we must be prepared for some of those in whom we have invested a great deal of love and life to be unable to confirm their faith in Christ. Like the rich young ruler, they will have pursued Christ up to a point and then, realizing what this will end up costing them, turn and walk away from him.

But Vincent Donovan reminds us that the potential for rejection must be a part of the gospel presentation if the acceptance of Christ is truly going to mean something.

> Perhaps the most important lesson I was ever to learn in my missionary life, I learned that day: that Christianity, by its very essence, is a message that can be accepted — or rejected; that somewhere close to the heart of Christianity lies that terrible and mysterious possibility of rejection; that no Christianity has any meaning or value, if there is not freedom to accept it or reject it. . . . It must be presented in such a way that rejection of it remains a distinct possibility. The acceptance of it would be meaningless if rejection were not possible. It is a call, an invitation, a challenge even, that can always be refused.[17]

Gradual evangelism is not about coercion, manipulation, or even, to some degree, persuasion. It is the presentation and demonstration of the truth we claim to possess and the love we contend that has come to possess us. More than anything else, it is people who have long been searching for peace and purpose assisting newcomers with their search. We come together as a community of passionate merchants all searching for the pearl of great price.

THINGS TO THINK ABOUT

1. Based on what happens in your ministry, what is your operational theology of evangelism? Where would unconvinced seekers plug in? What
   is the atmosphere in regard to the honest asking of questions and sharing of doubts? Once a confession of faith is made, how are these new
   believers initiated further into the complete rule of God?

2. What's your opinion of the concept of the bounded set versus the centered set? How might this perspective be problematic? Do you feel
   that the potential benefits might outweigh any inherent risks? Please
   elaborate.

3. Who are the people in your ministry that you believe would be effective
   guides for unconvinced seekers? Why do you believe they could come
   alongside people in nonconfrontational, engaging ways? How might
   they become vital resources for gradual evangelism?

4. What are some ideas for fresh approaches to introducing people to Jesus
   that are built on the theological premise of Christianity being a lifelong
   initiation process into the kingdom of God? What other resources exist
   that might also be appropriate for propagating gradual evangelism? How
   might you utilize them?

Chapter Seven

PREACHING HEART TO HEART

Sermons are like dirty jokes; even the best ones are hard to remember. In both cases that may be just as well. Ideally, the thing to remember is not the preacher's eloquence but the lump in your throat or the heart in your mouth or the thorn in your flesh that appeared as much in spite of what he said as because of it.   — FREDERICK BUECHNER[1]

We must recognize, first of all, that the aim of the popular teacher in Jesus' time was not to impart information, but to make a significant change in the lives of the hearers. Of course, that may require an information transfer, but it is a peculiarly modern notion that the aim of teaching is to bring people to know things that may have no effect on their lives.   — DALLAS WILLARD[2]

THE SEARCH FOR A BETTER WAY

Is there a better way to preach to Asian Americans, especially convinced and unconvinced Americanized ones? It would seem that most preachers involved in this unique ministry have never given this much serious thought. Like so many of their pulpit peers, Asian American preachers seem content to prepare and deliver their weekly messages in the styles modeled and taught in their seminaries even if their preaching has been ineffectual for years.

There is a lingering assumption that whatever is taught by a seminary, from how and what to think about God to how to herald the gospel, will work well in any and every setting. Conditioned never to question this modernistic mentality, no earnest effort to overhaul one's preaching style is undertaken. This is a far cry from the malleable, almost postmodern-like, attitude of the apostle Paul, who adapted his form to fit his audience, be they orthodox Jews in the synagogue or philosophical Greeks on Mars Hill.

117

Failure to discover the most effective way to reach the specific constituency you are serving will more than likely yield only years of frustration and frozen spiritual assets for both you and them. For even in preaching, the medium is the message.

An Awakening Awareness

My thinking on this subject began in earnest in 1982. At that time, IWA, Inc., the parachurch organization in which my wife and I were involved, embarked on an ambitious mission to survey the constituents of twenty-five Japanese American churches in Southern California. Curious if there were any cultural clues that might explain why these few had found Christianity meaningful, we hoped that some key insights might improve the ability to reach the scores of still-unconvinced Japanese Americans much more effectively. A total of 963 people responded to the ecumenical survey; 86 percent were Japanese Americans, of which 39 percent were Sansei and 34 percent were Nisei.[3] Some of the more significant findings of that survey will be expanded on below; what is pertinent for now is how that survey made me wonder whether there were culturally better ways to do Asian American ministry.

Having graduated from seminary at the end of 1980, I too had emerged thinking that we had all been the recipients of ministerial methods that were culturally transportable. As I embarked on my first year as a full-time pastor, I conscientiously constructed and delivered my monthly messages as if my homiletics professors were anchored there in our pews. Thus the premise of the IWA survey shook my seminary-honed sensibilities: Might there be superior ways to preach to Asian Americans that my otherwise learned professors were clueless about? What might they be?

The ensuing years saw me experiment with possible solutions to this nagging question. The ideas that follow this introduction came to life during that period. But even though the responses to some of these adjustments were both gratifying and validating, it was not until 1988 that I became forthright in my convictions about the unmistakable merits of culturally adjusted preaching to Americanized

Asian Americans (AAAs). That was the year I was invited to take part in a special consultation on the ethnic church in America, co-sponsored by World Vision International and *Christianity Today*. My ethnic preaching epiphany occurred during a memorable exchange between an administrator of a prominent East Coast Protestant seminary and the pastor of a renowned black Baptist church in Oakland, California.

The administrator, a white American, wanted to know why it was so difficult to get more black students to enroll in the nonblack seminaries. Although seminary officials were dedicated to engendering more diverse student bodies, they were frustrated by the lack of any real progress.

The pastor, an African American, responded by saying that while black churches appreciated this integrative intention, most balk at sending their brightest and best to predominantly white seminaries because in the past those students failed to receive the tools they required to minister in a black cultural setting.

As the pastor elaborated on this, the scales quickly began to fall from my eyes. "When they study American church history, how many books on African American church history do they read? None? That can't be because African American churches don't have any history in this country, right? It's because your church history scholars don't deem black church history relevant to the overall discussion of American church history, isn't it? And do you think that some white Presbyterian or Episcopalian professor is going to know how to train our people to stand in the pulpits of the black churches in this country? You've got to be kidding. After they earn their A's from mimicking their professor's style, they'll be laughed out of the black pulpits because they no longer know how to preach in a cadence or to stir the emotions of common people. The only place that our people can get equipped to minister in black churches is in black seminaries. The day when white-majority seminaries offer a variety of methods that more accurately address the needs of African Americans, that's when you'll see more African Americans signing up. Right now, frankly, we're not getting our money's worth at your schools."

The terse dialogue continued, but I slipped away to my own thought world to see if I could harness the ideas that were ricocheting in my head. I knew that there is a definite black preaching style. As soon as you hear it, you identify it as such. It is hard to imagine any other style being effective in an African American church. However, that raised two seminal questions: Is the style taught by the white seminaries one that is best suited for the white culture? and Is there a style of preaching that would work best with Asian Americans, specifically those Evergreen Baptist Church of LA is trying to reach?

Equipping Everyone

In answer to the first question, it is my belief that predominantly white-minded seminaries need to catch up to other institutions of higher education and make available courses that recognize the expanding plurality of people and their needs in our postmodern setting. In this sense, seminaries should train all potential ministers to be missionaries so that they know to use appropriate means to reach specific people groups. This is crucial not so much so divinity schools will attract more minorities but that they better equip those who come. Otherwise, blinded by their own denials, these institutions will continue to fail to fully equip anyone, not just nonwhites whom the Lord has called to minister to nonwhite populations. And unlike their African American brothers and sisters, Asian American graduates, by failing to recognize the unique bridges that God has already built into their respective cultures, will enter into ministry without even knowing that they have been shortchanged.

What about the second question? Are there better ways to preach to convicted and unconvinced AAAs? We believe there are.

MAKING THE FAMILIAR UNFAMILIAR

I believe that the greatest challenge to those called to fill today's pulpits is simply this: to make the familiar unfamiliar again. The gospel is essentially a story, one that has become all too predictable to the majority of those posing behind the pulpits and languishing in the pews. By living in our nation's marginally Christian culture, even unconvinced Americanized Asian Americans have been exposed to just enough of the gospel story, both in good and bad contexts, to be as jaded as any grim-faced churchgoer. Too many of us think there is not much new about the Good News. Familiarity has definitely bred contempt.

Mind you, this is not the same as shake-your-fist-in-God's-face rebellion; that much reaction might be a welcome change from the polite apathy that our sermons normally induce. No, this brand of contempt is not immediately noticeable. Everyone appears to be quite satisfied with the weekly dosage of doctrine or discipline the preacher dispenses. At least that is the gist of the comments habitually hurled at the preacher as the parishioners escape to the parking lot or the coffee hour. But where are the changing lives, the challenged consciences, and the ruffled concepts that are the evidence of the handiwork of God's Spirit?

To stand in the same pulpit, week after week, telling and retelling the same story has to be either one of the most stupefying or the most challenging tasks to undertake. If convinced and unconvinced AAAs are going to show up each week and give you thirty minutes of their precious time to let God speak through you, you owe it to them not to lull them all to sleep by going through the motions. This does not mean you have to entertain them, but it does mean that you must preach God's true story of redemption and atonement so as to make them sit on the edge of their seats, as if they were hearing that timeless story for the first time. I once heard a communications expert state that the truth isn't the truth until people believe you; and they can't believe you if they don't know what you are saying. And they can't know what you're saying if they don't listen to you; and they won't listen to you if you're not interesting. And you won't be interesting unless you say things freshly, originally, imaginatively. Given the twenty-first-century audience's severely truncated attention span, I cannot imagine more pertinent advice for today's preachers.

This has no chance of happening until you, the preacher, in the midst of your devotional and weekly preparation times, hear the gospel story as if for the first time. How easily the Word of God and all the sacred doctrinal trimmings become the tools of the trade for those of us whose profession it is to study and interpret it. We cannot hope to overcome the congenial contempt of the congregation until we manage to overcome our own.

To accomplish this we must jettison the subtle smugness and misguided arrogance that convinces us that we have little left to learn about God. For somewhere along the road of our quest, we began believing that we had this infinite God of the universe all figured out.

Once God becomes predictable, the Lord loses the ability to surprise or dumbfound us. Getting too chummy with the Holy Other will ultimately prove to be disastrous. To preach effectively, a paradox must be perpetuated: we cannot afford to lose sight of that which we can barely see — the mystery of God.

Walking in the Wilderness

The best place to confront God's mysteriousness is in the wilderness of our souls, that place in which we cannot hide from our fears, our doubts, our tormentors, our sins. It should come as no surprise that so few are found on the road that leads to this place of testing and refining, for it is an unpleasant place to be. How much easier to remain within the protective walls of our certainty, our community, even our Christianity than to choose to tread the road less traveled. But since the Lord Jesus made that choice, so must we.

In *Followed or Pushed*, Fuller Seminary's evangelism professor Eddie Gibbs asserts that it has never been more critical for modern Christians to maintain a growing edge to their belief in God:

> The Church has to take an unchanging Gospel to a changing world. This demanding task entails a constant rethinking of the Good News of Jesus Christ. How can it relate to different situations? Believers must continue to grow in their understanding of the message they convey and be prepared to face the challenge of applying it to their own lives in fresh ways.[4]

Contrary to modernistic assumptions, postmodern unconvinced AAAs do not need answers so much as they need to see believers still grappling with the synergism between faith and doubts. But we are apprehensive about showing this paradoxical face to them, thinking that seeing this will turn them off. But what is truly disgusting to them is our painfully flawed attempt at looking perfect. They do not want to believe that we are divine; they want to know that we are as human as they are. Like Thomas, they too need to see and touch the holes in our lives and in our faith in Christ before they will believe that they can believe.

To be effective preachers we must challenge ourselves and our people to lose our faith in order to save it, to go beyond the limits with which we typically shackle God. Not long ago I was introduced to a person who had obviously been in the wilderness of her soul for quite a few years. There were numerous times during our conversations that I felt threatened by her open-minded search for God. I obviously was not as adventurous as I thought I was. This was humbling. Several weeks after our time together, she wrote me a nice note and included her favorite quote. It read:

> You have to lose your faith continually if you want to save it. Not that it's possible to simply "lose your faith." But you have to lose the limits of your belief, that belief which is the support of your faith, which brings it to the point where you imprison your faith. It's a task you have to keep taking up always, a task which will make you pass constantly between the feelings of terror and liberation.[5]

She prefaced this sage advice by saying, "[This] gets me excited every time I read it." While some long-standing Asian American Christians may find those words threatening, the typical unconvinced AAAs would find great relief and validation in them. Why the difference?

Many Christians are afraid to venture into the wilderness of their souls — afraid of what they might find or of what might find them. In sharp contrast, typical unconvinced AAAs, not tormented by the neurosis that comes from trying too hard to preserve an airtight orthodoxy, find this troublesome wilderness to be a familiar place. They respond quite positively to desert-spawned preaching that is not afraid to present the many paradoxes of our faith in God and the battle to make this brief life mean something, for this is the substance of their own experience. Thus, they are drawn to sermons that bring the mystery of God a little closer to home.

Minister-author Calvin Miller is an avid proponent of this philosophy. In *Spirit, Word, and Story: A Philosophy of Preaching*, he
asserts that

> the sermon must make visible the unseeable realm.
>   ... Seeing the unseeable rouses this imperative mystery. What we can
> see may be interesting, but not for long; the things which are clear are
> soon only curios about which we are not curious. God's revelation of
> himself is real, but somehow shadowy. We only pry at it, having enough
> of it to convince ourselves that there is a God, but we never have all we
> want of God, and the sermon which makes real the hiddenness of God
> holds compelling interest. Oddly, to make his hiddenness real has very
> little to do with the sermon in either its preparation or delivery. The
> preacher's pilgrimage and his own hunger for his elusive God is what
> creates this alluring reach in sermons.[6]

To reach postmodern unconvinced people through the pulpit, there
must be a commitment to speak truth. About this mysterious yet personal God that we claim to know so well. About the effort it takes
to see this God more clearly. About the disappointments in life that
still befall believers. About the hypocrisy of Christians even when the
proclaiming of this truth may result in our being seen as flawed, fallible, ordinary sinners. But if they can see and sense that we too are
ordinary sinners yet we are loved by this extraordinary Supreme Being,
then postmodern unconvinced people, especially Americanized Asian
Americans, will be set free by that kind of truth. Free to draw closer to
the One in whom they might just barely believe. As Miller reminds us,

> the sermonic ideal is to talk from the silent center of the preacher to
> the silent center of those who attend the sermon. ... The preacher who
> clearly sees Christ will be able to project him on the screen of other
> searching lives. Great preachers are never those who have resolved every
> doubt or inner conflict, but those who remain honest in their intel-
> lectual conflicts and continue to grow as they preach with fervor such
> truths as they know to be redeeming.[7]

Filling Hearts, Not Just Heads

Many churches with ministries to various Asian American groups fall
into the same irresistible trap: the overemphasis of the intellectual, rational, modern approach to having faith in Christ. This might sound

a bit odd, seeing as how this criticism follows on the heels of a section that seemed to encourage a more cerebral approach to preaching. While the emphasis might have been on being more pensive about faith and the possible ramifications of living up to its challenges, it was not to be construed as promoting an approach that would be more rational than most already are. So much time and energy are spent preaching a logical apologetic message that may succeed in filling heads but not hearts. To reach today's postmodern unconvinced people you cannot afford to leave their hearts empty.

M. Scott Peck understands the primary place of appealing to people's hearts. He admits that it is so tempting to try to persuade by logic when the logic of the Christian vision makes so much sense to us who already believe in it. But to attempt to persuade unconvinced people with this same brand of logic is almost a waste of time. For even if you succeed in convincing them to convert, you may have merely won over their heads and missed their hearts.

> There are proofs of the reality of God. But to those who live within a godless state of mind, such proofs sound only like so much empty noise. . . . No, the transformation begins not in the mind, but in the heart. And if the heart is "hardened," no words can penetrate it. Conversely, when one has undergone what the pithy Old Testament Jews called a "circumcision of the heart," the words of the gospel message may fall upon the mind like the sweetest drops of living water (Deut. 30:6). Somehow, then, the successful evangelist must speak to the heart.[8]

So Peck believes that the way to a person's mind is through his or her heart. This is where true transformation must take place, for when the heart has been circumcised, the mind is more willing to embrace the message of Christ. This is especially true for Asian Americans, who tend to have overdeveloped heads and underdeveloped hearts, and we preachers are partly to blame for some of that. With the Asian Americans' natural propensity toward intellectual matters, it is so tempting to preach sermons that are more akin to seminary lectures or preparatory classes for a Bible trivia show. The congregants dutifully fill in their outlines and gamely attempt to keep up with their preacher's cross-referencing compulsion. For all of the details that are doled out, there is a certain deadness that prevails, for the transferring of information is not the same as transformation.

PREACHING FOR TRANSFORMATION

If we are going to appeal to twenty-first-century people's hearts, especially Asian Americans, we must prepare our messages with the goal of transformation, not merely the transfer of information, clearly fixed before us. As Miller says:

> The sermon joins with the other components of worship, seeking to build a nest where spiritual confrontation may hatch. By its conclusion, the sermon should create a *change matrix* in which individuals find themselves confronting important life issues. This matrix is mostly inward and psychological; it feeds on inner conversation that analyzes, questions, breaks status-quo-self-satisfaction. The sermon will only elicit the kind of response it demands.[9]

We must not just want our people to know about Christ and his forgiveness; we must want them to know Jesus and to allow his grace to give them real hope for living. How can we attain such a lofty goal?

I feel that one of the best books written on this subject is the aforementioned one by Miller, *Spirit, Word, and Story: A Philosophy of Preaching*. Anyone serious about learning to preach to people's hearts in order to see lives transformed must examine Miller's material. So much of what he advocates parallels what we have found to work with unconvinced AAAs. This merely underscores the fact that these methods are effective not only for reaching many different types of postmodern, secular, unconvinced people but also for impacting contemporary Christians who have been going to church for years and getting little out of the sermons. According to Miller, there are four keys to a vital sermon — inspiration, information, variety, and application.

Inspiration

Why would anyone give up a morning of golf or a leisurely Sunday at home to come to a place where the preacher either bores you to death, dangles you over the fiery pits of hell, teaches you the nuances of a foreign language, makes you feel like a guilt-laden pariah, insults your intelligence, tells you how to vote on issues, leaves you feeling hopeless and worthless, or all of the above? While faithful members may enjoy this sort of weekly diet, most unconvinced AAAs will not. They may come once, but they will not be back if this is the only type of food being served. Unlike so many of us, to their credit, they do not have the stomach for it.

Therefore, our messages, if they are anything, must at least be inspiring. "Generally, sermons should lift the spirit, not depress it." This is not to say that we steer away from confronting sin and calling people to repentance. Those are intrinsic parts of the gospel story that must be told. But if all we do is nail people to the cross, we then err by leaving them hanging there in despair and defeat. It did not end there for Christ; neither should it end there for us. We have not reported the whole story if we leave them without the resurrection of their Savior, of their hopes, of their strength, of their resolve, and most certainly of their faith in an almighty and all-loving God. All who come should leave inspired and renewed, eager to come again. "Preaching inherently must be positive in tone. . . . Sermons that focus on continual negativity and rebuke will fall at last on joyless, empty pews."[10]

And speaking of joylessness — do not be afraid to bring a sense of humor to the pulpit with you. Telling jokes, however, is not the same thing as having a sense of humor. People appreciate intermittent light-hearted cleansing of their palates before or after each main course is served up. Some preachers are afraid to elicit laughter during the worship service. But a wise preacher will use healthy humor to underscore difficult truths. Laughter can be quite disarming.

Information

"Information is the quality of teaching that a sermon bears. The sermon is to instruct, to teach new truth." If all sermons had to be were inspirational, they could easily deteriorate into positive-thinking pep talks. What makes our messages different is their inspirational content. In other words, the substantial message of the gospel should provide us with all the inspiration we need. But the challenge remains both to communicate the truth in new ways and also to reveal heretofore unseen perspectives on this truth, especially those emanating from cultural points of view.

Try not to belabor the obvious truth of a passage. Too many preachers merely paraphrase the thinking found in Bible commentaries. It may seem to be the safest way to go, but you will discover that your listeners did not swallow much of the truth you doled out. Why? It hearkens back to the point that familiarity often breeds contempt. If you present only the obvious, people will start to wonder why they had to let you speak for thirty minutes on something they could have read in two. Like it or not, there are much greater demands on today's preachers to be insightful and creative. If we cannot turn people on to the potency and relevancy of God's truth, they will turn us off.

We must never come across as if we have already unearthed all the riches from God's unlimited storehouse of treasures. We must keep both our listeners and ourselves ever curious.

Variety

Variety is not only the spice of life, it gives life to our sermons. People today, having been raised on a steady diet of television commercials, have notoriously short attention spans. Preachers must be prepared to change images every two or three minutes to keep their people from lapsing into sermon-induced comas. Variety, when it is used creatively and appropriately, can keep the listeners hanging on every word, not wanting to miss the next surprise. "When the congregation can guess what's coming next, the predictable preacher has failed; the Holy Spirit on such Sundays will be at work in somebody else's church." Remember: comfortable routines can soon become ruts. Predictability can render one's preaching powerless.

Application

"Application answers the all-important question: 'Why should I listen to you? What good will this sermon do me?'...The sermon's application determines its vitality." Before preparing any sermon, the preacher must remember who will be listening to the message. Determining the audience helps the application to be more direct. Most sermons are aimed at either mature believers or the unconvinced. But this bilateral definition of the audience is far from accurate.

What about the unconvinced person who is a single parent and has come to church the last several months in search of healing and wholeness? Why should she listen to your sermon? And then there is a medical professional sitting in the back row. He has had to deal with an overwhelming sense of inadequacy in the face of his patients' unrelenting suffering. Why should he listen?

Obviously, the list can go on and on. It is not possible to address every need every Sunday, but over the course of the year, we should address God's Word to all present and even to those who are not here that we wish were. This second aspect may seem to be a waste of time, but your members will soon begin spreading the word to those missing folks that their church is truly a place where their needs are also addressed.

This, however, is not claiming that our messages will provide the solutions and answers that everyone would love to have. As Miller writes,

> Most problems are not solved by listening to sermons. The sermon, no matter how sincere, cannot solve these unsolvable problems. So if the sermon is not a problem solver, where shall we go for solutions? Together with the Spirit, the sermon exists to point out that having answers is not essential to living. What is essential is the sense of God's presence during dark seasons of questioning. . . . Our need for specific answers is dissolved in the greater issue of the lordship of Christ over all questions: those that have answers and those that don't.[11]

To preach with an eye toward appropriate application, whether age/stage or culture/identity-related, is to preach for transformation. Even though we are not fixing everyone's problems, we are doing something infinitely better if we are doing it right: inviting them, once again, to place their heavy-laden or broken hearts into the gentle hands of the Father who sacrificed everything for them. And just as a frightened child can find sudden sanity and solace in his or her parents' arms, so also, in a similar mysterious and marvelous fashion, God's warm and promised presence makes all the difference in the world.[12]

HEART LANGUAGE

The idea of a father who willingly makes costly sacrifices on behalf of his children is a theme that speaks deeply to Asian American hearts. It is a silken thread that should be interwoven through the fabric of our messages, sometimes as an obvious feature and sometimes more as part of the background. It is a way to make the gospel more accessible to Asian Americans.

Those responding to IWA's 1982 survey claimed that the number one reason why Japanese do not become Christians is because they have little or no felt need for God.[13] If Japanese Americans are the vanguard of the Asian American movement, then the reason for their lack of response is representative of that of other Asian Americans. Why do you think having a felt need for God is such an obstacle for many Asian Americans? It might be because they cannot relate to how we have been trained to communicate what sin and grace are all about.

Quite often, Asian Americans have a difficult time grasping what it means to be sinners in need of God's forgiveness. Intellectually the concept of falling short of God's standards makes sense to them. But on a deeper, more visceral level, it does not register, because they believe themselves to be good people.[14] In general, some of this might be due to their being reared to live up to higher expectations and standards than most. Out of an indoctrinated fear of bringing shame on their family, especially their parents, many Asian Americans do their best to steer clear of trouble. Those who do get into trouble admit that they regret hurting their parents through their mistakes.

I believe this is one of the vital clues to salvation that God has planted in seemingly all Asian cultures. So in order to enable unconvinced Americanized Asian Americans to comprehend their need for Christ's forgiveness, we should use this bridge to reach their hearts.

Without the benefit of this insight, witnessing to postmodern AAAs, whether from the pulpit or one to one, can be both frustrating and fruitless. Coming at them with the concept of sin as doing bad things, we often find ourselves searching for ways to get them to confess to being rotten people: "So tell me, what are some of the bad things you've done that need Christ's forgiveness? Nothing comes immediately to mind? [With a practiced look of incredulity] You mean you've never taken office supplies home or failed to tell the truth EVER? Aha! So you do confess to being a detestable person in need of Christ! Let's pray." When you are dealing with unconvinced AAAs, it can get that ridiculous if you understand only the guilt side of sin.

Christian musician and author John Fischer also has a problem with the typical approach to sharing Christ that is based on getting someone to admit to being a wretched mess. This is how he describes the predicament:

> What happens when we find non-Christians who are disciplined, moral, generous, kind, and relatively happy? We immediately begin to hunt for that fatal flaw in their character which will prove that they really have been miserable, Christ-less wretches, and even their apparently good deeds have sprung from an evil source.
>
> Instead, we must realize every man and woman bears the image of God and as such is capable of producing some goodness on this planet. Christians must learn to appreciate the dignity of [people] regardless of salvation. Worth is not the result of salvation, it is the reason for it, and the reason hell is such a tragedy.[15]

Has God embedded a clue or two in Asian cultures, which are shame-based rather than guilt-based, that would facilitate more Asian Americans connecting with the meaning of the Good News? Think about it. Unconvinced Americanized Asian Americans already understand the concept of being unable to repay parents who have paid a great price to provide a better life for them. The Japanese even have a phrase for this: *kodomo no tame ni* (for the sake of the children). Using Matthew 7:7–11 as background, you could explain how our heavenly Father, motivated by unconditional parental love, gave up what was most precious to him: his only Son, so that God's earthly children could enjoy abundant and eternal lives. The Lord's only wish is that we would acknowledge this gift and respond by reciprocating God's sacrificial love. This is not a demand but a desire, for God cannot coerce or manipulate our response. God's love for us is the sacrificial, costly kind. We all benefit from it, but do we show our gratitude by loving God back?

We are free to rebuff the Lord and to live like self-made orphans, but this understandably causes God untold pain and shame. For to do this reflects poorly on our Maker and is to our shame. The realization that we have an unrepayable debt to the One who gave us breath is the awakening of a spiritual consciousness that can lead to restoration, deep healing, and salvation. If you want to speak to Asian American hearts, you must first learn the language of Asian American hearts.

THE POWER AND PLACE OF STORIES

The "for the sake of the children" theme is powerful because it is a commonly held story, both God's and ours. The gospel itself is primarily a story event, one that we are asked to believe in order to be saved. "This is how the birth of Jesus Christ came about: His mother Mary was pledged to be married to Joseph, but before they came together, she was found to be with child through the Holy Spirit" (Matthew 1:18). Doctrinal precepts are important, but they can come later. First we must believe that there is tremendous transformational power in this poignant story. And then we must believe that our lives are powerful stories, too. During the three-hundred-plus-year reign of modernity, facts, precepts, and the belief that we could know all the answers genuinely moved people. However, as we make the jump to lightspeed into the universe of postmodernism, stories take on a much greater role because of their simplicity and subjectivity. More and more people are moved by stories rather than precepts because stories always hold out the potential for childlike people to enter into them. Thus, whenever there is a coalescing of our own stories with God's there is always the potential for a mysterious melting of even the hardest of hearts.

Thus, we should bring together those converging stories more often from our pulpits instead of spewing out endless streams of precepts. This will never happen overnight. It first takes some effort and a creative eye to recognize the stories that are always there and then to juxtapose them. If we hope to reach postmodern Asian Americans and other people through our pulpits, we must become adept at both story seeing and story telling.

People the world over relish stories. This is no less true for Asian Americans. When IWA surveyed the constituents of those twenty-five Japanese American Christian churches in 1982, an odd bit of trivia was uncovered: the type of book they most enjoyed reading (40 percent) was biographies, true stories about people.[16]

At first this bit of information seemed to be of no great importance. But then it began to dawn on us that many in this same group of people who rarely displayed emotions (the Nisei) were addicted to the soap operas on Japanese-language television. These made-in-Japan dramas are simple, redundantly themed, slow moving, and English subtitled. Nevertheless, they never fail to elicit strong emotional responses from their ardent adult viewers, and this includes men.

Why was this? Is there a connection between this and their reading of biographies? Maybe, for in both cases, these were stories about ordinary people having to deal with the heartaches and setbacks of life. So the way to their hearts — to move them — was through those kinds of stories, not rational-sounding apologetics or doctrine-laden guilt trips. We decided that we needed to see and tell the stories that give substance and meaning to our lives if we were going to communicate with their hearts. And God's story is one of those.

Miller agrees. He puts it this way:

> Even as the Bible is replete with stories, our sermons will best reflect the narrative style of Scripture, as they also become narrative.... The Bible is literature ... it is a well-told story that makes us realize the kind of truth that matters most. The biblical story, however, also interacts strongly with our own.
>
> Why do the narratives of Scripture so enthrall us? I believe it's because the biblical stories are so germane to the life narratives we ourselves are writing. "Once upon a time ... Jesus," is a story that presupposes "Once upon a time ourselves."
>
> [The preacher] takes the stories of Scripture and feeds them homiletically into other life scripts.[17]

Becoming a pulpit raconteur is not the easiest thing in the world, especially for those who are more naturally inclined to be left-brain thinkers. Left-brain preachers tend to take a more modern, rational approach to sermons, serving up neatly packaged three-course meals that are liberally spiced with scholarly insights and step-by-step recipes for living more godly lives. Each point of their tripartite messages typically begins with the same letter (for better listener retention), and by including an outline in every program, each listener is tacitly encouraged to jot down as many priceless principles and sacred steps as possible in half an hour. "Where precept preempts stories, note-taking is vogue."[18]

But for all the feverish note taking that occurs in so many Asian American churches each Sunday, what percentage of that mountain of information do you suppose they actualize? People leave church each week with another page of notes stuffed inside the back covers of their Bibles, but how often do they also leave with hearts that are still aching and empty? How many of them have been so convinced of the rightness of an exclusively left-brain, lecture approach to hearing sermons that they do not even know enough to complain? Instead, the squawking erupts if their pastor fails to hand out a sermon outline or another simplistic recipe for solving one of life's complex problems.

While it may not be possible to measure the outcome of any message, the manifestations of lives being transformed become apparent over time: notes to the preacher expressing newfound hopes and redoubled efforts, reconciled relationships, an eagerness to worship, courage to fight injustice, and sometimes to keep on keeping on. Those kinds of changes are born in the heart when God has been experienced in a profoundly powerful way.[19] The genius of stories is that they succeed in disengaging the critical and sober-minded left-brained parts of us so that the wide-eyed innocence of the right-brained child can listen for the familiar timbre of the Father's voice.

Convinced that a story-telling style was the key to reaching the hearts of Asian Americans, I dumped the outline inserts in 1987, and I quit trying to preach as if my professors were there each week. Instead, with fear and trembling, I began to tell the story that God has spoken to us through his Word and our personal histories.

Being more of a right-brain person, I became acclimated rather quickly to the creative demands of being one of God's story tellers. Instead of isolating a passage's principles right away, I would attempt to enter into the narrative's moment in time. Reading descriptions of that place and time, imagining what the major and minor characters' states of mind might have been, I would work at it until I could smell the marketplace or feel the swell of Galilee's waves beneath my feet. I wanted the story to draw me in, to make me feel a part of it so that I could start to access its truth or its truth could begin to access me. This was also my desire for my congregation. To touch their hearts in a transformational way, they not only had to learn how God's story and mine converged; they also needed to hear how theirs came together with ours.

As we all learned in childhood, the best stories must not be overanalyzed and dissected. Their message is found in the sum total of all of the parts, and while there usually is a moral or main point to the story, what makes them so attractive and memorable is the beguiling way which they can speak so intimately to each listener. People listen to stories differently than they do lectures. Unconcerned about catching every detail, parishioners put down their pens and pencils and automatically switch mental gears when the preacher says, "There was a time in my life when I thought I knew all the answers and was calling all the shots. That was before I knew that I had cancer...." Within seconds, those left-brained graduate students have become awe-struck children again, having to deal with their own pain and powerlessness. They instinctively know how to place themselves into the story. In doing so, they identify more closely with the story's message.

No one understood this better than that master raconteur Jesus. Despite the disdain of his left-brained religious critics, Jesus preached in parables, stories drawn from everyday life to illustrate the timeless truths of God. In doing so, he spoke to the hearts of those willing to listen and drew them nearer to the kingdom of God. To those who would complain that preaching in parables leaves the truth too veiled, we should echo Jesus' reply: "He who has ears, let him hear" (Matthew 11:15). Stories, then as now, retain the all-important mystery of God and his kingdom.

To be a story teller in the pulpit demands that the preacher be an astute and accurate observer of life, for he or she must see how God is moving today as the Lord did in the past. As Miller writes:

We are gathering our art by being in the world and gratefully seeing all that is around us. Perceiving life is preparing to preach. When sermons come from men and women with no perception, the eye of the hearer is blinded, the ear is filled with the wax of oratory that never touched the world.... We who preach are the divine raconteurs, telling the "old, old story" by telling loads of new, new stories. These stories will get at truth, motivate the productive life, and drive out the demons of boredom as they do. Thus the world will learn of God and cheer that we have held its attention while it learned.[20]

With integrity and authenticity, we must look within ourselves for the stories. With compassion and grace we must look within the lives of our people for their stories. And with wisdom and objectivity, we must peer at the events of this world — especially the incarnation, death, and resurrection of Jesus — for the chapters in God's kingdom story. Then we must weave them together like a grand playwright, with humor and humility, with artfulness and authority, all the while drawing everyone into the drama that is the gospel. I know of no better way to reach Asian American hearts, especially the hearts of unconvinced AAAs.

THINGS TO THINK ABOUT

1. How predictable is the preaching in your church? What evidence is there of the preacher's growth since graduating from seminary? What evidence is there of an ongoing fascination with God's Word and with the pursuit of the Divine Fox?

2. What would it take in your church for God's timeless message to be communicated clearly, inspirationally, creatively, and relevantly? How enthusiastic are you about inviting postmodern unconvinced persons to come hear the messages on Sunday mornings?

3. What do you think about the author's point that there is a more fruitful way to preach to Asian American audiences? If there is, do you believe it is something that can be learned or can only be given by the Holy Spirit?

4. How fair is it to hope that every pastor of an Asian American church develop a more effective method of communicating God's true story? If it is something beyond our control, what advice would you give to a mediocre preacher or to one who is more comfortable sticking with the style learned in seminary? Is there too much emphasis put on the preaching event, to the detriment of the rest of the worship experience?

5. For pastors only: Styles aside, how effective a preacher are you? Are you still following the formula from seminary, or have you tried to forge a pulpit style that both fits who you are and transfixes and transforms your listeners? Do you aim your messages more at their heads or their hearts? Would your members agree?

Chapter Eight

ANTICIPATING THE UNCONVINCED

Worship is life.
— MELVIN FUJIKAWA, worship pastor, Evergreen Baptist Church
of Los Angeles

The Reformation was about returning the Word of God to the people of
God. The New Reformation is about returning the work of God to the
people of God.   — Cited by numerous current Christian sources

You may be wondering why the previous chapter was devoted solely to preaching and why this chapter has not one but two subjects: worship and shared ministry. There are several reasons for this.

The first is that I have more to say about preaching than these other areas because that has been the aspect of ministry in which I have had the most experience. The Lord has called me to proclaim the Good News, so much of my thought, time, and energy are devoted to honing my craft. And since preaching is a solitary art (i.e., it is one of the few types of ministry that cannot be directed or performed by a committee or group), any new ideas that I have can be put to the test immediately. Consequently, in a relatively short period of years, I have been able to experiment with quite a menagerie of culturally adapted approaches to proclaiming God's Word.

Another reason for this disparity is due to my steadfast belief that preaching occupies one of the most prominent spots in a church's public ministry. Other efforts and ministries are occurring, but there is a distinct tendency for people to associate the effectiveness of their church with the effectiveness of their church's pulpit. For better or for worse, much of a church's self-esteem is tied to what happens during those thirty-odd minutes that are given to each preacher to serve as a conduit of the Almighty.

Quite often, the first contact an unconvinced person will have with organized Christian faith is the Sunday morning worship service. And that first encounter may never transpire if the members of the church do not feel positive about the type of food that is being served up weekly (or maybe I should say "weakly") from the pulpit. They will not invite their unconvinced friends or family members for fear that they will have a bad experience. But when the messages are meaningful and are delivered in an inspirational and engaging style, the opposite holds true.

In this regard, the quality of the worship experience itself is also an exceedingly significant factor and will be addressed below. But even if the times of prayer, praise, and thanksgiving are vibrant and alive, everything can come to a grinding halt for what can seem like an eternity if the pulpit has been neglected. For this is the one stretch of time in the service when people must sit quietly (assuming this is a typical Asian American service) and listen, so whatever they are hearing had better be worth their undivided attention.

There may be those who believe that too much emphasis is put on the sermon anyway, and there is some credence to that complaint. However, until or unless things change radically in that department, serious efforts to enliven and enhance our Asian American pulpits must not stop. For it is when people esteem their pastor's preaching that they are more likely to invite others to join them for worship. As Eddie Gibbs reminds us, you cannot avoid the pulpit if you want to bring new people to the worship service:

> The majority of people who identify with this upfront model of ministry tend to be more of a clientele than a congregation. The focus of identity is with what happens at the front of the church rather than any sense of belonging to one another. They take pride in being associated with the celebrity. Such is their level of satisfaction and feeling of prestige that they become enthusiastic advocates of their church, serving as its promotional agents.
>
> The quality of the performance means that they are able to invite their relatives, neighbors and associates with confidence. They know that they will not be embarrassed. On the contrary, they are sure that if they can once get the person they are seeking to influence inside the church doors, their major problem is over: the chances are the newcomers will be suitably impressed to the extent that they will want to

come again. The major contribution of celebrity church members to the life of their church is that of recruiter of others to join the appreciation society.[1]

Having said this, we must shift our attention to two other general areas of ministry in the Asian American church, for even the most effective pulpits cannot support the weight of the entire church. Preaching needs to be a part of an overall emphasis on kingdom initiation and involvement if Asian American churches are going to make more room for postmodern-minded, unconvinced Americanized Asian Americans. In this regard, we will look at some of the more noteworthy adjustments that have been made at Evergreen Baptist Church of Los Angeles in the interrelated areas of worship and the ministry of the laity.

WORSHIP

What does it mean to worship the Lord? Minister-author Frederick Buechner defines this central devotional act of all Christians in the following manner:

> To worship God means to serve [God]....One way is to do things for [God] that [God] needs to have done—run errands for [God], carry messages for [God], fight on [God's] side, feed [God's] lambs, and so on. The other way is to do things for [God] that you need to do—sing songs for [God], create beautiful things for [God], give things up for [God], tell [God] what's on your mind and in your heart, in general rejoice in [the Lord] and make a fool of yourself for [the Lord] the way lovers have always made fools of themselves for the one they love.
>
> A Quaker Meeting, a Pontifical High Mass, the Family Service at First Presbyterian, a Holy Roller Happening—unless there is an element of joy and foolishness in the proceedings, the time would be better spent doing something useful.[2]

If poor preaching can be a detriment to an otherwise vibrant worship experience, a vacuous and petrified worship time can deflate even the most inspired proclaiming of the gospel. We can therefore ill afford to neglect this crucial aspect of the Christian corporate life.

I firmly believe that the ongoing upsurge in our attendance since 1987 is due to the combined effect of our efforts to adapt our preaching styles to match Asian Americans and to develop a worshiping style that takes the attention off of ourselves and places it back on the Lord. The overall vision was to see our services go from being staid, sterile, and predictable to uplifting, stimulating, transforming and awe-inspiring.

But we felt we could institute changes only if they did not alienate older members who had kept this church alive through the many lean times since it was founded in 1925. Far too often, necessary changes never see the light of day due to the strong resistance put up by long-time members. To their credit, the ones here at Evergreen-LA have demonstrated time and again a willingness to alter elements if that is what the Lord seems to be asking of them. And when it comes to the worship experience, the Lord apparently has asked a lot of them lately.

Creating the Right Atmosphere

One of the first elements to come under scrutiny was the atmosphere for worship at Evergreen-LA. All of us are more affected by our surroundings than we realize. Our environment has a profound impact on our sense of well-being and of worship. For example, if you have ever been shopping for a home or an apartment, why is it that some places feel right to you while others do not? The same can be said for different church sanctuaries: why do you resonate with some and not with others?

It is always possible for any believer to worship the Lord, regardless of what the surroundings might be. However, it is likely that the average Christian would find a shady spot next to a clear mountain stream more conducive to worship than the chaotic confines of a Chinatown restaurant's kitchen. When it comes to worshiping the Lord, atmosphere can make an enormous difference.

When we say "atmosphere," we are concerned with two separate elements: the physical and the philosophical. Let us begin by examining the adjustments made to the physical atmosphere of our worship service.

Just as there are architectural and aesthetic elements in the design of sanctuaries that are clearly identified with certain periods, places, and denominations, we believe that there must be a design to which

Asian Americans can best relate in the context of worshiping God. The majority of our Asian American structures are modeled after the American version of their denomination's typical church building. Stained glass, wooden pews, mystical symbolic emblems — except for signs in Asian characters, walking into an Asian Baptist church in America is no different from walking into a white Baptist church. It feels like a church; it typically does not feel like home.

One of the reasons for this is because many of our Asian American congregations either have bought an existing church building or are sharing another church's facilities. The design of the building and its decor were determined long before the Asian Americans came on the scene. If the new congregation effects any changes, they usually are more cosmetic than substantial — new carpet or a fresh coat of paint. That was the situation for Evergreen-LA when we were located on Second Street and Evergreen in East Los Angeles for many years.

The used building we called home was fairly typical in appearance for old, inner-city churches — amber-hued industrial windows, threadbare drapes, pileless carpets, rubber-tiled floors, and rows of rock-hard wooden pews and cold metal folding chairs. The only obvious Asian touch was the multicolored Japanese seat cushions that the members of the Women's Fellowship had crafted with love and care. The outside was stuccoed and painted a tired shade of beige — a perfect canvas for the local gang's graffiti — and the weathered entrance doors had received a fresh coat of chocolate brown paint. On hot summer Sundays, the lack of central air conditioning must have caused all but the most faithful to have second thoughts about worshiping the Lord.

Like countless other congregations, we learned to make the most out of what the Lord had provided for us, and in spite of our surroundings, we experienced sustained numerical growth. Many were the times when we would complain about the drab, non-Asian condition of our building, yet when we had the opportunity to move and erect a new facility, our first instinct was to design something that was merely a more updated version of the typical American church. At the time, we did not stop to think whether there was an Asian American alternative to the atmosphere that we had grown accustomed to seeing.

We eventually gave ourselves more permission to color outside the lines in this area. We decided to make our first building feel and look more Asian American. But we realized that we could not emulate the lines and colors of a typical non-Christian Asian church without losing our visual distinctiveness from them. It would have to be subtler if it was going to achieve the effect that we desired.

That this first structure was not supposed to be the permanent sanctuary gave us much liberty to break away from traditional church patterns. Most of the congregation did not expect this first building to look like a traditional church. In fact, they expected it to look more like a gymnasium than a sanctuary since that was its stated destiny. Why put stained-glass windows in something that will eventually be a gym? If this was going to be a transitional building, then it should be simple, flexible, and functional.

Simple, flexible, and functional — this was not only a good description for our multipurpose building but also the definition of one of the best elements of Japanese design. Operating with the premise that many of the elements of the Japanese American subculture are synonymous with the values and images of the emerging, merging Asian American subculture,[3] we chose to construct an environment that would emulate these elements of Japanese American design and aesthetics. We wanted Asian Americans, especially unconvinced ones, to have a sense that this was an Asian American environment. This, we believed, not only would help them immediately feel comfortable here; it also would enhance their worship experiences.

We worked together to translate these notions into our hoped-for reality. From the outside, the multipurpose building rather resembled a Costco warehouse store, with its simple rectangular shape and adjoining rectangular colonnade. We jokingly referred to it as Christco. There were not many options to play with due to the original plans to convert this into a gymnasium someday. Without a steeple or a cross, the building did not look like a church. But the real adjustments were made on the interior.

Using what we considered to be a Japanese palette, we had the sanctuary painted a cool shade of gray, with the glossy black doorjambs framing doors of darker gray. The wall-to-wall carpet is an eggplant purple, and the interlocking, ergonomic, light-colored birch chairs are upholstered in a neutral blue-gray fabric. The front of the sanctuary keeps with this simple, contemporary theme, consisting of a raised platform outlined on either side by stepped walls that are accented with large potted plants. The temporary baptistery is off to one side, partially hidden by a tall, multipaneled Japanese *shoji* screen and plants.

All eyes are naturally drawn to the prominent soffit with its front cutout in the shape of a cross. This overhang defines the pulpit area and conveys the light from the skylight above onto the custom-designed, minimalist, light-colored, wooden pulpit. The stark simplicity of this focal point is striking. A beautiful satin banner festooned with crosses hangs in the open space in the pulpit's center, offsetting the floor-to-ceiling giant banner that accents the back wall. All the lighting, whether natural or artificial, is indirect, producing a toned-down ambiance that blends nicely with the rest of the decor.

These details are not provided as a blueprint for the perfect Asian American church interior. They are provided so that you might appreciate the intention that was behind all of those choices. To the best of our ability, given the limitations of our space and budget, we wanted to create a room where Asian Americans, especially postmodern-minded, unconvinced ones, would feel free to worship God. When traditional forms did not support this goal, we created new ones. As much as possible, we did not want to be limited by our previous experiences with non-Asian church atmospheres.

Have we succeeded? The ultimate challenge will come when we are ready to construct the permanent sanctuary. At that point, any latent desires to have a church that looks like a usual church will surface. But this first building seems to have the atmosphere we sought to generate. We say this because it feels right to us, and, more importantly, it feels right to our target audience. Whenever they come to visit our church for the first time, they usually comment, "You know, this doesn't look like a church. I like it. It feels Asian. It's peaceful in here." As we hear comments like that, we know that we are on the right track. You might be curious to know that, as our demographics continue to expand, the consensus is still positive about this feeling like a good worship space. As more Korean Americans, Vietnamese Americans, Filipino Americans, Thai Americans, African Americans, Latino Americans, multiracial Americans, and white Americans join us, they all seem to embrace this Japanese-based aesthetic. That should hardly come as a surprise to anyone, since there has long been a widespread acceptance of Japanese design elements. That they work well to define a worship space for a multi-Asian and multi-ethnic congregation is a new application for them.

If a church wants to reach more Asian Americans for Christ, it would do well to consider making similar changes in the physical environment that is utilized for the worship service. Obviously, some situations allow for this better than others. At the least, you should critique your worship room as if you were an unconvinced AAA visiting for the first time. What may feel homey to you may look homely to someone not convinced that this is worth his or her coming back. While it may not be possible to Asianize the aesthetics, see to it that things are at least neat, clean, and in good condition. Sloppiness and shabbiness repel people looking for a quality church. And where possible, as you discard worn or no-longer-appropriate items, make an effort to secure replacements that will give your worship area a more Asian American atmosphere. You will be pleasantly surprised at the difference these alterations to your sanctuary's physical atmosphere will make, both to yourself and to the unconvinced. However, while much thought and prayer should go into creating a physical atmosphere where Asian Americans feel free to worship God from their hearts, without concomitant changes in your church's philosophical atmosphere, these physical changes will prove to be inconsequential.

Have you ever walked into someone's house only to find yourself wishing that your name was on the deed and not that person's? It is as if the architect and interior designer knew the desires of your heart when they put this house together.

I remember feeling that way once when I went to pick up my date at her parents' house. Everything was just the way I would have wanted it to be in my dream house. But even though I was surrounded by all of my favorite things, something was terribly wrong. And I knew exactly what it was. Although their words and expressions were congenial, I could sense that her parents were not thrilled to have their daughter going out with me (we will not waste precious space here examining their reasons). Needless to say, their negative attitudes soured my enjoyment of my surroundings.

That is an example of the power that an attitude or philosophy can exercise over any environment, no matter how perfect or pleasant. Thus, the wrong philosophical atmosphere during times of worship can distract from any ambiance you might have labored to create. But the appropriate one can work in concert with the right ambiance to produce an atmosphere that is primed for God to make God's presence felt in each worshiper's heart.

Unlike the suggestions for changing the physical atmosphere, the philosophy that we at Evergreen-LA try to bring to worship is not something that applies only to Asian Americans; we believe it should be present whenever and wherever any Christians gather to bring their offerings of worship before the Lord. The attitude we try to bring to worship now is that we are all sinners — broken, imperfect, perpetual — who come together because of common needs. We share a need to praise the God who sustains us. We share a need to express the thankfulness in our hearts. We share a need to have the Lord make us whole people again. We share a need to be filled with Christ's presence again. And we share a need to acknowledge our shame and continual requirement of God's cleansing love. We come to worship the Lord as people with needs that are familiar to us all. We do not so much come out of habit as out of necessity.

This profound sense of need is rarely evident in the typical church's carefully orchestrated worship times. All the regulars look so stable and clean, with nary a trace of dirt or doubt or death to mar their starched, spiritualized exteriors. Somewhere in the distant past, some misguided neurotic must have taught that this was the mask that every worshiper must don. And so our times of worship have disintegrated into a perpetuation of this sterile myth of human holiness. In the process, the faces behind those masks are mouthing silent screams of frustration and despair. This cannot continue.

We cannot let this philosophy prevail because it precludes the need for a Savior. Perfect people do not need Perfection. This is why so many worship services are hollow rituals rather than holy encounters, for there can be no encounter with the Lord if we push the Lord away. This denial of our true condition also prevents the formation of true fellowship among believers for much the same reasons: afraid to admit the sin and shame we share, we push each other away. So we physically come together each week, but we remain spiritually separated from God and each other.

It not only does not have to be this way; it should not be this way. Sanctimony has no place in the sanctuary: "If we claim to be without sin, we deceive ourselves and the truth is not in us" (1 John 1:8); "Therefore confess your sins to each other and pray for each other so that you may be healed" (James 5:16). Being a sinner is a lot like being an alcoholic — the struggle is never over. Both must acknowledge that the battle begins afresh every day. Like alcoholics, Christians are never "former sinners"; they are simply sinners who, appalled at their "addiction" and its destructive power, pledge to stop sinning. But the struggle not to "drink," not to "sin" is ongoing.

John Fischer's pastor is a recovering alcoholic. In comparing his pastor's ongoing fight with alcohol and his own daily struggle with sin, Fischer believes that his own problem is the more dangerous of the two. After all, his battle with sin can be much more easily hidden from view. If his pastor were to start drinking again, nearly everything about him would proclaim his failure: his face, his mannerisms, his lifestyle, his absence from Alcoholics Anonymous meetings. On the other hand, Fischer maintains that he could be saturated with hidden sin and the members of his church would scarcely notice.

> They won't even miss me at church because, unlike AA meetings, I can get away with deception at church. I don't have to worry about being found out at church because no one else wants to be found out either. We're easy on each other; we all put our best foot forward and we're all hiding — from the pastor on down.[4]

The philosophical atmosphere we are trying to promote at Evergreen-LA is that worship service should be more like a meeting of Sinners

Anonymous than of Sanctimonious Saints. While we cannot cause others to come sans masks, we can demonstrate that it is safe to remove them by daring to remove ours first. We do this by preaching messages fleshed out with stories of broken, fallible people being loved by a magnanimous and merciful God. We speak of ourselves not only as sinners but also as the "sinned against." The songs we sing and the prayers we lift up speak of a tarnished and tattered people wanting what only the Holy One can give: forgiveness, faith, strength for the journey, healing of hurts, God's own comforting presence.

Worshiping at Evergreen-LA is hoped to be not so much an intellectual experience as it is an inspirational one. Without denying the central place of solid biblical instruction, our overarching desire is to create an atmosphere of awe and wonder for those still willing to ask, seek, and knock. Whether or not they have confessed their faith in Jesus, we want everyone to leave the worship service certain that they have been in the presence of the Lord. Even as Jacob marveled, after awakening from his nocturnal vision of a heavenly staircase filled with the angels of God, so we too want to come away from each worship time thinking, "Surely the LORD is in this place, and I was not aware of it. . . . How awesome is this place! This is none other than the house of God; this is the gate of heaven" (Genesis 28:16–17).

There is a greater likelihood of this occurring when we acknowledge that the gate of heaven is open to imperfect people struggling to make sense out of a nonsensical world. We are then free to exclaim that the kingdom of God knows no boundaries. Divorced people are not singled out like leprous pariahs; single-parent families are treated with respect and dignity; the pain of being childless is acknowledged and addressed; single adults are seen as whole people; failure and faithlessness are treated as maladies common to all.

Calvin Miller recalls reading a parable by A. P. Gibbs that is a perfect illustration of how heartfelt worship arises out of heartfelt gratitude. Apparently, a pet dog has been abused, malnourished, forsaken, cold, and abandoned. A kind-hearted man happens upon this miserable creature and takes it home for the night. Because of his compassion, he ends up caring for the pet forever. As time passes, the pet becomes healthy and vigorous through its master's ministrations and comes to love him more and more. One night, while the master is in his study, the dog walks quietly over to his chair and gently licks his hand. The master looks down and sees the one-time mongrel gazing up at him with eyes brimming with gratitude. What that restored and loved dog is feeling, according to Gibbs, is worship.[5]

Since incorporating a philosophy of a common need for God and God's grace, the difference in our worship times has been remarkable. Strangers are coming who never before would have stepped foot in a church. Unwed mothers. Recovering addicts. Damaged couples. The wounded and the hopeless. More of us are coming forth now with real hurts, real failures, and real problems. Between the invocation and the benediction, there has been a growing humility among those who gather to worship the Lord. The sanctuary now is less a courtroom than it is an emergency room.

As the fear of being judged diminishes, the anticipation of receiving God's unconditional love increases. As Fischer points out, "Christians must realize that sin is not the problem. Sin was taken care of 2,000 years ago on the cross. The problem with Christians is getting up enough courage and belief in that cross to confess the sin and enough humility to accept the forgiveness that is offered."[6]

This is the essence of the Good News: we do not have to keep trying to take care of our sins because Jesus finished that burdensome task on the cross. All that is left is for us is to incarnate that truth with each other in the body and with the world. It is this renewed philosophy that continues to transform our worship services into corporate celebrations of God's gift of grace and truth. Each week, as we gather together as a forgiven community, we are grateful once more for the gift of Jesus. And it shows in our worship of him.

Worship by Design

Most of the people who show up for worship have no idea how much work goes into putting each service together. Those charged with this lofty responsibility must provide at least one service per week. And plenty of churches are responsible for providing multiple services every week, in different languages, in different genres, to different audiences. Quite often, under this relentless pressure, little thought is given to designing each worship service around a particular theme, let alone to designing a series of services. Instead, services are frequently slapped together from week to week, without much coordination and communication occurring among the leaders of the various parts.

I know from years of doing exactly that how easy it is to fall into this pattern. We start out with lofty plans for crafting weekly inspiring experiences. But the rest of the demands of ministry and the shortage of gifted and available leaders begin to take their typical toll. And before we know it, we are congratulating ourselves on Mondays for having survived another weekend of services.

Do you want to guarantee that the folks in your congregation develop low expectations about coming to worship God? All you have to do is perpetuate this pattern of haphazard and directionless worship. If it's obvious to everyone that worship is not going anywhere, either this week or the next several months, why should people do anything more than just show up?

One of the best decisions I have made thus far in my tenure as senior pastor was to call a worship pastor to join my staff right away. I realize that many churches are not in a position to hire a full-time worship pastor, but I am saying that churches cannot afford to have no one assigned to this weekly ministry that affects everyone. We could not afford to hire someone full-time our first two years after the hiving into two churches. We called someone we knew to have a deep love of God, a passion for worship, and a vision for what worship for Asian Americans might become. He began working part-time, but near the end of his second year with us, we made him three-quarter time, with the plan to bring him on full-time the following fiscal year. Given the size of our congregation, doing this was truly an act of faith. However, we are still convinced that the need to design our worship services — each week and overall — merits having someone in this capacity. Whether it is a lay person or a staff person, as long as that person displays a clear calling to lead people into the Lord's presence, you would do well to put that person in charge of the worship ministry of your church.

Having a gifted person overseeing worship has enabled us to step back on a regular basis to evaluate past efforts and to look forward to where the Spirit may be leading us as a people. As a result, we have been inspired to do things like redesign our worship bulletins, retrain our ushers and greeters, establish a repertoire of hymns and praise songs, and establish a rotation for our sound ministry people and worship team members. On a grander scale, we have been able to plan six to twelve months in advance, anticipating both the traditional seasons and critical seasons in the church's life cycle. Whether it is being able to look forward to Advent or Lent or to prepare us for a new challenge from the Lord, having a clear design and direction for our worship services has literally been a godsend.

For the Advent season of 1998, for example, we latched onto the theme of "The Unfolding Story." Equipped with this, our worship people got busy. A semi-original Christmas Eve cantata was written and rehearsed around the theme. A member who is an artist was consulted; based on her recommendation, she painted a progressive picture each week that was tied to the theme of that week's message. This, and the focus during our weekly home Bible studies, helped to build a mounting sense of anticipation throughout the church. People have expressed how much they appreciate the obvious design that is going into our worship services.

One of the design changes that we've embraced has to do with the basic flow of each week's service. On the recommendation of our worship pastor, we took nearly the entire worship ministry contingent to experience a show called *Cirque du Soleil*, a renowned French-Canadian traveling troupe that is much more theater than it is circus. Recruiting performers from around the world, the producers select one main theme, and through the original music, costuming, special characters, and so on, they draw the audience into that theme. From beginning to end, from the supple Chinese acrobats to the German artist who spins inside a giant steel ring, everything contributes to the show's premise. We came away inspired to achieve something similar with our weekly worship services.

There were times when what went on in our worship services felt like a three-ring circus, with the presiding pastor acting as ringmaster, trying in vain to hold it all together. Now we take great pains to design each element to enhance whatever theme is being advanced during that service. Most of the time, themes arise from the sermon's emphasis, which then guides the worship team leader in selecting appropriate songs and tempos. If there are baptisms, baby dedications, testimonies, communion, or commissionings, we tweak them so they obviously are a part of the larger whole of that service. An easy example is when we serve communion. Whoever preaches plans to finish the message at the Lord's Table, finding a way to tie in one of the message's main points with Christ's atoning sacrifice. Or if someone is going to share a portion of his or her testimony, we select a person whose story enriches and illustrates the service's theme. Sometimes it is not possible to fold everything into the chosen theme, but most of the time it works quite well.

Most people today, especially Americanized Asian Americans, prefer to have things well-planned and well-executed. Designing the worship services at your church takes a great deal more time and preparation and may occur only over the long haul if you call someone that God has gifted to craft worship services. However, let me assure you that the higher cost is absolutely worth it. We know that the Lord is worth the effort.

The Charismatic Third Wave

Without question, one of the major factors in improving our worship times has been the charismatic movement, specifically the Vineyard Christian Fellowship. Their artists write most of the new songs we sing, and most of our previous key worship leaders were strongly influenced by the teachings of the late John Wimber, the sometimes controversial founder of the Anaheim Vineyard, and his staff. Wimber began speaking out against the "cold and lifeless orthodoxy" of mainline churches in 1976 and motivated countless thousands of Christians to seek out a greater experience of holiness and the Holy

Spirit. Their emphasis on dynamic worship was a natural outgrowth of this pursuit.

The charismatic movement has come a long way since the first Pentecostal churches were born at the turn of the twentieth century. In those early years, they were looked upon with suspicion by the mainline churches, even listed alongside the Jehovah's Witnesses and Mormons in Christian books on cults. Today, it is hard to study the subject of church renewal without at least appreciating the pivotal role that the charismatic movement has played in revitalizing churches all over the world. That is true of the renewal that began at Evergreen-LA in 1978.

Church growth champion C. Peter Wagner, formerly opposed to Pentecostalism while he was a missionary in Bolivia, began to take another look at this movement when it was documented that their churches were exploding with unprecedented growth, especially in the Third World. As an ardent adherent of the radical pragmatism of church growth, how could he be against anything that was resulting in such spectacular growth of churches? Wagner began to assert that God was using the charismatic movement to revive the church in the twentieth century.[7]

In 1988 Wagner published his theories on modern-day revival in *The Third Wave of the Holy Spirit: Encountering the Power of Signs and Wonders Today*.[8] He labeled the turn-of-the-century Pentecostal movement the first wave of revival and the charismatic movement of the 1960s the second. Characterizing Wimber's movement as the third wave, Wagner believes that the Holy Spirit yearns to fall afresh on the mainline churches in a powerful display of what has traditionally been identified with overtly charismatic fellowships, for example, power evangelism and healing, miracles, prophetic utterances, speaking in tongues, without these churches releasing their mainline moorings, as happened so often in the second wave. The phenomenal growth of all three waves has been well documented. Look how far they have come since their controversial beginnings:

> In 1965 there were approximately 12,000,000 Pentecostals in the world. By 1977 there were over 50,000,000 Pentecostals and charismatics. By 1987, with the third wave giving added impetus, the total was estimated

at 277,000,000, including 20,000,000 in non-charismatic churches. In fact, Pentecostal-charismatic Christians now represent 17.5 percent of the world's 1,646,000,000 Christians.[9]

But is Wagner correct in saying that God's method for renewing mainline churches is to see that they develop a more charismatic emphasis? Rather than trying to answer this question, I will pass along some insights that we have gained in working through this question over the past several years.

I used to think that Evergreen-LA was on its way to becoming what Wagner calls a third wave church. A renewed interest in the spiritual gifts and the Holy Spirit was starting to spread throughout the church. A few people with prophetic gifts were emerging, and more and more worshipers were exercising their freedom to raise their hands or stand during the times of praise. I even found myself examining Wimber's writings on power evangelism and healing, wondering if there was a part of my own spiritual life that I had been neglecting or avoiding. It certainly seemed fitting at the time to assert that Evergreen-LA was fast becoming a third wave church.

Today, however, if you were to ask any of the pastors what kind of church Evergreen-LA is, they would tell you that this is not a third wave church, even though there continues to be an openness to incorporating some charismatic emphases in our worship times and ministries. So why the denial?

More than anything else, we are not convinced that mainline churches must become fully charismatic to experience renewal. Every church, regardless of denominational affiliation or history, has a de facto obligation as Christ's body to obey the directives that emanate to it from the head, Jesus Christ. Thus, there should be openness to the gifts of the Spirit. And not just that, but a willingness to move beyond the limitations of our biases, the courage to take great leaps of faith. There should be a zeal to sow the seeds of faith, a commitment to serve others in the name and spirit of Christ — in short, to be the body of Christ alive and at work in the world.

So, yes, we believe this means allowing for the current viability of some spiritual gifts that impassioned dispensationalists traditionally deny, but there can also be an overemphasis on these sign gifts to the detriment of the overall health and unity of the body. This is especially critical in an established church that is exploring ways to revitalize its worship times and general ministries. Much too often, a well-intentioned group within a church becomes charismatic (e.g., believes in a second baptism of the Holy Spirit evidenced by the speaking in tongues) and begins to lobby for the rest of the church to share their convictions. But everyone does not develop the same enthusiastic interest in healing and prophecy or singing Vineyard choruses and lifting up their hands, for example, and there soon is a polarization in the church that often leads to schism.

We at Evergreen-LA are very much aware of how easily an interest in improving the worship time can lead to this unfortunate factionalism in the church, and we hope it never happens here because we do not believe that this brings glory to God. Just before Jesus was arrested, he lifted up a long prayer that revealed his major concern about leaving this earth: the unity of his followers. Speaking of both his disciples and those who would eventually come to believe in him, he said, "Holy Father, protect them by the power of your name — the name you gave me — so that they may be one as we are one. . . . I in them and you in me. May they be brought to complete unity to let the world know that you sent me and have loved them even as you have loved me" (John 17:11, 23). While we believe that we must learn to honor the Lord better in our worship of him and service to him, we maintain that the highest priority is attaining unity in the midst of diversity.

Now in order to put the unity of the entire church first, everyone must be willing to die to something that is important. The unconvinced world is not impressed when we proclaim to be unified because of our unanimity. It is when we put aside our personal agendas on behalf of God's larger agenda that we cause heads to turn. Do you remember what Jesus taught us about how we are to relate to enemies?

> You have heard that it was said, "Love your neighbor and hate your enemy." But I tell you: Love your enemies and pray for those who persecute you, that you may be sons of your Father in heaven. He causes the sun to rise on the evil and the good, and sends rain on the righteous and the unrighteous. If you love those who love you, what reward will you get? Are not even the tax collectors doing that? And if you greet only your brothers, what are you doing more than others? Do not even

pagans do that? Be perfect, therefore, as your heavenly Father is perfect. (Matthew 5:43–48)

Those who would fervently pursue the charismatic side of the faith in search of God's perfection or holiness need to understand that God's perfection is made manifest when we die to ourselves — even some of our strongest convictions regarding the pursuit of God — in order to promote love and unity in the body.

There are several related reasons for this being true. First, any time we empty ourselves of power and glory on behalf of others, those are the moments when we identify most closely with Christ and what he chose to do in order to come to be with us (Philippians 2:1–11, esp. vv. 5–8). Insisting on your own way is not what Christ's love does (1 Corinthians 13:5); that easily turns into self-exaltation. God alone exalts, and then only those who, like Christ, learn to empty themselves first (Philippians 2:9–11).

Second, the gifts of the Spirit must always operate under the guidance of the fruit of the Spirit (Galatians 5:22–26), or else they will end up dividing the body, not building it up. Whenever there is an overemphasis on the gifts, the fruit of the flesh (Galatians 5:19–21) is manifested instead. We believe it is possible for the Spirit to abandon movements if the people involved lose sight of the bigger picture. So if the Spirit is truly in what people are doing, the Spirit's fruit should naturally be an outgrowth of what is happening. Humbly letting go of your agenda, especially when it feels costly to you, is clearly a sign that the Spirit is behind what you are doing. When push comes to shove, we look for the fruit of the Spirit over any gifts, no matter how powerful they might be. Love, after all, is "the most excellent way" (1 Corinthians 13:1; cf. Romans 8:5; 15:5–7; Philippians 1:27).

This whole subject of the third wave, I believe, is something that should be seriously explored by anyone called to Asian American ministries. There seems to be a growing fascination among churched Asian Americans with the signs and wonders movement as characterized by the Vineyard and other charismatic ministries. Many young adult Christians are elated over their newfound intimacy with God, and they are fervently pursuing the latest spiritual area that is being promoted. This is not necessarily negative, but things can get out of hand if the leaders are not prepared for what might happen.

This is not about leaders trying to manage or control God's Spirit; God's Wind blows whichever way pleases God (John 3:8). But God's shepherds have a responsibility to maintain the flock, to keep it safe and together (Numbers 27:16–17). Therefore, if you are a shepherd, you must be aware of some of the factors that might be fueling this interest in signs and wonders so that you can give proper guidance to the members of your flock.

For instance, I believe that many Asian American Christians are pursuing signs and wonders partly out of a reaction against the over-emphasis on intellectualizing spirituality that has gone on for decades in both conservative and liberal Asian American churches. Fed only a modernistic diet of apologetics, piety, and morality, many of these Christians are starving for a closer, more personal experience with God. The charismatic paradigm promises this. Many times, it is like water being dropped on a dry sponge when these left-brain believers are introduced to the right-brain side of God. They often testify to feeling close to the Lord for the first time since becoming Christian. While the Lord, in most cases, is probably truly doing something wonderful, the church must shoulder some of the blame for this need being so extreme. This is all the more reason to learn how to reach Asian American hearts and not just fill their minds with information (see chap. 7).

Another consideration is the idea that our *Zeitgeist* has manifested itself as a hunger for ecstatic experiences. Our society has become so materialistic and impersonal that many people are reaching out for ways to balance their lives and relieve their boredom. It is hardly a coincidence that the decade of the 1980s saw the emergence of New Age mystics and a renewed interest in the occult that continues unabated through the end of the 1990s. Is it possible that the church, as it has done so often with other fads, has come up with its own version of New Age thinking with this ongoing obsession with signs and wonders? While this question may offend some charismatics, those charged by God to look after the church nevertheless must pose it.

There is, and always has been, a place in the life of the church for irrational, supernatural experiences.[10] At least, there should be if the church is open to all that God has prepared for it. As mentioned earlier, there would be less of a need for ecstatic experiences if there were not such a heavy emphasis on the rational and the natural. But ecstasy, if it is going to build up the body of Christ, must be tempered with maturity.

Mature believers know that there is a valid need to get lost in the Lord during worship in order to take the focus off of them. But they also know that God is equipping them to live out their faith in a complex, sinful world where people still lose their jobs or do not get healed, where evil often holds the trump card, where all the pieces do not fit and all the answers are not there. Yet mature believers can still believe in a sovereign God. And they can live with the fact that other authentic believers may not share their convictions or passions yet are equally, if not more, involved in the serious pursuit of the Lord.

Mature Christians know that ecstasy has a place in their lives, but it is not meant to be an excuse to escape having to deal with the often harsh realities of their lives. We all need to be taken up to the seventh heaven to commune with the Almighty, but it is so that we can return to earth better equipped and more committed to claiming more of it as God's kingdom. Ecstasy and maturity need each other: by themselves they can lead to harmful extremes, but together they can help both individuals and churches to excel.

With this in mind, let's turn our attention to the issue of shared ministry.

SHARED MINISTRY

If it is true that many Asian American Christians are susceptible to pursuing ecstasy to the point of excessive self-absorption, this alleged tendency also might have something to do with how their churches have traditionally defined ministry and ministers. In other words, their hunger for more frequent and potent experiences of God using them may stem from the paucity of primary opportunities of this nature in their churches Here again, the Asian American church must do some soul searching.

Week after week, year in and year out, these people have been taught that God works through the lives of ordinary sanctified sinners to reconstruct lives, systems, and societies. It is only natural, then, that they begin to look forward to being the conduits of God's mercy and power in the world, to carry on Christ's ministry as God's ministers. This is all well and good. But disillusionment and disappointment begin to displace their determination the longer they participate in church life.

They eventually discover that, despite all of the inspirational rhetoric, their direct involvement in ministry comes down to their being more like vassals of the church rather than vessels of the Spirit's presence and power. Most lay people who express a desire to participate in ministry are deposited in a committee or elected to a board, where they will then spend the next several years making motions, approving minutes, and learning about church politics. There is no getting around the business of the church, and those who answer the call to serve faithfully in this capacity are to be commended. However, no matter how essential this business might be, it does not even come close to providing lay people with the empowering experience of seeing the Lord use them to make a difference in a sinful, suffering world. In so many churches, these experiences are reserved for the ordained pastors.

In the recent past there has been a groundswell of interest in churches developing a healthier concept of lay ministry. Each year there are conferences to attend and new materials to study that should be a part of every church's agenda. What we are about here, though, is a chance to come at this issue from the point of view of the Asian American church. What kind of changes need to take place in these churches so that the lay people are given more opportunities to participate in hands-on ministries? What are some of the ways that Evergreen Baptist Church of LA has been moving toward establishing a healthier sharing of ministry?

Changing the Pastor's Role

In far too many churches there exists an unhealthy codependency between the pastor and the congregation. Author Greg Ogden calls this a dependency model of ministry, in which the image of the pastor is that of the caretaker and the people are cast in the role of passive consumers of the work of 10 to 20 percent of the congregation. The pastor always performs real ministry while the members of the church are the grateful recipients of his esteemed care. "Pastors are construed to be the experts in spiritual things, while the people view themselves as objects receiving what they are not qualified to give one another."[11]

For the church to recapture its vibrant heritage of ministry, it must be willing to dispose of this dependency model in favor of the biblical model of interdependency or equipping. Ogden shares this quote from Elton Trueblood:

> The ministry is for all who are called to share in Christ's life, the pastorate is for those who possess the peculiar gift of being able to help other men and women practice any ministry to which they are called.[12]

While it is never a simple task for any pastor to switch from being the doer to being the equipper of doers, I would surmise that this is especially difficult for pastors of Asian churches, especially Chinese, Korean, and Southeast Asian ones. In churches such as these, with their strong immigrant constituencies, there is a pervasive Confucian mentality that wants to preserve the pastor's role as the venerated minister of the church. What this means is that anyone trying to promote the ministry of the laity in one of these churches should be prepared to be met with great resistance.

Asian pastors may not want to step back from their very visible roles of being primary caretakers for the congregation, fearing a diminishing of their authority and status. They also may have to overcome a basic disbelief that the lay people are capable of ministering to the sick, bereaved, or confused: But if this does not begin in the pastor's heart, it does not have much of a chance of taking place. Each pastor must be willing to become one who prepares "God's people for works of service" (Ephesians 4:11–12) beyond the mere stating of that overused phrase as an intention. That means a different role than what they have been trained or expected to fulfill.

I hope that more Asian American believers will begin to experience the joy of the Lord working through them to minister to people living in a world of pain and alienation. As they do, maybe they will come to esteem their pastors for a new and more biblically based reason — not as the sole caretakers but as the ones who equip and encourage them to share in the ministry of caring for others. This can even become a much more meaningful and satisfying ministerial role for the pastors. But it must first begin in their hearts.

One powerful way that the Lord planted the seeds of shared ministry in my heart was by getting me to believe that the Spirit of God was busy forging another kind of major paradigm shift for the Christian church. The first generations after Jesus were part of what author Loren B. Mead calls the apostolic paradigm. Numbering just a handful and huddled in tight-knit faith communities, the first several generations of Christians faced a world that was overwhelmingly pagan. There were no ordained clergy; neither were there any lay people. All Christians were convinced that Jesus had called and commissioned them to be ministers and missionaries, and they saw the mission field beginning outside their front doors. Commitment to pursuing the priceless pearl of God's kingdom was high, as was their commitment to the quality of life together. As Mead describes it, "The early church was conscious of itself as a faithful people surrounded by an hostile environment to which each member was called to witness to God's love in Christ. They were called to be evangelists, in the biblical sense of the word — those who bear good news. Their task was to carry into a hostile world the good news of healing, love, and salvation."[13]

Following Mead's model, the second paradigm took centuries, not generations, to shift. Called the Christendom paradigm by Mead, it began when the emperor Constantine converted in 313.[14] With Constantine's conversion, Christianity grew in stature and power throughout what became known as the Holy Roman Empire. Hierarchical structures crystallized, clergy were ordained, and they demarcated the realm of ministry for themselves, not the masses. The laity were given the responsibility of being good citizens of the empire, supporting the clergy and perpetuating the institutional church. And the mission field? If the empire was officially Christian, then the mission field was beyond its borders, on the frontier but not across the street. And who were the missionaries? A select few professionals that the Lord had called to sacrifice themselves in order to seek and save the lost.

The paradigm's importance for us lies in the fact that most of the generation that now leads our churches grew up with it as a way of thinking about church and society. And all the structures and institutions that make up the churches and the infrastructure of religious life, from missionary societies to seminaries, from congregational life to denominational books of order and canons, are built on the presuppositions of the Christendom Paradigm.... We are surrounded by the relics of the Christendom Paradigm, a paradigm that has largely ceased to work. But the relics hold us hostage to the past and make it difficult to create a new paradigm that can be as compelling for the next age as the Christendom Paradigm has been for the past age.[15]

There is a small but determined cadre of Christian leaders who are convinced that the Spirit of God is slowly but surely bringing about the third major paradigm shift in church history. Called the new apostolic paradigm by Mead, it appears to be a return to the key characteristics of the apostolic paradigm. Once again, every believer is a minister and a missionary, and the mission field begins outside your front door. The church is not so much a self-perpetuating institution as it is a kingdom community known for loving God and loving people. And what of the clergy? The clergy are learning the importance of sharing the ministry with the laity.

I found Mead's model to be a profound validation of the newfound challenges of ministry in the twenty-first century, amid the effects of postmodernism. Many baby boomers and most Gen-Xers are not satisfied being told what is true; they want to experience the truth firsthand. They also have little interest in perpetuating institutions. They want to roll up their sleeves and experience ministry for themselves. They are not content to be armchair ambassadors, studying the Bible in safe and sane environments. They would rather study the Bible in the midst of ministry and missionary work. If the Lord calls them to go to some faraway place to be and do this, they are willing. But they also realize that, in sprawling metropolises like New York or Los Angeles, the world has parked itself outside their front doors.

If you want to be a vibrant twenty-first-century church, you must give serious consideration to the idea of the new apostolic paradigm. Think about this: are the young people from your church that are involved in campus ministries being discipled in the Christendom paradigm or the new apostolic paradigm? I have met so many alumnae from ministries like InterVarsity Christian Fellowship and Campus Crusade for Christ who have yet to connect with a local church. Is it any wonder? After serving God's purposes as ministers and missionaries on their campuses and around the world, they graduate and find that the typical local church seems more interested in perpetuating its kingdom than God's. That's a little harsh, I know, but I want to make sure that you understand what's at stake here. We are not talking about how to attract the next generation to ensure the survival of our churches. No, we are talking about becoming the kind of churches that are ready to receive and release this next generation of ministers and missionaries.

Let me share with you the mission and vision that the Spirit of God has brought to fruition from those seeds of shared ministry that were planted in my heart. Embedded in these two brief paragraphs is my conviction to pursue the new apostolic paradigm through the ministry of Evergreen-LA.

Our Mission — Loving, Growing, Serving
To be a passionate faith community where each person is unleashed to LOVE God and people, to GROW into a gracious, inspired minister and missionary of Jesus, and to SERVE people, both near and far, to the praise and glory of God.

Our Vision — Living Sedaqah Everywhere: Loving God, Loving People
Jesus has called us, Evergreen-Los Angeles, to demonstrate his passion for reconciled relationships through our becoming a multi-Asian/multi-ethnic, multisocioeconomic, multigenerational Sedaqah[16] Community and by reaching out as his grace and message to the unconvinced and the overlooked so that together, we will be living proof that loving God and loving people matter most.

Broadening the Scope of Ministry

A critical element of Evergreen-LA's philosophy of ministry is that "every believer is a disciple, and every disciple is a minister and a missionary." However, it is one thing to make that claim and another thing to forge the needed links between people who want to be in ministry and people who are in ministry.

Having just finished saying that the pastor is not the only minister in the church, I would like to add that ministry is not limited to
what the typical pastor does. I must confess that when I first began to
consider the issue of lay ministry, I mistakenly thought that it meant
training lay people to do what pastors normally do. While it does include the aspect of caring for the members of the church, ministry of
the laity should also reach far beyond the parameters of the church
community. But this will require a broadening of our concept of what
ministry is and where it takes place.

The Lord has equipped some believers to take over many of the primary caregiving roles that pastors are normally expected to fill. These
people will require encouragement and modeling if they are going
to become sensitive undershepherds, if you will, who can look after
the needs of the rest of the flock. If the church is growing numeri-
cally, this is an eventuality that it will have to face. Better to pursue
this as an appropriate goal for the body than to back into it out of
necessity!

One obstacle that you will encounter in attempting to establish this
new emphasis in an Asian American church is the resistance by some
of the older members. While many of them might accede that this
new approach is more biblical than the old one, when it comes time
for them to be in the hospital, they still expect, or at least prefer, to
have one of the pastors of the church pay them a visit. In fairness to
them, they grew up under the old system, and it is hard to ask them in
their later years to alter their expectations. Laying out a clear biblical
apologetic for the new approach may not accomplish very much, for
this is more of a visceral issue than a rational one. To many of the
older folks, it does not feel the same if the pastor does not come and
pray with them.

With this in mind, we have taken a two-pronged approach at Evergreen. When one of the older members requires a visit, we try our
hardest to send one of the pastors. At the same time, we are raising up
the younger generations to have a different set of expectations when
it comes to receiving care from the church. They have a much easier
time feeling cared for when lay ministers come alongside of them. But
we also realize that, if this is going to be the wave of the future, we

must invest heavily in training those lay ministers so that they are confident and capable.

The older Asian Americans also have a hard time making the "minister" label stick to them. They automatically think of the pastor when they think of a minister, and since they are not the pastor, how can they be ministers? Here again, we are trying to be sensitive to their needs, but we have not given up trying to broaden their concepts of ministry.

But what about those who are not called to be ministers within the church? This group probably constitutes the lion's share of the congregation. How can they fulfill their calling to serve the Lord and others? Where will this take place if not within the programmatic structure of the church?

I now have come to understand that much of what constitutes lay ministry will happen outside of the church, many times far beyond the control of the presiding boards and committees. This is a new concept for many of us. In fact, it is a bit unsettling to think that most of the ministry should be taking place outside of the sphere of influence of the power structures of the church. While this may provoke anxious feelings on the part of those called to minister without a net, financial or otherwise, it also offers unprecedented freedom to shape and direct various ministries.

What we are talking about is the vision of growing a ministry wherever the Lord has seen fit to plant you in the world. It may be in an office, a warehouse, a fitness center, a supermarket, a classroom, a hospital, or your own home. These are places where you are called to be like Christ, to incarnate God's presence and teachings, to make Jesus real. Being there is not being a minister. But being there with the eyes and ears of Jesus is what will cause you to discover your unique calling.

Sometimes this will entail organizing a support group at work, where you may be able to introduce the important part that Scripture plays in your life. But it may also never take the shape of a Bible study. Instead, it may mean coming alongside a co-worker or relative who appears to be in need of "a friend that sticks closer than a brother" (Proverbs 18:24). Or it may mean treating your charges, be they employees or children, in the self-giving style that Christ commended to us all. In other cases, you may be called upon to assert the kingdom's values in your company's policies and practices. Or you may sense the Lord challenging you to tackle tough social issues, such as drugs, teen pregnancies, homelessness, and the like. In any case, most of these ministries will never require board approval. Your church may not even be aware of how you are called to serve. What is important is that every believer has identified his or her calling and is pursuing it.

Even so, the churches must make a concerted effort to find out what their people are doing for the Lord out in the world. In order for believers, particularly Asian Americans, to become convinced that these kinds of activities are bona-fide ministries that the Lord is calling them to pursue, they must be recognized and promoted alongside the ministries within the church that already predominate.

With so many Asian Americans involved in professional and technical careers, we must start to highlight how they are learning to bring Christ and God's kingdom into the marketplace if they are ever going to equate this type of calling with those that involve serving through the church or overseas. What message are we sending if the only ministers we laud are the pastors, those serving in some capacity in the church, or short-term and career missionaries? Deliberate efforts must be made to put the spotlight on some of the lay ministers who have already discovered and developed their ministry niches to the point where they can testify to how the Lord is making his presence known or felt through them.

Under the able direction of our outreach pastor, himself a former InterVarsity campus minister, Evergreen-LA has created a monthly support group for its public school teachers. We hold a special commissioning service for them in the worship service annually, to reinforce the message that they are Christ's ministers in the schools. We also have made it a yearly practice to commission our church school facilitators, our newsletter staff, and all the members of our Body Life Team (our governing board). It may not seem like much, but it is a way of keeping a fundamental part of our philosophy of ministry before the congregation. "Every believer a disciple, every disciple a minister and a missionary."

It has never been more important than it is now to destroy the archaic and illegitimate dichotomy between those who work for the Lord and those who work. Asian Americans in particular need to move past the venerating of their pastors that has produced such a sterile brand of spirituality for them and begin to risk being God's beacons in otherwise dark corners of the world.

Making Ministry More Accessible

So how do you go about getting more lay people involved in these broader applications of ministry? You must remove the barriers that might keep them from discovering their true potential to make a difference for the Lord.

The first barrier that must be removed is that of having the wrong idea about ministry and ministers. That was the purpose of the previous sections. This can be accomplished through a sermon series, an emphasis in the weekly Bible studies, and other such avenues. However, teaching alone will not remove the obstacle of a closed or narrow mind. Asian people especially like to hear how other people have fared; thus the encouragement to get some of the lay ministers who are serving the Lord outside the church to share their stories. It is important that the congregation is presented with a wide variety of people and approaches so that they do not think that ministry always has to be something on a large scale or with fabulous results. Some of the most inspirational testimonies come from simple people doing the small things that God asks of them.

But after you have taught them about their all being called to minister in Jesus' name and after they have heard how others have responded to this challenge, there is still at least one more step in removing the obstacle of their old thinking. You must give them opportunities to discover and cultivate their spiritual gifts, and you must assist them as they attempt to define their ministry.

Some form of discipling is called for. As more of the lay ministers are highlighted, make it easy for those who want to explore these same areas to connect with them. Another idea is to stage a ministry fair at least once a year, rather like the career fairs on college campuses for graduating seniors. Promote it widely and see to it that a healthy cross-section of ministries, both inside and outside the church, is well represented. This would be a place where they could ask questions, get ideas, and, more importantly, become part of a supportive network.

This last idea begins to address one of the biggest obstacles to releasing the ministry potential God has built into every church, and that is the problem of ignorance. It might be more accurate to call this being out of the information loop. This problem is less noticeable in smaller churches, but it does not mean that it does not exist there as well. Where it becomes painfully obvious is when a church's weekly attendance grows larger than two hundred. At that point, the grapevine approach to disseminating vital information is usually overtaxed, and increasing numbers of people are left in the dark as to what is going on and the ministry opportunities that are available.

What is called for is a formal reorganization of the flow of information in the church. Some will resist this attempt to modernize and streamline, citing how much more personal the old word-of-mouth method was. Asian Americans, with their natural propensity toward being more relational, may be particularly hard to convince of the need to change. They need to appreciate that, while the old way might have been more personal, it was becoming unwieldy and nonfunctional. Too many new people are being left out of the loop. Unconvinced new AAAs, with their lesser degrees of sticking power, need to have greater, quicker access to the pulse of the church, or they may not come back. Therefore, every effort must be made to make the church, and especially its ministry and growth opportunities, more accessible to everyone. While it is more work and more costly, it is all a part of being better hosts and encouraging people to become more involved in God's activities.

Even with between five hundred and six hundred people, it takes a committed, concerted effort to create an accurate, accessible information system. We talked about the critical need to create some kind of ongoing infrastructure that was responsive to malleability of ministries and the constant influx of new people. But the sheer scope of the project always overwhelmed us and nothing on a large scale was ever accomplished. The strategic hiving from a church of around a thousand people into two more manageable churches gave us at Evergreen-LA a new reason to attack this looming problem. As of this writing, we have established a fresh monthly newsletter, are overhauling the printed ministry materials, installing software that will allow us to build personal profiles of our members, and designing a church website as well as a coffee bar / information center for our new Ministry Center. Most importantly, we have identified gifted and concerned lay ministers who are even more passionate than us pastors about putting this system in place. Amazing things can happen when you unleash the rest of the ministers in your congregation!

Improving the quality of your worship services and practicing shared ministries will not only bless your members. Making those two changes will also bless the unconvinced Americanized Asian Americans and others who drop in to check things out. For though they do not believe in Jesus, they will be surrounded by people who obviously do. And if perchance they do not believe in the church, there is a great likelihood that, if they experience a people are drawn to ministry and missions out of their worship of the living God, they might change their minds about joining a community like that.

THINGS TO THINK ABOUT

1. On a scale of one to ten, with ten meaning like being in throne room of the living, loving Lord and one meaning like being in line at the Department of Motor Vehicles, how would you rate the typical worship service at your church? What factors contributed to your rating?

2. If you did not already have commitments, connections, or a hunger for the Word, would you go out of your way (e.g., give up golfing, pancakes at home with the family, sleeping in) to attend your church's worship service? What might be obstacles or turnoffs to unconvinced people coming at all or coming back? Atmosphere? Overt attitude toward obvious sinners?

3. How does your church look at the influence of charismatic churches like the Vineyard? What kind of instruction has been given regarding the balance between the fruit of the Spirit and the use of the gifts?

If there has been any friction over charismatic/noncharismatic issues, what were they, and were they ever resolved?

4. Who do you think would put up the most resistance to the idea of shared ministry? Why? What steps are you willing to take to move the church in this direction?

Chapter Nine

REJUVENATING SICK BODIES

In the final analysis, the issue is one of mission. How do we as Christians whether mainline or sideline, liberal or conservative, connectional or free find a community that forms and sustains us in an authentic faith and move out bearing that faith into the structures of our ambiguous society? How do we pass those forms of community on to the next generation?
— LOREN B. MEAD[1]

Asian churches in America are not the only ones that might benefit from the remedies and approaches prescribed in chapter 8. Undoubtedly these prescriptions could prove to be life-giving ones for ailing churches from a considerable cross-section of categories, both here and abroad. But, since this book is about growing healthy Asian American churches, the critical question is whether or not they can rejuvenate your particular Asian American church body. If your church wants to have a ministry to members of this emerging, merging Asian American subculture, could these correctives be just what the doctor ordered? Let's examine the possibilities.

SICK CHURCHES

Untold thousands of churches in America need to be either rejuvenated or finally laid to rest. The percent changes displayed in figure 9.1 indicate that mainline churches in particular are most in danger of going the way of the dinosaurs. Most mainline Protestant churches have been in serious decline since the 1960s, having lost nearly 20 percent of their combined membership. Mainline Asian American churches have been a part of this downturn.

In the same time frame, many evangelical denominations have been growing like weeds (fig. 9.2). "During the past two decades,

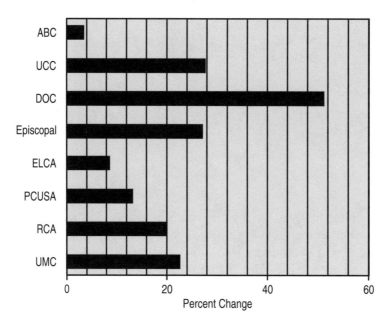

Figure 9.1
Mainline Membership Decline, Percent Change 1965–94

Source: *Christianity Today,* August 11, 1997

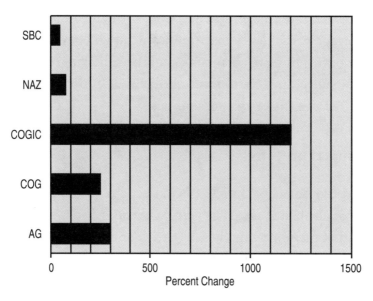

Figure 9.2
Evangelical Membership Surge, 1965–94

Source: *Christianity Today,* August 11, 1997

black Protestant groups have gained, Roman Catholic membership
has grown a solid 16%, and the boom in the conservative evangelical
churches (including Fundamentalists, Pentecostals and charismatics)
has caused some to envision a religious revival."[2] If these other
churches are thriving, why are the mainline ones wasting away?

Many theories abound. Some say that Americans are tired of the
traditional trappings of churched Christianity. In offering his explanation for the widespread decline of mainline churches, Peter Morgan
apparently validates the main thrusts of the previous two chapters:

> We may be living in a time of a paradigm shift in mainline congre-
> gations. People in our congregations now express a hunger for vital,
> authentic religious experiences. They come to church with an innate
> longing to experience the presence of God. They believe that such ex-
> periences are possible and that they give joy, meaning, and guidance to
> life. In recent years, many have left our mainline congregations with the
> hunger unfulfilled.
>
> John Biersdorf comments, "...people do not seek theological talk
> about how one can discuss the experience of God. They hunger for the
> actual presence of God...one has to have experience before guides and
> judgements about experience make any sense....Theory is not an end
> in itself, but a means to more faithful practice....People today hunger
> for the experience of reality out of which life's meaning may come, not
> for discussion of reality."[3]

Then there are those who claim that people relocate too often to
become established in a local church, while others contend that the
mainline churches lack the marketing and communication savvy that
the evangelicals employ to win new members. Support for this last
supposition is the fact that "a contingent of prospering evangelical
congregations exists within each of the mainline denominations."[4]

I think that the best explanation for the decline of mainline
churches in particular, and of numerous other ones in general, is what
I have been arguing in various forms throughout this book: that too
many churches, mainline or otherwise, have lagged behind people as
they have experienced cataclysmic cultural paradigm shifts. As their
social and religious values and thinking shifted, they dropped out or
they will not come because what some of our churches are about
and how we go about it is a poor fit with who they are or who they
have become since the 1960s. Truth be told, many of us have been

so busy serving the needs of our institutions (i.e., denominations and churches) that we have failed to deal with three huge social factors that have emerged since the 1960s. Like it or not, these three factors have drastically transformed the ethos of the American people.

What are these three challenges? Television. The culture of narcissism. And the culture wars.

Television has forever changed people's expectations regarding satisfactory communication. While it has always been bad to be boring, in the days before television, most people did not know that many of us preachers were boring. Or they knew we were, but they still came because church was the only thing to do on weekends. The television revolution has changed that forever. People have learned to crave excitement and stimulation. Cable and the remote have taught them that something more interesting is a few clicks away.

Since the 1960s, humanistic psychology has established itself as the pseudo-religion of America. Its major tenets — namely, radical self-centeredness and seeking personal happiness first — have taken over the psyches of most Americans to some degree. "If it feels good, do it." "You deserve a break today." "Have it your way." In light of the constant barrages to pursue self-actualization that people receive, Jesus' call to lay down our lives for others and to lose ourselves in order to find ourselves must sound pretty harebrained.

Finally, too many mainline and ultraconservative churches allowed themselves to get caught up in the culture wars over abortion, homosexuality, and the role of women. They have focused so much on these three divisive issues that they ultimately demonized each other, overlooked people's basic needs, and lost sight of their core business: saving souls and pursuing God's kingdom on earth until Christ returns.

Whatever the cause(s) may be, the chronic illness that has dogged us and our brethren should cause mainline and other dying churches to ask two questions: Why do we exist as a church? and Do we want to be healed?

Many fine groups and organizations in this country frequently outdo the church when it comes to helping the needy or fighting the evils of society. But none other than the Christian church has been charged with the responsibility to initiate people into the kingdom of God through their faith in Christ. We might be performing many wonderful deeds of Christian charity, but if we are not reaping a continuous harvest of new believers, we may be failing to be the church. If that is the case, it is no wonder that we are wasting away, for any time a mission is merely temporal, it is most likely to be a temporary one.

For their part, scores of Asian churches in this country, while unencumbered with the same kind of faded prominence and success as the white mainline churches, must contend with their own types of sickness. As a result, for instance, a growing number of the more liberal Asian American churches have been showing an unprecedented interest in evangelism these days, now desperately seeking a cure for their dying congregations. Even so, there have always been many theologically conservative Asian churches in America, and they have consistently stressed evangelism and outreach. Yet, except for the Korean Christian churches, a number of which are bursting at the seams, Asian churches in America have generally failed to produce the kind of fruit in keeping with their convictions. Except for the steady flow of immigrants in search of community and services, many Asian churches in this country do not attract many newcomers, especially the more Americanized ones. And of the latter, if the Chinese American church is any indicator of a wider trend, those that are either born in the church or who come later fail to stay; well over 75 percent of the ABCs (American-born Chinese) end up leaving the Chinese church.[5] For all that is healthy about the Asian churches in America, something is not right.

Even though matters such as irrelevance, cultural mismatching, and differences in values and outlooks can be said to be what has caused their widespread failure to attract and retain more Americanized Asian Americans, what Asian churches in this country are sorely in need of is a distinctive kind of rejuvenation. There needs to be renewal.

SPIRITUAL RENEWAL

"Truth without enthusiasm, morality without emotion, ritual without soul, are things Christ unsparingly condemned. Destitute of fire, they are nothing more than a godless philosophy, an ethical system, and a superstition."[6] Without authentic renewal, using the best methods in the world will be like recommending a corpse for a promotion. Any efforts to make a dead body more productive are a waste of time. Life, not just the appearance of it, is the prerequisite for the successful application and adaptation of anything suggested in this book. And the only way for a church to be alive is through its desire to be renewed, both spiritually and in its sense of mission.

When we speak of the need for Asian churches in this country to experience spiritual renewal or rejuvenation, we are not saying that they have to become charismatic (i.e., believe in a second baptism of the Holy Spirit that is evidenced by the speaking in a heavenly language, or tongues), although there are those who would disagree.[7] Rather, many of our Asian churches in America need to be spiritually rejuvenated because they have come to take their relationship with the Lord for granted and have become too complacent and self-reliant. Just as any human relationship tends to get stale over time, so does our relationship with the Lord. What was once exciting and full of promise becomes predictable, dreary, and yes, even pathetic.

When the church loses touch with the Ground of its being, it easily can stray from the unique course that God has set before it in this world. At some point, you might even say that the church might wander so far from God that the Lord then removes the Spirit from it.[8] As the psalmist wrote, "Create in me a pure heart, O God, and renew a steadfast spirit within me. Do not cast me from your presence or take your Holy Spirit from me" (Psalm 51:10–11). Unless this was merely poetic license, it appears that without a continuous pursuit of God, there is the danger of the Lord taking away the Holy Spirit.

When a church body gets too caught up in its own rituals and religion, it risks falling out of favor with God (i.e., if it will not look to the Lord for sustenance and guidance, then the Lord will not be found in what it does). The prophet Isaiah recorded just such a period in the relationship of the people of Israel with God:

> He said, "Surely they are my people,
>   sons who will not be false to me";
> and so he became their Savior.

In all their distress he too was distressed,
　and the angel of his presence saved them.
In his love and mercy he redeemed them;
　he lifted them up and carried them
　all the days of old.
Yet they rebelled
　and grieved his Holy Spirit.
So he turned and became their enemy
　and he himself fought against them. . . .

Look down from heaven and see
　from your lofty throne, holy and glorious.
Where are your zeal and your might?
　Your tenderness and compassion are withheld from us. . . .

Why, O Lord, do you make us wander from your ways
　and harden our hearts so we do not revere you?
Return for the sake of your servants,
　the tribes that are your inheritance.
For a little while your people possessed your holy place,
　but now our enemies have trampled down your sanctuary.
We are yours from old;
　but you have not ruled over them,
　they have not been called by your name.[9]

Or, as A. W. Tozer once wrote, "Until self-effacing men [and women] return again to spiritual leadership, we may expect a progressive deterioration in the quality of popular Christianity year after year till we reach the point where the grieved Holy Spirit withdraws — like the Shekinah from the temple."[10]

So what is a church to do if the Lord's Wind seems to have been removed from its sails? The answer is not found by attending the latest church growth seminar or trying to mimic all the aspects of a successful church down the block. It is as simple and profound as falling in love with the Lord all over again.

Just as some married couples wisely carve out some time to ignite again the spark of love that first warmed their hearts, churches too can rediscover their First Love. Lulled into a savorless stupor through years of sterile preaching and stale worship, longtime churchgoers need to soak their hearts all over again in the teeming depths of God's grace and love. And this can slowly take place through heart-to-heart preaching, worship, and other experiences in the church.

But preachers, worship leaders, and the like cannot direct others to this place of rediscovery if they have not been there recently themselves. The way to this place is illumined by the lamp of the Lord, probing the innermost parts of those willing to take this path of renewal (Proverbs 20:27). And the first step of this journey is taken with a humble heart. "For this is what the high and lofty One says — he who lives forever, whose name is holy: 'I live in a high and holy place, but also with [whomever] is contrite and lowly in spirit, to revive the spirit of the lowly and to revive the heart of the contrite'" (Isaiah 57:15).

The process of renewal begins with the simple acknowledgment that there is a need for renewal. Denial is just another form of spiritual pride and arrogance. But even a timid yes given in reply to the question Do you want to be healed? will give the Great Physician permission to operate. Confession will overflow into repentance, and repentance eventually into renewed life.

As each Asian church in America is endowed with a revitalized fervor for the Lord, there will be a spontaneous upsurge of zeal to bring others into a life-giving relationship with Jesus. Alive again with faith and fire, the rejuvenated church will be eager to explore the course that the Lord will set before it.

MISSION RENEWAL

Spiritual renewal is both an end and a means. Having a rich relationship with the Lord is not simply a prerequisite for greater things; it is the greatest thing. But those who are awash in God's forgiveness and love cannot help but want to pour the overflow of God's abundance into other parched lives. Thus, genuine spiritual renewal will create an intense desire to be a more integral part of the Savior's will and work in the world. It leads to the renewal of the vision for the mission of the church.

What was the original vision for your church's mission? In other words, why was the church started? Whom was it trying to reach with the Good News? For a good number of Asian churches in this country, you need look no further than the name with which each church was christened. Obviously, the charter members of the First Chinese Baptist Church felt led to make God's presence felt among the Chinese, more specifically the Cantonese-speaking immigrants and their families. This would differ from the intentions of the Filipino Christian Fellowship or the Korean Gospel Mission.

Ultimately, this book is for churches that are interested in ministering to Cell B Asian Americans, saltwater fish who are culturally more marginalized. I am assuming you are reading this because you share that vision. But that may not be the case. The spiritual renewal of an Asian church in America does not mean that it must switch its vision from what it was originally to the one that constitutes the theme of this book. After all, a rejuvenated church, after examining its original intentions in light of what is valid today, may feel led of the Lord to redouble its efforts in the same direction. The Lord wants dynamic ministries aimed at every segment of the Asian population in this country.[11] We desperately need to have vital churches all along the flow of the generations of Asian Americans.

However, it may be that as your church discovers a revitalized enthusiasm for bringing in the harvest, it will sense God's Wind blowing it in the new direction of a more blended Asian American ministry. If that is the case, then there needs to be a clear restating of the church's mission. Some may balk at this, believing that it is enough to invite different Asians and others and to be more accepting of them. But that is not enough.

In order for the whole church to get behind this new vision, there should be a formal acknowledgment of reaching out to unconvinced persons, especially AAA ones. Laid out by the pastor and church leaders, this new intention must be affirmed by everyone as a sacred summons from God. This is critical not only for creating a new corporate purpose for the rejuvenated church, but also because it will establish a bias for future decision making related to staffing, programs, facilities, policies, and ministries. Having a new vision to build a church for unconvinced AAAs is a tremendous challenge not only because it must be established on virgin soil but also because it may prove to be quite costly.

COUNTING THE POSSIBLE COSTS

What might it cost your church to forge ahead in this new mission-ary endeavor to reach unconvinced AAAs? Depending on whether or not you are attempting to convert an existing mono-Asian church or to start an Asian American or multi-Asian/multi-ethnic church, the following considerations will have varying applications.

As mentioned in chapter 5, when the apostle Paul embarked on his mission to establish authentically Gentile Christian churches, he first had to resolve critical issues that carried over from the mother church, such as circumcision and a very Jewish way of perceiving Christianity. His solutions, while disturbing to many of the tradition-alists, enabled him to bring the gospel to the Gentiles within their own societies and cultures. In attempting to move beyond the somewhat concentric circles of the churched and the tradition-bound, certain cir-cumcision issues must be addressed and resolved if the new ministry to unconvinced Americanized Asian Americans is going to be effective.

Expanding the Role of Women

Your church must be prepared to have a more egalitarian attitude in regards to men and women if it hopes to connect with unconvinced AAAs. While it may strike some as being rather incongruous to re-fer to the role of women in the church as a modern-day circumcision issue, I believe that this issue will soon become much more of a sore point than it already is. In contrast to many of their denominations' white churches, which have already seen fit to confer equal status on women, more than a few theologically moderate and conservative Asian churches in America continue to preach and teach variations on the principle of the authoritative-male/submissive-female model.

True, these unresponsive Asian congregations cite that they are only acting in accordance with the teachings of Scripture, and there is certainly biblical substance to their argument. However, lest we forget, the Judaizers who were accusing Paul of liberalism also had a scrip-tural leg to stand on in regard to circumcision. Yet Paul pointed out an even more substantive but implied biblical principle: the circumcision of the heart that they were not seeing in arguing for the validity of his teaching. In any case, he did not tell them to stop practicing circumcision; they were doing it based on their interpretation of God's law. However, he wanted them to understand that physical circumcision was not only unnecessary but also an impediment to ministering among Gentiles. Could it be that this issue of women's roles in the twenty-first-century church falls into a similar category?

Most of the Asian cultures tend to be quite chauvinistic toward women.[12] This may be why numerous Asian American Christian women and men have such a hard time with egalitarianism and mutual submission. There may be conflicting issues of power and servanthood that they are not yet ready to face. Please understand that my purpose here is not to convince the proponents of a strict hierarchy to change their belief. That is something they must work out with the Lord. What does concern me is that many of the people we want to affect are quite comfortable with women, including Asian American women, being educated and professionals. When so many Asian American women have been reared to be assertive, independent, and competent, how can they fit into churches that relegate them to subservient, passive roles? Listen to what former Apple Computer's CEO John Sculley has to say about the impact women are having in the highly charged arena of the high-tech marketplace:

> As we shift toward a work world which learns to leverage intuitive and creative skills, women will emerge as the country's most important hidden resource. Some 30 percent of the students in the nation's top business schools today are women. A disproportionate share of them also is getting the high honors and distinctions in our universities. At Apple, where 50 percent of our managers are female, some 70 percent of our performance awards for management last year went to women.
>
> If creativity and innovation are important in regaining our world competitiveness, women leaders may prove ideally suited for our own country's renewal. Many of the characteristics of the new-age leader are the typical personality traits that women possess.[13]

Myriad Asian American women have already shown themselves to be of this caliber. So any church that wants to reach them and the growing numbers of Asian American men who are comfortable with the success of these women cannot afford to dodge this bullet much longer. If the apostle Paul were alive, he would probably be wrestling with this issue as it relates to evangelizing a large population of unreached people.

There is also the related issue of what the Asian churches in this country are going to do with the growing numbers of high-caliber women coming out of the seminaries. An article in a 1990 issue of *The Atlantic Monthly* contained the following provocative comparison:

> The academic and intellectual level in seminaries would be mediocre indeed were it not for the ever increasing numbers of women, who, as their denominations began to allow their ordination, started coming to the seminaries in significant numbers in the 1960s. . . . Women students consistently score higher than men. One recent study showed that women aged twenty to twenty-four entering theological training in all denominations scored twenty points higher in the quantitative section of the Graduate Record Exam than men in the same age group. In contrast, women in professions other than the ministry score on the average eighty points lower than men on this portion of the GRE.[14]

If it is true that the quality of Asian American male seminarians is declining and *if* it is also true that the current crop of Asian American females in seminary are there because the Lord has called them to be there — to become clerics, not just because they are intelligent — then what should our response be? Asian American pulpits either sit vacant for years or are inadequately filled by less gifted males while more Asian American, seminary-trained females are forced to figure out creative ways to confront the sturdy walls of opposition. If the Lord Jesus is truly calling these sisters into the ranks of the ordained, could it be that too many of our languishing or dying Asian American churches might be ignoring an important part of the Lord's provision for their rejuvenation? In the end, your personal convictions may still prevent you from affirming female pastors and church leaders. At least appreciate that there are scores of God-fearing, Word-honoring brothers and sisters who do, and the Lord is blessing them, too. For without fellow Christians who are led to remove this barrier, countless unconvinced, postmodern-minded AAAs males and females will probably never come to embrace Jesus.

Issuing Altar Calls Less Frequently

In some churches, every sermon leads into an impassioned appeal for any unconvinced persons present to make an on-the-spot conversion. Many longtime Christians may argue loud and long for this practice to be perpetuated, but they need to consider the possibility that this is no longer the best way to present the invitation of the gospel (see chap. 6).

In actuality, it may serve to detour people in the process of searching for the pearl because it demands a public demonstration of a commitment that they might still be deliberating. This is not to say that altar calls should be eliminated; they should definitely be given as the Spirit leads. But the Spirit may also lead the pastor to issue other kinds of calls to commitment, ones that are directed at mature Christians. Do not be surprised if the basic issue of decreasing altar calls provokes some strong reactions.

Allowing Visitors More Anonymity

While this may seem relatively innocuous when compared with the previous issue, it will also prove to have its share of impassioned supporters. Nevertheless, your church must consider ways to help make new people feel welcome that do not put them on the spot. Many of the unconvinced AAAs that we see are coming to church because they find themselves in the middle of a crisis and have decided to give God a chance. They are usually the last to arrive and the first to leave. Most seem to want to preserve their anonymity in the larger gathering.

It is crucial that the pastor who preached that day is free to spend some time with them immediately after the service. We have found that this makes them feel significant, and there is a greater chance that they will return. But this means that the regulars must give the pastor a wide berth on Sundays so that he or she can do this. This may also cause a commotion among some of the members, but it is a related cost of ministering to those who have little commitment to returning.

Replacing the Hierarchy with a Network

If your church hopes to affect the increasing numbers of Asian American young adults, it must alter the process of decision making and the
concomitant distribution of power. People who have been highly educated and reared with an anti-authority attitude in society will respond
more favorably to churches that employ a networking concept for
decision making and ministry than those that use the traditional hierarchical method.[15] Christian young adults frequently complain about
feeling locked out of the power structures and the decision-making
processes in their Asian churches. It is interesting that this same transition is also taking place in the secular workplace, largely due to the
fact that,

> for the first time, alumni of the sixties generation and the Vietnam ex-
> perience are moving into the ranks of business leadership. They are
> loosening the bonds of leadership from a hierarchical to a network
> model. . . . Why is the network so important? Because that is the natural
> course of how ideas flow.[16]

The great thing about a network is that it has no center. Rather
than being a structure, it is a dynamic process in which modular
ministry teams come and go, mix and match, depending on what is
most needed and where. Coordination and cooperation, rather than
competition and control, become the buzzwords among the leaders of
various ministries. Ministry leaders, including pastors, function more
like coaches, keeping the vision and mission of the church clearly in
focus for those entrusted with being ministers. Postmodern people, in
the main, are much more relational than are modernists. Quite often
the process matters to the former much more than the outcome. Networks are much more empowering than are hierarchies. They are what
make shared ministry possible.

Admittedly, this changeover can be a particularly thorny issue in
churches where the leaders come from a more immigrant-oriented
value system. The vast majority of our Asian churches in America fit
this description to varying degrees. In such instances, I believe that
the persistence of the hierarchies of power and authority stem from
a latent adherence to a Confucian mentality. Having this traditional
value of filial piety, most Asian churches are run (or ruled) by a cadre

of older people, many or all of them men. The pastor, by virtue of his or her office, is usually afforded automatic membership in this group, but there are exceptions.

Again, I am not trying to threaten churches that operate like this. I am merely indicating that it is naive to think that churches set up to meet the needs of Cell D Asians (low assimilation, high ethnic identity, or imported bass) will also be attractive to Cell B Asians (high assimilation, high ethnic identity, or acculturated cod).

Churches for Cell B Asians must operate much more out in the open, so that more people feel that they are a part of what is happening. In the case of mono-Asian churches trying to become multi-Asian, more of the marginal adults, including the single adults, must be elected to the governing bodies. But since people reared on thirty-minute television programs tend to think of life and its commitments in shorter segments, the church's by-laws may need to be changed to allow for shorter commitments in some offices. This also goes for commitments for certain roles and groups. Those who feel that the willingness to make long-term commitments is a sure sign of the spiritual maturity necessary to serve on the board or council will have a hard time with this cost. But the infrastructure of Asian American churches must reflect the kind of people that make up the body.

In making the transition from a hierarchy to a network, what may prove to be the biggest obstacle is the reluctance of the older leaders to pass the baton of power and influence to the succeeding generations. Fuller Seminary's Bill Pannell, in writing about this unwelcome transition in the broader context of evangelicalism, defines the problem:

> Hundreds of great "athletes" are standing out on the track, waiting for a tired evangelicalism to catch up. Eager, proven talent has been in place for years, shifting from one foot to the other, waiting for the hand-off. Many are still waiting. Others have given up and wandered off to find another event where they'll get a chance to run.
>
> Which leads to the real issue with batons: someone's got to let go. It's hard to give up power. It's even harder to admit that power is what this whole baton-passing thing is about. Once you pass the baton, you have no choice but to trust the next runner. You've lost control....

> ...I would not try to pass the method, but something of the spirit, the ethos, the passion. Older leaders do have a great deal of power to invest in new leaders, encouraging and legitimizing them.[17]

Asian American churches must have a much more decentralized mode of operating. More people need to be entrusted with more responsibility. This supports the previously mentioned concept of shared ministry, rather than a pastor-based one. If these churches are truly going to be new, then there must be regular transfusions of new blood, new ideas, and new leadership.

Abolishing the Small-Church Mentality

A lot of people feel comfortable in a small church, one that averages between seventy-five and one hundred worshipers per Sunday. And there are pastors who are called to this scale of ministry. However, in order to reach the scores of unconvinced Americanized Asian Americans, the church must overcome its fear of growth, for the indications are that people like unconvinced AAAs prefer going to large, nontraditional churches.[18] For example, the fastest-growing types of church in the United States are large interdenominational churches. "In 1984 only 100 American churches averaged more than 2,000 worshipers on Sunday; that number has doubled, and some 10,000 churches now have an average attendance of 1,000 or more."[19]

Numbers like these boggle the mind of most Asian American Christians. The exception would be the Koreans, who are familiar with their churches in Korea normally exceeding 2,000 or more people.[20] But some of us recall growing up in Asian congregations of about 50 to 150, led by one bilingual pastor or one pastor for each language group. So whether we are pastors or lay ministers, we are overwhelmed by the notion of being a part of a sizable church. We feel this way because of our lack of prior experience and because of our concern about the quality of intimacy that is possible in a church of 500 to 1,000. But according to Fred Smith, a leading consultant for large churches, one thing they deliver better than small churches, oddly enough, is intimacy. "Large churches are honeycombed with small groups — cells, sharing groups, discipleship groups — organized around a subject such as caring for small children or growing older."[21]

Of course, we are not considering how small churches might become large churches because we believe that churches with more people are somehow superior to those with less. That is obviously false. Rather, this is brought up in the context of what it might cost a church to minister to unconvinced AAAs. To the degree that the pundits are correct, having a larger church makes it easier to attract these people. Our experience at Evergreen Baptist Church of Los Angeles since 1987 has shown this to have some validity.[22] As for how to grow your church, in both depth and scope, that is what this book is all about. A church that is excited about being a part of God's kingdom should attract new people. What I want you to realize here is that, if the Lord begins to "add to your numbers daily those who are being saved," you should not stand in the way of the church's growth.

To resist the growth of your church may sound ludicrous, but there are many, for good reasons, who would prefer that their church stay small or, at most, medium-sized. Current facilities and staff will soon be overtaxed, and the budget will have to be increased to meet these greater demands. The informal lines of communication will have to give way to more efficient means of keeping everyone abreast of what is happening. And the senior pastor will have to change from being the shepherd who does all the tending to being the primary visioncaster who motivates and unleashes the staff and lay ministers.

There are many more reasons that would give pastors and their church members cause to resist growth. But if you feel called to reach unconvinced AAAs, you should at least be prepared to pay this particular price of pursuing this ministry.

Improving the Church's Name

Everything about the church should serve its God-mandated mission. So if the church's name no longer seems to reflect that mission, it should be changed to something that does. Here again, we may be treading on what some might consider holy ground. Nevertheless, since a church is clearly identified by its name, that label must not be an obstacle to accomplishing the mission.

For example, Evergreen used to be called Nisei Baptist Church, but some visionary leaders in the 1950s realized that a name that emphasized only the second-generation Japanese Americans would not sound inviting to future generations of Japanese Americans. So the decision was made to name the church after the major street where it was located. Who could have guessed then that such a generic-sounding name would come to be associated with not just different generations of Japanese Americans but with a new, emerging, merging Asian American subculture? During the 1980s, when our church began to grow rapidly, a non-Japanese Asian American had no need to explain why he or she attended Evergreen. As we enter the twenty-first century and are intent on becoming more multi-Asian and multi-ethnic, someone without any Asian heritage will not have to explain why he or she is a member of Evergreen — all because some insightful church leaders were willing to make a difficult decision nearly fifty years ago.

In a similar vein, there has been a much-chronicled move away from churches with names that are either too jargony (e.g., Church of the Holy Ascension, Mount of Olives Christian Church) or too closely identified with mainline denominations (e.g., First Chinese Baptist, Glendale Lutheran). In this sense, Evergreen Baptist Church of LA has been blessed. As it has intentionally become more contemporary, greater numbers of people have come to refer to it without the Baptist appendage. If your church is genuinely moving away from being so traditional, then you might seriously consider giving it a new name that reflects that shift (e.g., Hope Chapel, Sacramento Asian American Ministries, Grace Point Fellowship). This is not to say that being associated with a mainline denomination is an automatic liability. On the contrary, denominational churches can truly benefit from the greater accountability that comes with being part of a larger and more diverse family. Evergreen-LA has not dropped Baptist from its name for that very reason, and this decision has not hindered our ability to attract people who are supposed to have mainline phobia.

Just remember: a new name without a matching new ministry is false advertising.

Upgrading the Church's Self-Understanding

This last possible cost is sort of a potpourri of things that have to do with changing the church's self-concept. Bringing up items like restructuring the decision-making process and changing the church's name has already alluded to some of this. But there are other issues that need to be considered if the church is going to be a relevant force in the twenty-first century.

I firmly believe that Asian American churches can glean many valuable lessons from leading edge corporations like Apple Computers and become third-wave churches in the process. In applying this term, I am coming from a different direction than the charismatic usage of it. Before explaining what I mean by this, let me first review the roots of this terminology in order to keep the confusion to a minimum.

Alvin Toffler, futurist and author of the best-selling *Future Shock*, was the first one to peer into the future and foresee what he called the managerial third wave. In describing the evolution of civilization, he pictured it as a progression of waves or phases. He called the first wave the Agricultural Age, the second the Industrial Age, and the third the Information Age. This last wave was something that Toffler predicted would happen. Amazing developments — the microchip and the personal computer, fax machines, copiers, cellular phones, satellite technology, and fiber optics — prove Toffler was right. In this age of instant access to information, organizations and institutions must be retooled, or else they risk being left behind as the tempo of change keeps accelerating.

The church is no exception. First-wave churches were established during the Agricultural Age. A pastor was called to look after all the needs of the members of a small community. Life was simple and predictable. Unfortunately, too many of our Asian churches in this country are still operating in this mode. They have not even advanced to being second wave yet.

Second-wave churches were built around the model of the Industrial Age, intended to grow but with a more-of-the-same attitude, not an appreciation for change. Growth was expected to happen; it did not have to be planned. Like many second-wave corporations, churches like this are self-contained, with few outside dependencies. Operating in this mode, second-wave churches see little need to form a network of support and resources with other churches. Each church is bent on becoming an institution, and it is almost as if the other churches are competitors. Plenty of Asian American churches are a combination of the first two waves, but unless they evolve into third-wave churches, they run the risk of becoming overinstitutionalized anachronisms. In describing the problems of stagnant industrial companies, analyst John Childs inadvertently paints a fairly accurate picture of the situation in many of our dying first- and second-wave churches. "Among the features which so often mark the struggling organization are low motivation and morale, late and inappropriate decisions, conflict and lack of coordination, rising costs and a generally poor response to new opportunities and external change."[23] So what does it mean for Asian American churches to become third wave? The answer to that question is far from complete because this new form of managing and imagining an organization is still slowly taking shape itself. Sculley writes:

> Third-wave companies are the emerging form, . . . for all institutions. . . . [T]he source of their strength lies in change — in the ability to transform their products and organization in response to changes in the economy, in social habits, in customer interests. By contrast, the source of strength in industrial-age companies is stability. Everything about them is geared to establishing stability including their emphasis on title and rank rather than on making a difference, on structure over flexibility, on putting the institution's needs before the individual's. No wonder the second-wave company is slow to respond to external change.[24]

Sculley's description of a second-wave company strikes me as an apt illustration of our typical church. Differences are minimized and new ideas or concerns are often swallowed up in the overarching concern not to rock the huge institutional boat that the second-wave church has become. And what institution other than the church better epitomizes the zealous desires to perpetuate tradition? It is just this type of atmosphere that will suffocate any serious attempt to bring a relevant ministry to unconvinced Americanized Asian Americans.

All but a few of the books that I have seen in print regarding third-wave churches are those that promote a strong charismatic emphasis for mainline Protestant institutions. While there do seem to be some parallels between the two uses of the term (e.g., openness to change, acknowledgment of diversity) the charismatically oriented books (by the likes of C. Peter Wagner and John Wimber) do not address this issue from a management point of view. Mead's book, *The Once and Future Church: Reinventing the Congregation for a New Mission Frontier*, however, is an excellent treatment of what it will take to move from being a Christendom paradigm church (second wave) to a new apostolic paradigm church (third wave). I hope more books of this nature will emerge in the next few years. Until they do, my nascent images of the third-wave Asian American church will have to suffice.

The vision Jesus has set before my eyes is that of the church as an open campus instead of an insular institution. People, whether staff or lay, could join a third-wave church for a while, knowing that the church is more interested in contributing to their lives than in their contributing to the church. There would be less stress on institutional loyalty and more on the church's commitment to its people.

This investment on the church's part would come with no strings attached, so that people know that they are free to take what they have gained and move on to the next stage of their pursuit of the pearl of ultimate value. What matters most is that their time spent with the church, be it short or long, proves to be a consequential part of their equipping and refining to be more like Jesus Christ. According to Fred Smith, this emphasis on the growth of people will result in the growth of the church: "These churches grow because they have identified their business differently. They see themselves as delivery systems rather than as accumulators of human capital."[25]

The third-wave Asian American church would also weave mutual networks of support and resource sharing with other churches. As it is now, every church must strive to be a complete unit on its own. The smaller churches, with fewer resources available to them, cannot keep up with the larger ones. But other churches are not the competition; they should be cohorts. Realizing this anew, the larger third-wave churches like Evergreen-LA will make every effort to serve smaller or newly planted churches, sharing insights, programs, staff time, or equipment. Far from being threatened if these churches begin to thrive, third-wave churches will rejoice that there are that many more dynamic churches that can influence the diverse community for Christ. Many of us at Evergreen-LA are convinced that the true measure of our faithfulness and stewardship is to share our insights and ministry teams with other churches, across generational and even denominational lines, until the Lord revitalizes and restores them. We believe that the Lord wants what is happening at our church to be a movement, not a moment.

Finally, third-wave Asian American churches would have a greater variety of ways to get things done. People who see a need would be given the primary responsibility to respond to it instead of having it assigned to a subcommittee and then having it take a year or so to get back to the now-deflated people. Those who are given the power to make a difference are also given the freedom to fail so long as they learn from their mistakes. For the abundant grace of Jesus is readily available for those who take risks in trying to get at needs or solve problems.

Everything that was laid out above in the section on confronting the church's hierarchy applies in a third-wave church. The process of getting things done would become more decentralized and less organized. The pastor would not need to have a hand in everything that occurs in the church, and the ruling boards would no longer feel the pressure to repress change for the sake of keeping the church stabilized. Instead, everyone in leadership would feel responsible for unleashing the limitless potential of a God-equipped, Spirit-led church on an unsuspecting world.

In some ways, it would seem that Toffler did not invent the concept of third-wave management, at least not when it is applied to the church. For it would seem that a long, long time ago, when the world was still in the midst of the first wave, the church skipped the first two waves and began with the third. The world has changed drastically in two thousand years, but the idea of an open, caring community that values every person and quickly responds to needs is as valid today as it was in the first century. We need to learn how to harness high technology to serve this new direction for the church.

You might be thinking that all this talk of creating a third-wave Asian American church is a pipe dream. By the grace of God, since I became the senior pastor in March 1997, we have put into place almost every one of the third-wave elements prescribed above. Has it been easy? Not on your life. But it has been worth all the pain and problems of figuring it out. My staff has exceeded nearly all of my expectations. Led by a common mission and vision, the church's leaders have learned to work alongside each other. The people in the pews, captivated with a compelling vision of God and whom God has called us to be, are becoming ministry entrepreneurs. And me? I would not want to trade places with anybody. So you see, I am not promoting a pipe dream. I practice what I proclaim.

OPEN LETTERS TO THE THREE TYPES OF FISH

Change often feels far too fast to those who helped carve out the status quo and much too slow to those whose needs are no longer well served by the status quo. I would like to address open letters to each of the three types of fish in my rivers>bay>sea model.

To the Imported Bass/1.0 Generation

You imported bass were the pioneers, the first ones to come across the vast expanse of the Pacific in your pursuit of the pearl: the vision of a better life for you and your loved ones. Whenever and however you came, you should long be remembered and revered for your pluck and courage, for your tremendous faith in the face of adversity and obstacles. You made great sacrifices for your progeny because of your great love for them, and they should never forget this.

In planting freshwater churches or by joining one, you also established that faith in Jesus Christ was one of the anchor points in your adopted homeland. You have left a legacy of leadership and faithfulness to the legions of Asian Americans that have come after you.

After everything you have done for the sake of the children, I can

well imagine how hard it must be to see so many of the second generation and beyond leave freshwater churches. Given your core belief
that one's family should be the center of a person's universe, it must
be painful and frustrating as you watch the ongoing decentralization
of Asian American families, even churched ones. To have come this
far, to have given so much, only to see this happening.

As you chide your children and grandchildren for leaving their families and their churches, please remember that you were the first ones
to leave your families and your countries. Whether or not you anticipated this, what they are doing is an outgrowth of your difficult
decision to relocate to America. It is a fact *and* a fact of life in this
country for every group of immigrants, regardless of origin. The strong
undercurrents of acculturation and assimilation are sweeping along
your offspring toward a culturally pluralistic and ethnically diverse
future.

You must come to accept that the first-generation Asian church
cannot function like a dam, halting the flow of acculturation and
Americanization while forming a giant multigenerational lake behind
it. You keep thinking that the younger people will stay and serve if you
call a second-generation youth pastor or English-speaking associate
pastor to speak their language and meet their needs. Some will stay,
especially the second-generation ones. But most will leave, not because
yours isn't a Spirit-filled, Word-centered, Jesus-preaching church but
because the freshwater conditions there make it nearly impossible for
them to breathe. As each generation comes of age in America, they are
less equipped to survive and thrive in the freshwater conditions that
you and your pastor(s) enjoy.

My prayer for you is that you will continue to make great sacrifices on behalf of those you love. Give the next generations your best
blessing by passing the baton of leadership to them. Support their efforts to create new ministries with your fervent prayers. Invest God's
money in their dreams to have churches and ministries that are appropriate and relevant to whom God has created them to be. You and
your ministries will always be a locus for immigrant groups (with the
exception maybe of the Japanese American churches; see the section
that follows these letters). And that's always going to be a wonderful

and crucial mission! I sincerely hope that, as sad or mad as you might be at the changing faces in your family portrait, you would rejoice at the glorious opportunity being afforded you to launch the next several generations of Christian risk takers. Unlike you, most have never known the pain of deciding whether or not to come to America. But much like you, many of them have left familiar people and surroundings in search of deeper truths and greater opportunities. Point the generations that came after you in the direction of the ultimate Pearl and tell them to go for it! It is their time to become pioneers like you.

To Salmon / 1.5–2.0 Generation

Typically bicultural and bilingual, you salmon are much like the middle child in a family of three children. As the middle child you intuitively understand the concerns of your older sibling (1.0 generation), yet you are quite sympathetic with the complaints of your younger sibling (3.0 and beyond). If anything, you are much more comfortable with your older sibling than your younger one. You often find the former's values comforting while you often question the latter's, as much as you sometimes hate to admit it.

Most likely you grew up as the dutiful children of observant or at least concerned parents. You went to church or were sent to church not only to learn about God but also to be indoctrinated with good morals and to mingle with other nice Asian young people like you. Being bilingual, you were able to sit through bilingual worship services and understand what was going on. The freshwater Asian church has never been a perfect match for you, but due to strong family ties and a familiarity with immigrant culture, many of you have toughed it out. If you have been blessed with children, however, you must have started to wonder if there is a future for them at your freshwater or bay multilingual, immigrant-oriented church.

Your children probably have been complaining ever since they were pre-adolescents. In the ensuing years, their ability and desire to embrace the Asian-centric culture of your church has waned even more.

It's not because they are rejecting you, their forebears, or their rich heritage. It's because they are so Americanized.

This is not simply about the different ways in which they adorn their bodies. It's about the vastly different ways they see themselves, the world, Christianity, even God. It's about their diverse choice of friends and spouses. It's about the racially ambiguous faces of their children, your grandchildren.

My prayer is that you would embrace as fact that your generation occupies the critical transitional spot in the entire generational flow scenario in America. Since God has positioned you as a unique bridge between the older and the younger siblings in this multigenerational scheme, are you willing to serve as active peacemakers between the two? With your ability to speak or at least understand the mother tongue and your natural close ties to your cultural roots, who better to appreciate the unspoken expectations and deep concerns of the first generation? In your natural role as parents and mentors of more Americanized Asian Americans, who better to empathize with their frustrations and to imagine with them how they need the future to look? And who better to understand the influential currents of acculturation and assimilation since it was your generation where they first began to take effect?

Bay of Transitions churches and ministries, by definition, are inherently short-lived. The succeeding generations of Asian Americans, by virtue of how much further along they are in the ongoing acculturation process, will not find your freshwater/saltwater combination suitable or relevant. Thus, your contribution to the overall mission to see many Asian Americans become followers of Jesus is to equip, bless, and empower the third generation and beyond to build the churches and ministries that will best match their needs. Your legacy, in part, will be the spiritual viability and vitality of those who came after you.

To Acculturated Cod/3.0 Generation and Beyond

If there are going to be vital churches all along the generational flow of Asian America, you and your acculturated cod colleagues will have to step out in faith and create them. Ones that are for fresh combinations of several adjacent Asian American groups. And multi-Asian / multi-ethnic ones that are living proof of Jesus' ability to mold hopelessly diverse people into close-knit faith communities. However, before you do that, I believe that God wants us acculturated cod to be reconciled to a portion of our pasts.

If you (like me) grew up in an ethnic specific freshwater church, you've already accumulated your laundry list of complaints. You are tired of jousting with the older people who occupy most of the power positions in the church. They seem set in their ways and in their expectations of the younger generations. They may have even sinned against some of you in trying to prevent what you may now accept as inevitable. Wherever possible, try and come to a place of reconciliation before you embark on your mission.

Put yourself in their place. If you had risked everything to pursue a better life for your offspring, wouldn't you feel threatened and alarmed if they declared that they were leaving to start their own church or to attend one that was a better fit? This was not supposed to happen. Or at least it was something you never anticipated. And so you do everything in your power to stem the tide, to halt the silent exodus, even if it means withholding blessings or not sharing leadership. They assumed that the pursuit of the pearl was going to be costly, but they never dreamed that one of the costs would be the sanctity of their beloved families. Whether or not they ask you for forgiveness, Jesus will show you how to forgive them before you leave them. Or if you have already left them, to forgive them in your hearts.

For as acculturated cod you must still follow the generational flow out toward the Sea of Inevitability. You must still find the same kind of courage and faith that buoyed your forebears here from distant lands across the vast Pacific. To survive and thrive as Americanized Asian Americans — many a fusion of ethnicities and cultures and many married beyond the bounds of your own heritage — you must learn to create vibrant faith communities that love and serve the living and present Jesus in the midst of a postmodern new world.

THE UNIQUE POTENTIAL OF JAPANESE AMERICAN CHRISTIAN CHURCHES

I want to conclude this section on rejuvenation by returning to one of my favorite subjects: the unique position of Japanese Americans to be able to impact culturally marginal Asian Americans.

As we discuss the idea of rejuvenating Asian churches so that they can take up the challenge of ministering to Cell B Asian Americans, I would like for us to revisit my earlier assertion that Japanese Americans represent the vanguard of this newly emerging, merging subculture (see chap. 4). If what I believe is true, then many Japanese American Christian churches should be giving serious consideration to writing a new chapter of ministry, one that they might be able to author with significantly less effort than other Asian American groups. In short, I believe that if Japanese American churches experience renewal, many of them would have the foremost potential to become new Asian American churches.

I have been saying all along that culturally marginal Asian Americans need multicultural Asian churches that correspond with who they are. This is because identity is a life issue. In speaking to this, Calvin Miller contends that

> we spend all of our lives looking for people "like" ourselves in communities "like" our own with doctrines "like" the ones that we believe. Churchmanship in America is composed of a broad pluralism where many different kinds of churches are divided by only the tiniest shades of differences. Still, we want to go to the churches that are "like" us.[26]

But who is going to establish the churches with which culturally marginal Asian Americans will be able to identify? Here again, the Japanese Americans, led by the younger Nisei and older Sansei, are presented with an opportunity to lead the way. But if they have been oblivious to this vanguard role as a whole, the Christian ones are even more unaware of their potential to lead the way in the developing of intentionally Asian American churches.

Whereas, intentionally or not, they have been at the forefront of the movement to create an Asian American identity, when it comes to embracing this new direction in their Christian churches, they have been lagging far behind. To be sure, there has been an almost imperceptible move in this direction by a slowly increasing number of Japanese American churches over the years, for they are not immune to the forces of acculturation that are prodding their group as a whole. However, most of them do not seem to acknowledge this movement in their midst, or they are choosing not to encourage it. In either case, they are missing a novel opportunity to expand their mission to include other Cell B Asian Americans who can identify with the subculture they already have.

Unlike other Asian ethnic churches, Japanese American churches are facing a different situation as far as immigrants go. Large-scale immigration from Japan effectively ended with the arrival of the last of the Issei two generations ago. Thus, generally speaking, the present Japanese-speaking component of their congregations is dying out with the Issei. By 2010 there will be no more Issei pioneers.

The new immigrants from Japan, consisting mainly of businessmen and their families, will not mix as well with the Nisei, Sansei, and Yonsei because they do not share the Meiji-era culture with them as the Issei pioneers did. So for those who do resettle in America, there must be separate ministries. It is just as unrealistic to expect these modern arrivals from Japan to mix with the Meiji-era, acculturated Japanese Americans as it is to try and blend immigrants from the People's Republic of China with third-generation ABCs. Therefore, the Japanese American Christian church is looking at a future that will be monolingual, that is, English. No other Asian church is faced with this uncommon scenario so soon.

But how many Japanese American churches are reading the bold brushstrokes that are already on the wall? Over the past fifteen years or so, non-Japanese Asians have been infiltrating their congregations and conferences in increasing amounts, drawn to their attractive brand of Asian American subculture. As an example, in sponsoring the nation's largest Japanese Christian family conference at Mt. Hermon, California, since 1949, the Japanese Evangelical Missionary Society (JEMS) has seen more and more interracial couples, ABCs, and various other Asians in attendance. To their credit, JEMS has always awarded a warm welcome to these people. But even so, there is a pervasive sense that this is still a Japanese conference that just is not averse to other Asians coming to be a part of it. Of course, JEMS is a parachurch organization and Mt. Hermon is a once-a-year conference, but on a smaller scale in Japanese American Christian churches across the country, this same scenario is occurring.

While it may be difficult officially to broaden the mission of a parachurch organization that was founded to minister to Japanese, it would seem that individual churches would be more able to accomplish this transformation. Granted, those that are a part of conferences that were established to reach the Japanese (e.g., the Japanese Free Methodist and the Japanese Christian Churches [formerly O.M.S. Holiness]), would have many more obstacles to surmount. They would have to secure the formal blessing of their conferences before setting forth on this new path. But those with traditions of local church autonomy and self-determination (e.g., Baptists, Congregationalists) should be able to pursue this ministry as long as it was determined that this issued from the Holy Spirit.

This is not an easy, one-step task that can be accomplished overnight. But we should not allow the difficulties to daunt us if we are convinced that this is what the Lord wants for Christ's church. I know that this is feasible because this remarkable transition is continuing to take place at Evergreen-LA.

Evergreen Baptist Church of Los Angeles was a fairly typical Japanese American church. The only major departure in its long history would have to be the mutual decision to separate the two language groups into independent churches in the early 1950s. But that one deliberate decision could almost be called a precursor of what is naturally going to happen in most other Japanese American churches, namely, the emergence of an all-English-speaking ministry. Whatever the motivations were for their decision, the English-speaking contingent at Evergreen-LA had unknowingly launched themselves as a prototype vessel into yet uncharted waters.

Other Japanese American churches, with vision and commitment, can follow in Evergreen's wake. If they are willing to recognize their unique place in society and to affirm the ethnic blending that is so evident in their relational circles, they can reach out and begin to touch tomorrow today.

The leaders should get together and begin to ask the Lord to give them a vision for their church's mission ten and twenty years from now. They will need to agree that this is their new mission from God and be willing to pay the price of this pioneering ministry. Consideration must be given to the hiring of non-Japanese Asian staff in order to show the seriousness of their intentions. And they will have to learn more about the subtle differences between the different Asian cultures so that theirs will no longer predominate. Above all, they must approach this new and yet familiar mission as a sacred calling from the Lord.

Evergreen-LA is proof positive of what the Lord can do as the Spirit of Christ rejuvenates a church. Is it possible for Jesus to do something similar in your church?

THINGS TO THINK ABOUT

1. One writer believes the following to be characteristics of renewed churches: participation of the laity; a sense of expectancy for both the presence and the power of God; evangelism and church growth; youth as an integral part of the church; warmth and fellowship; biblical preaching; joyful, exuberant (even spontaneous) worship; concern for world mission; focus on both the gifts and fruit of the Spirit. How does your church compare with this list? Where might there be need for serious spiritual renewal and why?

2. What was the original vision for your church's mission when it began? In other words, why was the church started? Whom was it trying to reach with the Good News?

3. What do you think some of the costs for rejuvenating your ministry might be and why? How willing and able is your church to pay these costs?

4. What is the official church position on women in leadership and on women as pastors? What effect, if any, has this had on attracting unconvinced AAAs of both genders to become a part of your community?

5. According to the manner in which your church operates and sees itself, would you classify it as being first, second, or third wave? In regard to church renewal and effectively reaching unconvinced, turned-off Asian

Americans, how critical do you think it is for more churches to think of themselves in more third-wave concepts?

6. If you are part of a historically Japanese American ministry, where do you think it will be in twenty years? Where do you sense God wants it to be in terms of its location and facilities, and more importantly, its scope of ministry? What needs to change in order for your church to become a genuine, blended, Americanized Asian American or multi-Asian/multi-ethnic ministry, rather than a Japanese American church that is open to other Asian Americans coming?

Chapter Ten

WHAT WILL ASIAN AMERICA LOOK LIKE?

Asian Americans have become a crucial barometer of the contemporary racial climate.
— MICHAEL OMI[1]

The Asian American identity as we now know it may not last another generation.
— ERIC LIU[2]

Around 1990, *Time* featured a face on the cover that was touted as the face of twenty-first-century America. The product of a special computer morphing program, the face was a combination of photographs of all the different ethnic women who have come together to form the country's new population in proportion to the size of their respective ethnic groups. The unadorned face that stared back at me from the cover, though ethnically fairly nondescript, possessed Asian-influenced features. Is it possible that Asian Americans are truly going to help shape the face of twenty-first-century America?

THE SIREN SONG OF THE SEA OF INEVITABILITY

Dean Cain (star of the television series *Adventures of Lois and Clark*) is part Asian. Keanu Reeves (star of the movie *Speed*) is too. So are Ann Curry (morning television host), Paul Kariya (professional hockey player), Tia Carrera (star of the movie *Wayne's World*), and Russell Wong (*Joy Luck Club, Vanishing Son*). And lest we forget, a significant portion of Tiger Woods's (golf professional) genetic heritage is from Thailand and China. As we head into the twenty-first century, each of these persons occupies a prominent niche in the American populace.

And each personifies the future face of not only Asian America but America itself.

Think back to the rivers>bay>sea model that I presented at the beginning of this book. As the relentless forces of acculturation pull on each of the three kinds of fish, they are all moving downstream, with each successive generation hearing the siren song of the sea louder than the next. From the freshwater Rivers of Dreamers (immigrants) into the co-mingled waters of the Bay of Transitions (1.5 and 2.0 generations), Asian Americans are flowing further and further out into the briny and mysterious depths of the Sea of Inevitability. What will life be like in the place where all manner of people mix and match? What will Asian Americans look and think like in the future? How should Asian American churches and ministries begin to prepare for the metamorphosis that has already begun?

The Current Is Moving Faster

One of the most noteworthy factors to keep in mind is that the pace of acculturation and assimilation is much faster than it was before World War II. People are arriving in the Sea of Inevitability much faster these days because of how fast the current of acculturation and assimilation is flowing. As obstacles to joining with the mainstream of American life have continued to collapse, it has become far easier for many immigrants and their families to acquire wealth, education, status, and access. This rapid pace is one of the main reasons Eric Liu believes that Asian Americans will not have the opportunity to reshape American culture on a large scale.

> It is perhaps unfair to expect Asian Americans to influence American life in the same fashion, to the same degree, as the Jews have. One reason is the ever-quickening pace of assimilation. For all that we hear about the "disuniting of America," the truth is it has never been easier to assimilate than it is today. Ever since the 1960s, new arrivals — at least those with some education — have faced gradually fewer barriers to social entry. They do not have to ghettoize. They are not forced, by the ostracism of others, to sustain and draw sustenance from their heritage. They are freer to adopt other styles, to invent their own.[3]

In the 1950s an Asian immigrant to America might never wander far from the familiar freshwater surroundings of his or her Filipino-town or Little Tokyo. Lack of English-language skills, workplace prejudice, and segregated housing practices must have seemed like impenetrable barriers to ever being able to move out and move up. Marrying a non-Asian was frowned upon, too. The twenty-first century, although far from ideal, will find many Asian immigrants who arrive quite fluent in English, who are welcome additions to most workforces, who own some of the finest homes in prestigious neighborhoods, and who have graduated with advanced degrees from top-flight schools. Add to this composite the much more lenient attitudes not only toward intermarriages but also toward the children of those diverse unions, and it makes perfect sense that, these days, it is not just the more Americanized Asian Americans who are willing to swim out into the deep, uncharted waters of the Sea of Inevitability.

A Multi-Asian Mix

When I first answered the call to pastoral ministry in 1977, I thought that the Lord was directing me to pastor only English-speaking Chinese Americans (CA). Three years later, when I relocated to Southern California to complete my degree at Fuller Seminary, God amended my understanding to include English-speaking Japanese Americans (JA). Nine years after my first call, the Lord again amended my understanding, this time to include English-speaking Korean Americans (KA). Not long after that, I concluded that my original interpretation had been too narrow, that all along God had called me to pastor English-speaking Americanized Asian Americans (AAA). Thinking then that the issue of whom I was called to pastor was finally settled, for the next nine years I set my sights on helping to create a ministry that would specialize in reaching that specific population. You can imagine my initial consternation when, soon after the strategic hiving of our church, not only did a much wider array of Asian Americans start showing up, but a healthy portion of these newcomers were from overseas (freshwater fish)!

As I explained in chapter 2, the fact that our ministry was attracting both immigrants and AAAs was at first inexplicable to me. You might recall my saying that, while acculturated cod (3.0–6.0 generations) will not survive in freshwater ministries, there are some imported bass (1.0 and 1.5 generations) who not only can survive in saltwater ministries but are committed to adapting successfully. Having the opportunity to observe this phenomena every week at Evergreen Baptist Church of Los Angeles, I believe that this is more evidence that people are acculturating and assimilating at a faster and faster rate.

If you relocated yourself and started a new life in America, why would you spend the rest of your life in a poor facsimile of what you left behind? Coming to a more Americanized church like Evergreen-LA for many of these first-generation folks is, to their way of thinking, a step toward the future rather than a step back from it. It may be another way that they are pursuing their pearl, a quality of life that would probably never happen in the homeland. Given this, I predict that more and more first- (imported bass) and second- (salmon) generation people will spend less and less time in organizations like churches and cultural groups that are not clearly moving toward the Sea of Inevitability.

In order to send a clear message of affirmation to all our first-generation people, we decided to drop the phrase "Americanized Asian American" from our church's new vision statement. Not because we no longer felt a burden to see more unconvinced AAAs become faithful followers of Jesus. It should be obvious that that is not true. But we felt that having that phrase in our new vision statement would automatically and unnecessarily disenfranchise a precious new part of our faith community. So instead, we coined the terms *multi-Asian* and *multigenerational*.

The first term is much more encompassing, gathering our ever-widening menagerie of Asian and Pacific Islander Americans into a unified whole. Now, whether they hail from Singapore or Seoul, whether they were born overseas and came here as a youngster or were born in Boston to third-generation parents, there is a greater chance that they will all feel loved, wanted, and included.

The second term, *multigenerational*, carries a dual meaning. It is there to reiterate our welcome to Asians of any generation. However, it is also there to affirm the fact that this is a church for people of all ages, because we believe that the richest kind of faith community is one where many generations interact with each other. Unlike many new AAA churches, Evergreen-LA consists of people in their eighties all the way down to newborns, with every kind of age and stage in between. More significantly, people have begun to cross the various generational and life-stage lines to befriend one another. We think that this is getting much closer to the biblical concept of family, that is, a sedaqah faith community, than focusing on nuclear families. We believe that it does take a spiritual village to rear a child, especially if that child is going to learn to pursue the true pearl of inestimable value — God and God's heart to restore creation.

Pastoring a church that used to be just Chinese-Japanese-Korean American but is now multi-Asian poses some difficult challenges for us. The greatest one is to recognize our latent Chinese-Japanese-Korean bias and to rid ourselves of it. It is easy to expand terminology without expanding the breadth of your embrace.

For example, how many times do we ignore the fact that some of the Asian Americans in our group are not Chinese, Japanese, or Korean? I know that, as a Chinese American, I do not appreciate it when I am at, for instance, a gathering that was promoted as being for Asian Americans but every speaker or leader is Korean and everything they say or do assumes that everyone else is Korean. So why is it, when it is my turn, do I speak as if there are no Thai, Filipino, Indian, or multiracial people in the room? Even if there is only one person who is not from the predominant and prevalent Asian American group(s), that person was created in God's image and deserves to be recognized for who he or she is. All of us who are minorities should know how awful it is to feel invisible or overlooked. We should know better, but many times our own experiences of marginalization do not open our eyes when we sin against Asian Americans who are minorities within our own groups.

A Thai American college student named Jenifer Wana gave up fighting for the Asian American cause when she finally realized that this cause excluded Asian Americans who were not from one of the predominant groups. She writes:

It's bad enough that Asian people continue to be marginalized by white society. But when the Asian American community marginalizes its own people, it creates a double standard that undermines the entire movement. . . .

Whether you're reading a book, taking an Asian American studies college course, or reading a list of the heads of Asian American organizations, only a few ethnicities seem to represent the entire community — namely, Chinese, Japanese, Korean, Filipino, and (sometimes) South Asian. . . .

Until the Asian American community shakes off its ethnocentrism, members of certain groups are going to be hard-put to identify with the term "Asian American." Those who try to participate by joining organizations will feel excluded and unwelcome when they realize how little place they have in the dialogue about Asian America, and how few of the role models in the community look like them.[4]

Are you, like me, guilty as charged? If so, are you now willing to be like Jesus and empty yourself of your power and control so that the overlooked and those feeling insignificant will be lifted up? Until and unless every member of the fellowship, Asian or otherwise, is made to feel fully recognized and affirmed, we dare not claim to be a kingdom community, let alone a truly multi-Asian / multi-ethnic one.

One sure way to meet this challenge is to school yourself and your leaders in the unique histories and cultural nuances of the new Asian Americans and take the time to teach them yours. Before they started joining our church, I never used to read articles about Koreans, Filipinos, Vietnamese, or Malaysians. Now that I am their pastor, I find myself collecting stories and items that explain things like the Vietnamese lunar New Year or traditional Indian attitudes about male / female relationships. Here also is where partnerships with freshwater Asian churches that minister to these various minorities among Asian Americans could be helpful. Once we realize how much we need to learn, we are much more apt to seek out resources, mentors, and appropriately attuned ethnic consultants.

I remember deciding to investigate Japanese American history and culture after I married my wife, who is Japanese American, and when I first joined the staff of Evergreen-LA, a historically Japanese American church. One year, my wife and I subscribed to a season of plays at East-West Players that focused on the unjust incarceration of Japanese

Americans during the Second World War. It was not until the last play that it suddenly hit me: because I had married a Japanese American and because I now pastored people who had been imprisoned in those camps, this history was now my history, too. In 1998, a book called *Triumphs of Faith* was published; it detailed how Japanese American Christians dealt with the injustice of the camps. I was enthralled when many of the non-Japanese Asian Americans in our congregation lined up to purchase copies. I pray that this continues, for when various unfamiliar persons decide to become a part of our faith communities, there should come a point where all of us want to connect with one another's histories and stories.

One final challenge of pastoring a multi-Asian mixture that I will mention has to do with what often occurs when people from different Asian backgrounds fall in love and want to get married. When it is between Chinese Americans and Japanese Americans, these days that hardly ever poses any problems. If the families of one or both are from overseas, though, and there had been conflict between the countries within the last hundred years, there can be problems. Quite often, since the couple is in love and did not have to live through a war, they cannot fathom why their families are being so prejudiced. We must try and help them appreciate the kind of suffering and loss members of their families might have had to endure at the hands of people from the other country.

I knew a Chinese American man who could not understand why his family would not accept his girlfriend because she was Japanese American. Their relationship went forward without his family's blessing, but it was not until several years later, while attending a special memorial service for the Forgotten Holocaust, that he uncovered the explanation for his family's feelings. Until then, he had never heard of the Forgotten Holocaust. Thus, he had not known that, prior to America's entrance into the war in December 1941, the Japanese Imperial Army had invaded China and slaughtered close to thirty million Chinese before the war officially ended. Japanese soldiers had killed three of his father's older siblings. His father had never talked about these uncles that he had never known. I cannot predict whether their relationship will ever be resolved. But at least now he is more able to appreciate that his family's ongoing ambivalence toward his girlfriend may have less to do with their being sinners and more to do with their being sinned against.

Much more innocuous issues arise when someone from one culture marries someone from another. There could be as many issues for someone born and raised in Japan marrying a third-generation Japanese American from Detroit as there might be between an American of Filipino ancestry and an American of Korean ancestry. Once again, if these elements are now part of the multi-Asian matrix of your congregation, you had better start broadening and intensifying your understanding of the sundry parts of your charges. With the increase in the speed of acculturation and assimilation and with the wider range of associations that Asian Americans are forming, we need to be prepared to minister to a multi-Asian, multigenerational blend.

A Multi-Ethnic Future

Before we get into the subject of multi-ethnicity, let me offer a brief explanation as to why we decided to announce that we are a multi-Asian/multi-ethnic community. To the uninitiated, the combining of these two phrases seems needlessly redundant. Why not just say that we are multi-ethnic? Doesn't that cover all the bases? Why include multi-Asian at all if we are comfortable with being a multi-ethnic ministry?

First of all, we feel that we are breaking new ground by becoming a congregation consisting of not only English-speaking Chinese, Japanese, and Koreans, but also Indian, Vietnamese, Thai, Laotian, Cambodian, Malaysian, Filipino, Hawaiian, Guamanian, Burmese and/or various combinations of Asian/Pacific Islander ancestries. To say only multi-ethnic glosses over something fresh and probably trend setting. Our other reason is because holding off just using multi-ethnic still gives us room to grow. There may well come a time when we will have sailed so far out to sea that the most accurate description of us would be multi-ethnic. That remains to be seen.

So why add the multi-ethnic tag now when the multi-Asian paradigm is just getting off the ground?

Following the dual new apostolic (see chap. 9) mandate, that every disciple is called to be a minister and a missionary and that the mission field begins outside our front door, we have found it impossible to sidestep the issue of multi-ethnicity any longer. If your church is like ours, we are located in an ethnically diverse community. While it is true that a high percentage of Asian Americans live within a fifteen-mile radius, our immediate neighbors tend to be mid-to-lower-income Latino Americans and white Americans. As we began reaching out to them with various ministries, it got to the point where it was too awkward saying that was an exclusively multi-Asian church. Thus, in 1997 we opened the gates to all of our neighbors by adding multi-ethnic to our vision statement.

The response since then has been dramatic. Even though as of this writing probably 90 percent of our people are Asian American, those who are not have fewer qualms about becoming active members and leaders. As the non-Asian American portion of our body continues to grow, we realize that we will be able to come together as a kingdom community only so long as we are not afraid of addressing or confronting the cultural clashes that are already occurring. Rather than pretend that differences are not there, we plan on sponsoring sensitivity-raising workshops, for example, in the foreseeable future so that hidden concerns can be shared and mutual solutions can be found. Becoming more of a multi-ethnic church will, in the long run, provoke us all to describe unique aspects of our respective cultures that would otherwise remain concealed. I know this sounds paradoxical, but by becoming more multi-ethnic, we will probably become more Asian, too.[5] And by increasing the potential for tension and misunderstandings, we will also be increasing the possibility for a deeper intimacy.

The majority of our congregation that is Asian American does not seem to mind our concurrent embracing of multi-ethnicity. They know that this goes hand in hand with our commitment to reach our neighbors across the street, not just across the ocean. For those discipled by campus ministries during their college years to have a new apostolic outlook, they find Evergreen-LA's premeditated inclusiveness to be more in accordance with what they have learned about pursuing the pearl of greatest value. They too resonate with pursuing a vision whose supreme value is loving God and the person in front of you.

As the pace of acculturation and assimilation continues to quicken, more people, especially in Southern California, are finding themselves in much more ethnically diverse settings. Whether it is the software division at the high-tech company where they work or their bunch of friends from school, people are intermingling much more frequently than before. Thus, it is only natural that they would want a church that embraces each member of their circle. We have embraced multi-ethnicity because it also enables our members not to have to compartmentalize their relationships.

As people begin making friends with persons from a wider array of backgrounds, it is not long before God's Spirit is able to dismantle long-standing prejudices and stereotypes. It is then only a matter of time before some of these people begin to date, fall in love, and get married. Table 3 (in the Appendix) shows generations and numbers of in-marriages and intermarriages by gender of Chinese, Filipino, Japanese, Koreans, and Vietnamese in Los Angeles County in 1989. Harry H. L. Kitano, Diane C. Fujino, and Jane Takahashi Sato, the compilers of this data, concluded the following in regard to the trend of Asian American intermarriages:

> The data indicated that (a) generation was related to [intermarriage] for all of the Asian groups and that (b) with the exception of the Japanese, the Chinese, the Filipinos, Koreans, and Vietnamese who were married in 1989 came primarily from the first (or immigrant) generation.... The results indicate that generational status was the strongest predictor of [intermarriage] for both women and men. Compared to first-generation Asians, second-generation Asians were more than three times as likely to [intermarry], and third-generation Asians were approximately five times as likely to [intermarry].[6]

The fact that generation turned out to be the most important predictor of intermarriages only underscores the potential for acculturation and assimilation to radically alter the future. Acquisition of language and social skills; exposure to American culture; loss of family control over marriage; growing independence of children; value changes; mobility in housing; and occupational, social, and educational integration all increase dramatically with time lived in this country. The researchers summarized their findings by stating that even though the five Asian American groups are different,

> it appears that length of time, exposure to American society, and acculturation all related to generation begin a process leading to higher rates of [intermarriages]. The Japanese Americans, primarily a third-generation group, had the highest rates of [intermarriage]. The Koreans, primarily a first-generation immigrant population, had the lowest rates. Females, especially of the American-born generations, also were more likely to marry non-Asians than were those who were born in the old country. . . . Although [intermarriages] are quite common, there has been a strong tendency for Asian Americans to marry other Asian Americans rather than to choose interracial partners.[7]

Ministries like ours that continue to emphasize reaching the more Americanized generations are going to experience not only expanding numbers of intermarriages but also an attendant increase of multi-racial children and adults. Just because there may not be more than a handful in your ministry does not mean it is appropriate to pretend that they are Japanese or Filipino because they manage to fit in. They deserve to be identified accurately and afforded the dignity all people deserve.[8] As their numbers continue to swell, however, it will become even more critical for multi-Asian/multi-ethnic ministries to recognize them as fellow members of God's family, made in God's image like all the rest. Finding ways to incorporate their unique backgrounds into church school lessons, youth group studies, and sermons will go a long way toward fully embracing these precious persons.

As the number of Asian intermarriages continues to swell, the number and variety of multiracial persons in society will also grow significantly. Beyond the formal programs of the church, it is imperative that the Asian American members confront their own prejudices early on in the church's history if they hope to retain any people of mixed heritage. When a multiracial person either is part Asian but does not look Asian and/or comes to the church while a teenager or older, it is especially difficult for that individual to feel accepted and embraced if the majority of the congregation is and/or looks Asian American. Even though we promote ourselves as a multi-Asian/multi-ethnic congregation, some multiracial Asians and non-Asians report that they do not feel fully welcomed by the rest.

As God has diversified my own extended family to include multi-racial, white, Guamanian/Filipino/Spanish, Korean, Japanese, and African American/white, God's Spirit has been enabling me to embrace more readily people of similar backgrounds in our congregation. I find myself now thinking, "There is someone in my own family just like you. So since I have learned to embrace that person in my family who looks like you, I am going to walk across the room and learn to embrace you, too. Why? Because we are members of the same family." Jesus died to make us all blood relatives and members of God's family. Yet until this sinks in so that God's Spirit is free to alter our racist attitudes, ethnocentric cliques and contradictory behaviors, especially toward multiracial Asians, any talk of being multi-Asian or multi-ethnic is just that: talk. The future of multi-Asian and multi-ethnic churches is directly linked to the degree that this ongoing marginalization and alienation is confronted and healed.

The anticipated increase in multiracial Asians presents us who are called to some form of Asian American ministry with a vexing question: What will "Asian American" describe fifty years from now? Or, as author Eric Liu asks,

> What will "Asian American" mean when a majority of the next generation is of mixed parentage? Will membership in the race depend more on heredity or on heritage? Chromosomes or culture? Will it be a matter of voluntary affiliation, a question of choice? Or will the one-drop rule that makes American blacks black make anyone with an Asian ancestor Asian? Who will pass for white — and who will want to? . . .
>
> It is possible that the Asian American identity, fragile invention that it is, will simply dissipate through intermarriage. . . . On the other hand, it's possible that the Asian identity will intensify in the next generation. Sometimes the most fervent believers in the power of colored blood are those of mixed ancestry. Meanwhile, intra-Asian marriages among Indian and Filipino and Korean and other Asian Americans are also dramatically on the rise. The old borders are shifting. Where they will settle or whether there is simply no way to predict.[9]

A sea of new faces, new families, and new combinations is filling fast. Will there be enough relevant churches and ministries to ensure that Jesus and God's kingdom are important parts of that future blend as well?

VITAL CHURCHES ALONG THE ENTIRE FLOW

We are called to face this unpredictable future together, with devotion, faith, boldness, and vision. No matter how many of us may want to return to simpler times, we can only move forward. We cannot allow ourselves to be overwhelmed by paradigm shifts like postmodernism, third-wave management styles, new apostolic mandates, and ministry conditions that are getting more complex by the minute. God has called all of us into relationship with Jesus, to be Christ's ministers and missionaries at exactly this time in the world's history. We can only go forward. We must proceed with being Jesus' body on earth.

Figure 10.1 is a bit more graphic depiction of the flow of generations model. Minimally, it demonstrates the simple truth that none of us involved in Asian American ministries can afford to be so focused on the matters at hand that we neglect to see where our ministry is heading. It is not for me to say how long each of these transitions will take, for there are numerous variables having to do with things like geographic locale, density and diversity of Asian populations, availability of gifted, clear-minded leaders, a ministry's history, and enough funds.

Most Asian churches in this country are situated along the various Rivers of Dreamers. Others are making valiant efforts to extend the ministry into the Bay of Transitions. And a small but growing number of churches are attempting to make sense of ministry in different places out in the Sea of Inevitability. While I hope it is obvious that we need more saltwater churches and we are going to need lots more of them tomorrow, Jesus wants there to be vital, vibrant ministries all along the flow of generations. Since there is never going to be a super-church that can meet everyone's needs, all of us need to join hands and work to ensure that every generation has the opportunity to meet Christ within its most comfortable context.

Not Enough Viable Churches

This may come as a shock to some of you serving in half-empty Asian American churches, but we need more churches. The fact that

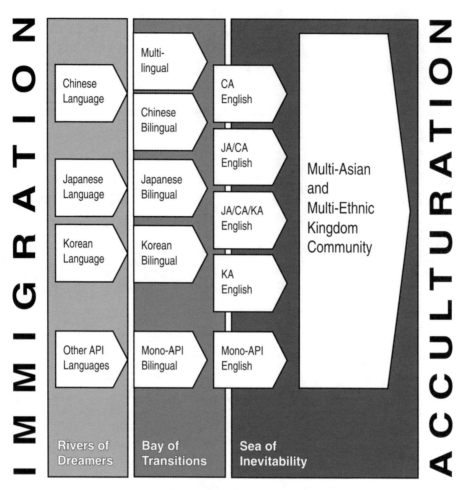

Figure 10.1
Charting a Course for the Future of Asian Churches in America
Using the Flow of Generations Model

Source: Kenneth Fong

unconvinced AAAs and/or unchurched Asian American Christians are joining the church where you serve does not mean that they are not looking for a church. For reasons that we have already gone over, they may never consider darkening your church's doorway. As Asian America continues its rapid growth (fig. 10.2), we must have many more vibrant, forward-looking ministries to embody and proclaim the Good News of Jesus to its ever-diversifying population.

Data from the 1990 census underscores the great need for scores of viable new Asian American churches:

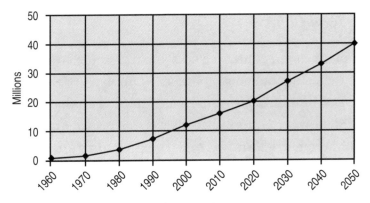

Figure 10.2
The Growth of Asian America

Source: "Asian American PERSPECTIVE: Intercultural Resources Newsletter," Asian American Ministry,
Campus Crusade for Christ (winter 1990): 1; and *The State of Asian Pacific America – A Public Policy Report:
Policy Issues to the Year 2020* (LEAP and UCLA Asian American Studies Center, 1993).

- Since 1965, the Asian American population has grown from just under 1,000,000 to well over 7,000,000. They are the fastest-growing minority group in the United States.

- Although they comprised only 2.9 percent of the total United States population in 1990, they increased in size by 95 percent from 1980 to 1990. During that same decade, whites increased by 6 percent, African Americans by 13.2 percent, and Latinos by 52 percent. Only an extraordinary growth rate has allowed Asian Americans to go from being only 0.7 percent of the population in 1970 to 2.9 percent twenty short years later.

- In California, where 40 percent of Asian Americans reside, their population has almost tripled since 1980. As of 1998, Asian Americans represent 12 percent of California's population, a sprawling, combined community of 3.8 million.

- By the year 2040, the U.S. Census Bureau estimates that Asian Americans will become 8 percent of the total population.

- By the year 2020, now less than a quarter century away, there will be approximately 20,000,000 Asian Pacific Americans. By 2050, there will be 40,000,000 Asian Pacific Americans, 10 percent of the total population.

- As a percentage of the total population, the foreign-born population will show a decrease. In 1990, the foreign-born population is 64 percent of the total Asian Pacific U.S. population; by 2020 this percentage will be between 54 and 56 percent, the majority of whom will be the elderly.[10]

Planting New Churches

However many Asian churches and ministries there are in this country today, there are not enough of them to minister to the gargantuan population of future Asian Americans. Given the projection that by the year 2020, a little more than half of the Asian American population will be foreign-born, we must keep planting more freshwater churches for them. But who is going to reach the other 10,000,000, some of whom will be salmon but most of whom will be acculturated cod?

For the longest time, new Asian churches were aimed at reaching the first and second generations. Preoccupied with this enormous task, planting new churches aimed at the third generation and beyond has been sorely neglected. Given the projection that in twenty-one years more than half of the Asian population is going to be Asian Americans who were born here, we must ramp up our efforts to plant churches for unchurched and unconvinced AAAs. If the Lord has burdened you with a desire to see more relevant Asian American churches, the Appendix contains tables 4–6 to assist you in determining where these churches are most needed. In any case, at least three things will have to happen if there is going to be a flurry of new church starts for Americanized Asian Americans.

First, a good number of first-generation churches will need to be convinced of the futility of the plans to reach saltwater generations by offering them variations on freshwater themes. The leaders must have enough clarity of vision to know that Asian Americans from the third generation and beyond will best be reached with pastors and churches that naturally resonate with the themes and issues of more Americanized Asian Americans.

Second, once these freshwater leaders see the handwriting on the wall, they should remove any and all obstacles that would prevent or bog down the launching of these new ministries. Many of the would-be pastors of these new churches speak to me of great personal discouragement. Beaten down and battered after years of lobbying for the legitimacy and urgency of AAA ministries, by the time they leave the staff of a bilingual or multilingual church, many of them are not sure they still want to pastor a church, let alone plant one without any kind of substantial support and blessing. It would make a world of difference if first-generation pastors and their congregations would sponsor new works, offering spiritual and financial support for up to five years, with no strings attached. Unfortunately, too many new churches aimed at AAAs flounder and even fail for lack of real support during those crucial first years.

Third, I believe that AAA churches that have already established themselves should expect to be the primary sources and/or training grounds for the needed acculturated cod pastors and lay ministers. This might mean establishing a thoroughgoing and rigorous internship program for prospective pastoral candidates, giving these budding leaders plenty of opportunity to learn from those who are already doing this kind of work. Teams of lay ministers need to be equipped as well, in preparation for being a part of a church plant. Experience has shown us that it jumpstarts the ministry if there is a pastoral team (two or three) and a solid core of lay ministers (at least fifty) when the new church is birthed. This can be expensive for one church, even a fairly large one, to do all the training, launching, and sponsoring. But what if several churches within the same denomination or conference worked together to achieve this worthy goal?

Without a doubt, the need for more new churches is staring all of us in the face. We cannot afford to focus only on the primary ministry the Lord has given to us. Our vision for reaching Americanized Asian Americans must definitely go beyond what is familiar or comfortable.

Restocking Some Existing Churches

In consulting with pastors of recently planted churches aimed at AAAs, I keep hearing about how the need for property crops up. During the first year or so, people are so excited about the new work that they could care less about owning a building or having office space. After a while, though, the weekly setup of the worship space and classrooms becomes a chore, staff are frustrated with having to work out of their homes, and families in particular begin to long for a sense of permanence. On top of this, more schools now will not issue long-term leases to churches, so even if the congregation is comfortable where they are, they still may have to relocate. Once they start searching for a site, they discover that a frightening number of municipalities will no longer issue permits that would allow churches to renovate office or warehouse space. It is not so much that these small cities have a thing against churches; they have a thing against reducing their tax revenues. As we pray about starting hundreds of new churches aimed at reaching unconvinced AAAs, we should remember to count the cost.

Starting new churches, especially ones that begin with more than one staff person, can easily cost the sponsoring church or churches one hundred thousand dollars for the first three years. Even if the new church finds an available site to purchase, they will then need to raise at least a million dollars or more. While I am all for starting new churches, especially for AAAs, I also think that we must be working on additional plans that would result in more vital churches to meet the future demand.

One idea that intrigues me is for already established churches like Evergreen-LA or Evergreen-SGV to identify existing churches that seem to have great potential for reaching unconvinced AAAs. Some might have been planted less than ten years ago. Others, like our church in the 1970s, might have decades-long histories but seem to possess a special spark that may ignite if only they got some out-side help. Most of these churches would already own property and be in buildings. Granted, some of the neighborhoods may have changed drastically, but I am guessing that a fair number of them would still be able to function as a center of spiritual life and vitality.

Without paying attention to denominational boundaries, wouldn't it be great if thriving churches could invest in existing churches that seem to need a little extra help to get over the hump? What if larger programs, like the ones we have at both Evergreen-LA and Gardena Valley Baptist Church, worked out a rotation for the pastoral interns? If any of them were going to end up planting a church or joining the staff of an existing church, it would aid in their preparation if they spent a year serving at a smaller church.

Or why, for instance, should Evergreen-LA want to plant churches for unconvinced AAAs in West Los Angeles or the South Bay when there might already be some Asian American churches there that could benefit from a partnership with us? What if we were willing to share a staff person for a certain period of time or if some of our trained lay ministers who lived in the vicinity were willing to invest six months or more at the other church, equipping others and maybe even staying there? And what about sharing resources too with nearby freshwater churches that were planted recently to reach immigrants from Indonesia or Vietnam? They could offer cultural insights to multi-Asian churches while the latter could help the former minister to their more acculturated youth and young adults. Some of you probably think I should have my head examined for daring to think that churches could co-operate instead of compete, but with what it costs to start churches from scratch, we need to come up with other ideas.

One thing is sure: we are going to need more vital churches all along the flow of generations. God only knows how we are going to be able to do it.

PURSUING THE PEARL IN A RAPIDLY CHANGING WORLD

My family's portrait on our wall speaks of the velocity of the cultural current that is moving all of us toward the Sea of Inevitability. There are the obvious Asian American faces staring back at the camera, but those of us with indiscreet Asian features hail from at least three different Asian ethnic groups, with most born here but one from overseas. And interspersed among us now is a fair-skinned blonde as well as three dark-haired members with naturally curly hair and coffee-ice-cream complexions. And there are young new faces among ours, never-before-seen combinations that speak a little of partial Chinese heritages and volumes of the sheer creativity of God. The future faces of Asian America stare back at us in many of our family portraits.

The future is arriving every day, bringing with it a world that is further and further removed from the church, posing both a terrible threat and a tremendous challenge to those of us who refuse to believe there is a better way to embody Jesus Christ than the church. If we are going to gain an audience, however, either as ordained or lay ministers, we must face up to the changing world in which we now live. People are just as needy. They are not as easily convinced that their needs will be met by and in the church. One secular writer portrays the present context for our ministry efforts as follows:

> [Seminary graduates today] face us, a postmodern populace that wonders if it may have evolved beyond the religious institutions that sustained this country for more than 200 years. At a minimum, the past few decades have made it clear that many Americans look at formal religion, churches, and indeed, the ordained ministry with no small measure of unbelief. Many Americans would not concede — except perhaps in the darkest hours of a restless night — that they want religion to shape their lives.
>
> This "us" that future clerics will be dealing with is as fragmented as the clergy itself, but we are united by a few strands. Religion is just one of many options we are offered if we seek self-knowledge and inner peace. If we choose to follow a religious faith, no longer do we join or stay with a church because it was where our family worshiped. We go not out of a sense of obligation but, so we claim, because we have picked and chosen, and are discerning consumers about even this. It may be the childcare offered, the music or level of preaching or social commitment, the charisma of the pastor. But all of those incidentals break down, I think, in the face of some simple persistent truths: many go out of naked need, and of those of us who don't go on Sabbath or Sunday, most have the same need and don't know what to do about it. Perhaps our religious commitment is deeper because it is no longer expected or demanded of us. But we know, as a certainty, that it is hard to be a self-made good person. And we sense that secular morality and the laws of the marketplace lack something basic.[11]

If this is an apt description of the postmodern mindset, then it is clear that though there has been a diminishing of confidence in the church, the hunger for transcendence, meaning, and wholeness has not ebbed. Some have maintained that, in spite of the apparent rise of paganism and atheism, the residents of this land are yet longing for God. Mike Yaconelli delivers these words of optimism and opportunity:

> I am convinced that just underneath the surface of most Americans is a deep sense that something is wrong — very wrong — with our culture. They know in their hearts that their lives are meaningless, that their relationships are empty, and that their possessions possess them. They are lost, aimless, and they are longing for a rudder, a map to tell them

where they are and where they are going. They are sheep in search of a Shepherd.

This is the moment many of us have been waiting for. This is the moment of evangelism. The American culture has never before been more ready for evangelism.

But where are the evangelists?[12]

Where indeed are the evangelists? And where are the believers who will answer the missionary call to incarnate Christ to unreached people groups, especially in our own country? Where are those who will beseech the Spirit to grant them the eyes to see and the ears to hear the clues to salvation that the Lord has already deposited all around us? Who is willing to make the paradigm shifts in how we understand the nature of our mission and the purpose of our ministries? Who will courageously step out beyond the present limitations of tradition-bound mentalities and methodologies to dream new dreams and forge new, more appropriate tools to initiate the increasing numbers of unconvinced or unchurched Americanized Asian Americans into the kingdom of God? Who will lead the way and who will plant the much-needed new churches? Who will provide the resources and people power to energize existing ministries with much potential? Where are the evangelists and the pastors and the churches ready to embrace the swelling sea of unconvinced and overlooked people?

Of the legions still trying to find the answer to the nagging emptiness inside of them, many are Asian Americans who do not identify with the majority of Asian American Christian churches that are bent on preserving the purity of their Asian heritages and the orthodoxy of their Christian traditions. If we are going to come alongside them in their pursuit of the true pearl of great price, if we hope to initiate them into the kingdom of God, then we must let God's Spirit first teach us new ways to accomplish this. For it is my fervent conviction that we must come up with fresh ways to present Christ's invitation to abundant and eternal life, with new and renewed churches that are more accurate reflections of who these people are. We must acknowledge the lingering uncertainty that lurks in the shadows of our own faith in Christ. We must break our own shame-induced silence. And we must approach them as fellow sinful and sinned-against seekers.

The world outside of our churches is perpetually changing. Instead of building more impregnable walls around our churches to keep it out, we need to punch more holes in the walls so that we, as ministers and missionaries called by Jesus to that world, can go out to it and embrace it as Christ did and still does. That embrace not only has the potential to transform the world; it also has the power to renew and transform us, Christ's church.

I hope this book has served to stimulate your thinking about what it is we are all trying to do and whom it is we are trying to reach. Although it feels much safer to proceed without having to challenge some of our basic premises, it is much more perilous to avoid this than to face it. For only by struggling to make the familiar things unfamiliar again will we be able to deliver a message and a Messiah that will capture unconvinced people's time and attention. Only then might they believe that the Pearl we are pursuing is more valuable than the one that they are pursuing.

THINGS TO THINK ABOUT

1. How apparent to you is it that the speed in which Asian Americans are acculturating and assimilating is picking up? How has your own family been affected by the mixing and matching of diverse people? If your ministry is seeing the effects of greater ethnic intermingling and intermarrying, how is it changing to address this shift in the makeup of your people?

2. How has the Lord been speaking to your heart and mind as you have studied this material and thought about your own church/ministry situation?

3. If you believe there is a need for a ministry for unconvinced AAAs in your locale, what first steps might you take? Whom else do you know who shares this burden? What churches might be willing to help launch something like this? What paradigm shifts might be required before anything truly different from the status quo could materialize?

4. What are the practical alternatives facing you if there do not seem to be any AAA ministries/churches on your horizon? Is there a fruitful future for you at a bilingual or multilingual Asian church? For your children? Your grandchildren?

APPENDIX

Table 1
The Asian Pacific American Population of the U.S., 1990

Ethnicity	1990 Population	Percent of Asian/ Pacific Islander Population
Chinese	1,645,472	22.6
Filipino	1,406,770	19.3
Japanese	847,562	11.7
Asian Indian	815,447	11.2
Korean	798,849	11.0
Vietnamese	614,547	8.4
Hawaiian	211,014	2.9
Laotian	149,014	2.0
Cambodian	147,411	2.0
Thai	91,275	1.3
Hmong	90,082	1.2
Samoan	62,964	0.9
Guamanian	49,345	0.7
Tongan	17,606	0.2
Other Asian/Pacific Islander	326,304	4.5
Total	7,273,662	99.9

Source: U.S. Bureau of the Census, 1990 Summary Tape File C

Table 2
The Japanese Segment of Asian America Is Shrinking Rapidly

Ethnicity	1980 Population	1990 Population	Percent Change
Chinese	812,178	1,645,472	+50.6%
Filipino	781,894	1,406,770	+44.4%
Japanese	716,331	847,562	+15.5%
Asian Indian	387,223	815,447	+52.5%
Korean	357,393	798,849	+55.3%

Source: U.S. Bureau of the Census, 1980 and 1990 Census

Table 3
**Percentage of In- and Intermarried Asian Americans,
by Gender in Los Angeles County, 1989**

	Female		Male	
	In-Marriage	*Intermarriage*	*In-Marriage*	*Intermarriage*
Chinese				
First Generation	68.2%	31.8%	78.0%	22.1%
Second Generation	35.3%	64.7%	52.9%	47.1%
Third Generation	13.4%	**86.6%**	35.7%	**64.3%**
Filipino				
First Generation	53.1%	46.9%	77.5%	22.6%
Second Generation	34.2%	65.8%	51.2%	48.8%
Third Generation	14.3%	**85.7%**	51.5%	**48.5%**
Japanese				
First Generation	59.0%	41.0%	71.7%	28.3%
Second Generation	50.0%	50.0%	51.7%	48.3%
Third Generation	37.1%	**62.9%**	45.5%	**54.6%**
Korean				
First Generation	86.7%	13.3%	96.3%	3.7%
Second Generation	37.5%	62.5%	66.7%	33.3%
Third Generation	00.0%	**100%***	31.6%	**68.4%**
Vietnamese				
First Generation	74.5%	25.5%	75.7%	24.3%
Second Generation	66.7%	33.3%	100%	00.0%
Third Generation	00.0%	**100%***	33.3%	**66.7%**

Bold figures highlight intermarriage rates of third-generation couples. Asterisks (*) denote figures that should not be taken at face value because of the extremely low numbers of raw data.

Source: Harry H. L. Kitano, Diane C. Fujino, and Jane Takahashi Sato, "Interracial Marriages: Where Are the Asian Americans and Where Are They Going?" in *Handbook of Asian American Psychology*, ed. Lee C. Lee and Nolan W. S. Zane (Thousand Oaks, Calif.: Sage Publications, 1998), 254

Table 4
**Top Ten States with the Largest 1990
Asian Pacific American Population**

Rank	State	APA Population	*Percent of State Population*	*Percent of National Population*	*Cumulative APA Percentage*
1	California	2,845,659	9.6	39.1	39.1
2	New York	693,760	3.9	9.5	48.7
3	Hawaii	685,236	61.8	9.4	58.1
4	Texas	319,459	1.9	4.4	62.5
5	Illinois	285,311	2.5	3.9	66.4
6	New Jersey	272,521	3.5	3.7	70.1
7	Washington	210,958	4.3	2.9	73.0
8	Virginia	159,053	2.6	2.2	75.2
9	Florida	154,302	1.2	2.1	77.4
10	Massachusetts	143,392	2.4	2.0	79.3
Total		5,769,651		79.2	79.3

Source: U.S. Bureau of the Census, 1990 Summary Tape File 1C

Table 5
Top Ten Cities with the Largest 1990
Asian Pacific American Populations

Rank	State	City	1990 APA Population	Percent of Total County Population	Percent of State Population
1	New York	New York	512,719	7.0	73.9
2	California	Los Angeles	341,807	9.8	12.0
3	Hawaii	Honolulu	257,552	70.5	37.6
4	California	San Francisco	210,876	29.1	7.4
5	California	San Jose	152,815	19.5	5.4
6	California	San Diego	130,945	11.8	4.6
7	Illinois	Chicago	104,118	3.7	36.5
8	Texas	Houston	67,113	4.1	21.0
9	Washington	Seattle	60,819	11.8	28.8
10	California	Long Beach	58,266	13.6	2.0

Source: U.S. Bureau of the Census, 1994 City and County Book

Table 6
Top Ten Counties with the Largest 1990
Asian Pacific American Populations

Rank	State	City	1990 APA Population	Percent of Total County Population	Percent of State Population
1	California	Los Angeles	954,485	10.8	33.5
2	Hawaii	Honolulu	526,459	63.0	76.8
3	New York	Queens	238,336	12.2	34.8
4	California	Santa Clara	261,466	17.5	9.2
5	California	Orange	249,192	10.3	8.8
6	California	San Francisco	210,876	29.1	7.4
7	California	San Diego	198,311	7.9	7.0
8	California	Alameda	192,554	15.1	6.8
9	Illinois	Cook	188,565	3.7	66.1
10	New York	Kings	111,251	4.8	16.0

Source: U.S. Bureau of the Census, special tabulations of the 1990 Summary Tape File 3A

NOTES

Chapter 1: Why Specifically Target Asian Americans?

1. Edward Iwata, "Race Without Face: An Asian American Male Confronts the Cultural Demons of White America and His Own Psychic Surgery," *San Francisco FOCUS*, May 1991, 132.

2. Throughout this book the term *Asian American* will be used as a synonym for Asian Pacific American, even though the latter label is the one that appears frequently. I hope that my use of a term that is more familiar to me does not offend any of my Pacific Islander brothers and sisters.

3. Since Buddhists never refer to Christians as non-Buddhists and since those we refer to as nonbelievers do have beliefs (not ours), I have decided to refer to those who are not Christians in a less presumptuous and/or pejorative way. Saying that they are unconvinced or overlooked puts the onus where it usually belongs: on us who claim to follow in Jesus' footsteps.

4. Donald A. McGavran, *Understanding Church Growth* (Grand Rapids, Mich.: Eerdmans, 1970).

5. C. Peter Wagner, *Your Church Can Grow: Seven Vital Signs of a Healthy Church* (Ventura, Calif.: Regal, 1976).

6. Donald A. McGavran and Winfield C. Arn, *Ten Steps for Church Growth* (New York: Harper & Row, 1977), 59.

7. McGavran, 209.

8. Ibid., 183–97.

9. Quoted by C. Peter Wagner, "Your Church and Church Growth, Part 4: The Sociological Foundation" (D.Min. course at Fuller Theological Seminary, Pasadena, California).

10. Matthew 28:19's "all nations" *(panta ta ethne)* literally means this.

11. McGavran, 223.

12. William J. Abraham, *The Logic of Evangelism* (Grand Rapids, Mich.: Eerdmans, 1989), 85.

13. McGavran, 242–43.

14. Revelation 7:9–10.

15. This an estimate. Although there are no hard figures, this is based on the overwhelming preponderance of Asian Christian churches that are devoted to specific Asian ethnic groups, rather than to the blended, more Americanized Asian American population that is the topic of this book.

16. We will deal with this in much greater detail in chapter 2.

17. McGavran and Arn, 53.

18. The term *assimilate* has long been interpreted by ethnic sociologists as a negative term, connoting the intentions of the majority culture to swallow

up all minorities. It is regularly read as denying minority persons the freedom to maintain their own uniqueness, even in the face of overwhelming
pressures to conform. I will occasionally use it when I feel it is the most accurate way to describe some Asian Americans' desire to become a nondescript
part of the majority white American culture. However, most of the time I will
employ the more acceptable term *acculturate*, which usually means that the
minority person is choosing to make certain cultural adjustments rather than
being made to disappear.

19. Diana Fong, "America's 'Invisible' Chinese," *New York Times*, May 1,
1982, as quoted in Harry H. L. Kitano and Roger Daniels, *Asian Americans:
Emerging Minorities* (Englewood Cliffs, N.J.: Prentice-Hall, 1988), 50.

20. Howard G. Chua-Eoan, "Strangers in Paradise," *Time*, April 9, 1990, 34.

21. William A. Henry III, "Beyond the Melting Pot," *Time*, April 9, 1990,
30–31.

Chapter 2: Pursuing the Pearl through the Flow of Generations

1. Dallas Willard, *The Divine Conspiracy: Rediscovering Our Hidden Life
in God* (San Francisco: HarperSanFrancisco, 1998), 26.

2. K. Connie Kang, "At a Crossroad: Rising Numbers and Influence Bring
Greater Success and Greater Problems for California's Asian Americans,"
Reaching Critical Mass: Asian Americans in California series, *Los Angeles
Times*, July 12, 1998.

3. For one of the best treatises on kingdom living, see Willard's *The
Divine Conspiracy*, which *Christianity Today* voted its 1998 book of the year.

4. Matthew 18:20.

5. Matthew 16:24–28.

6. For more on this, see M. Scott Peck's *Further Along the Road Less
Traveled* (New York: Simon & Schuster, 1993), 119f.

7. Kang.

8. Japanese, Chinese, Taiwanese, Korean, Vietnamese, Indonesian, Malaysian, Burmese, Laotian, Pacific Islander, East Indian, white, black, Latino,
and multiracial people, ranging from first-generation immigrants who speak
English with accents to fourth-generation Marginal Ethnics.

Chapter 3: Emergence of a Merging Minority

1. Eric Liu, *The Accidental Asian: Notes of a Native Speaker* (New York:
Random House, 1998), 56.

2. Molefi Asante, chairman of the department of African American studies, Temple University, Philadelphia, as quoted in William A. Henry III,
"Beyond the Melting Pot," *Time*, April 9, 1990, 29.

3. Ibid., 28.

4. Megan Garvey and Patrick J. McDonnell, "Jose Moves into Top Spot in Name Game," *Los Angeles Times*, January 8, 1999.

5. Ibid., p. 31.

6. Ronald Takaki, *Strangers from a Different Shore: A History of Asian Americans* (Boston: Little, Brown, 1989), 5–6.

7. Harry H. L. Kitano and Roger Daniels, *Asian Americans: Emerging Minorities* (Englewood Cliffs, N.J.: Prentice-Hall, 1988), 191.

8. Ibid., 191–92.

9. Of course, many Latinos walk across our southern border, too.

10. The Chinese term for California that was coined at the time of the Gold Rush. It eventually came to refer to America in general.

11. Most early immigrants came as sojourners, planning to amass a sum of money and then return to their families and their homelands. This was true even of numerous non-Asian immigrants.

12. All these figures would be higher if the individual Asian and Pacific Islander groups were looked at separately (e.g., 50 percent of Asian Indians are college graduates to only 13 percent of Vietnamese; median income for a Japanese family is $27,400 [highest], Vietnamese was $12,800 [lowest]).

13. Peter Y. Hong, "Reaching Critical Mass: The Changing Face of Higher Education," *Los Angeles Times* special report, July 14, 1998.

14. Excerpts from "We, the Asian and Pacific Islander Americans," a booklet published by the Commerce Department's Census Bureau, December 23, 1988. Information is based on the 1980 census and appeared in the *Pacific Citizen*, February 24, 1989, 5.

15. Henry, 31.

16. Howard G. Chua-Eoan, "Strangers in Paradise," *Time*, April 9, 1990, 33–35 passim.

17. Dr. Rose Hum Lee, cited by Kitano and Daniels, 41.

18. Ibid., 73.

19. Although the Chinese as a group have been here longer than the Japanese, the Japanese have almost a 20 percent greater rate of intermarriages. More of this will be discussed in chapter 4.

20. Harry H. L. Kitano, W. Young, L. Chai, and H. Hatanoka, "Asian American Interracial Marriage," *Journal of Marriage and Family* 46, no. 1 (1984): 179–90, as cited in Kitano and Daniels, 178.

21. See chapter 1.

Chapter 4: Japanese Americans — Vanguard of an Emerging Subculture

1. Bill Watanabe, quoted by K. Connie Kang, "At a Crossroad," *Reaching Critical Mass: Asian Americans in California* series, *Los Angeles Times*, July 12, 1998.

2. Howard G. Chuan-Eoan, "Strangers in Paradise," *Time*, April 9, 1990, 33.

3. Thomas Sowell, *Ethnic America: A History* (New York: Basic Books, 1981), 155.

4. Ibid., 156–57, 164.

5. Composer unknown, from a set of Cantonese songs entitled "The Prisoner in the Wooden Shed Suffered the Utmost in Hardships," 1911 or 1912, from Him Mark Lai, "The Chinese Experience at Angel Island, part III," *East West*, February 25, 1976, 1, quoted in Diane Mei Lin Mark and Ginger Chih, *A Place Called Chinese America* (Dubuque, Iowa: Kendall/Hunt, 1982), 144.

6. Ronald Takaki, *Strangers from a Different Shore: A History of Asian Americans* (Boston: Little, Brown, 1989), 180–81.

7. Sowell, 140–41.

8. Since 1950 the Chinese American population has made up for lost time, doubling in every decade. From 117,629 that year, the number was 237,292 in 1960, then was 435,062 in 1970, and was 806,027 in 1980. For the first time in seventy years, the Chinese had replaced the Japanese as the largest subgroup in the Asian American populace. But they could not catch up to the advanced stage of acculturation the Japanese Americans had already achieved.

9. It is important to note that not all Japanese Americans were evacuated and placed in one of the concentration camps. Some 10,000 living east of the prescribed areas and 150,000 in Hawaii were allowed to remain where they were. Nevertheless, the shocking removal and incarceration of more than 110,000 of their brethren, two-thirds of whom were American citizens, deeply affected their self-concepts and feelings of security.

10. Harry H. L. Kitano and Roger Daniels, *Asian Americans: Emerging Minorities* (Englewood Cliffs, N.J.: Prentice-Hall, 1988), 61.

11. Harry H. L. Kitano, *Japanese Americans: The Evolution of a Subculture*, 2d ed. (Englewood Cliffs, N.J.: Prentice-Hall, 1976), 75.

12. Ibid., 75–77.

13. Masayo Duus, *Unlikely Liberators*, as cited by Gary Libman, "Battle Zone: Veterans' Group Disagree about Who Should Be Listed on a Proposed Monument to Japanese-American Soldiers," *Los Angeles Times*, June 28, 1990, section E, 1.

14. There may be some question as to why the Hawaiians are not being factored into this discussion. They, having roots in Polynesia and not Asia, tend to be on a separate path from the Asian groups when it comes to merging into a new subculture. There are exceptions (see chap. 3).

15. Kang.

16. John W. Conner, *Tradition and Change in Three Generations of Japanese Americans* (Chicago: Nelson-Hall, 1977), 309–10.

17. Ibid., 318–19.

18. Kitano and Daniels, 133.

19. While Filipinos can trace their ethnic roots to Malaysia, their culture

has strong Spanish overtones due to their being a Spanish colony from the late sixteenth century onward. This, together with the fact that they have had a constant American military presence there since the turn of the twentieth century, gives a definite non-Asian shading to their culture.

20. The Cell D Asian American students typically join more immigrant-dominated Asian ethnic organizations (e.g., the Chinese Club, the Korean Christian Fellowship). If the name of the group is ethnic-specific, that is usually a give-away that the group is more for Cell D types than Cell B. If the name of the group contains the words "Asian" or "Asian American," that is an indicator that the group is for more Americanized Asian students.

21. Kitano and Daniels, 105–6.

Chapter 5: Coloring outside the Lines

1. Mike Regele with Mark Schulz, *Death of the Church* (Grand Rapids, Mich.: Zondervan/HarperCollins, 1995). From the subtitle for the book.

2. Acts 15:6–35.

3. *Webster's New Collegiate Dictionary* (1976), s.v. "culture."

4. Vincent J. Donovan, *Christianity Rediscovered*, 2d ed. (Maryknoll, N.Y.: Orbis, 1978), 29.

5. Ibid., 29–31.

6. John Huey, "Nothing Is Impossible," *Fortune*, September 23, 1991, 135.

7. Adapted from Joel Arthur Barker, *Future Edge: Discovering the New Paradigms of Success* (New York: William Morrow, 1992), 35.

8. Huey, 140.

9. Anne Wilson Schaef and Diane Fassel, *The Addictive Organization: Why We Work, Cover Up, Pick Up the Pieces, Please the Boss, and Perpetuate Sick Organizations* (San Francisco: Harper & Row, 1988), 33–34.

10. Edward Iwata, "Race Without Face: An Asian American Male Confronts the Cultural Demons of White America and His Own Psychic Surgery," *San Francisco FOCUS*, May 1991, 52.

11. Eric Liu, *The Accidental Asian: Notes of a Native Speaker* (New York: Random House, 1998), 49–50.

12. Rudy Busto, "The Gospel According to the Model Minority? Hazarding an Interpretation of Asian American Evangelical College Students," *Amerasia Journal* 22, no. 1 (1996): 133–47.

13. Regele with Schulz, 204–5.

Chapter 6: A Shared Pursuit of the Pearl

1. Keith Miller, *The Scent of Love* (Waco, Tex.: Word, 1983), 13–14.

2. George Gallup Jr., and George O'Connell, *Who Do Americans Say That I Am?* (Philadelphia: Westminster, 1986), 88–89, as quoted in William J.

Abraham, *The Logic of Evangelism* (Grand Rapids, Mich.: Eerdmans, 1989), 12–13.

3. Abraham, 38–39.

4. Ibid., 95–96.

5. Ibid., 93–94.

6. Ibid., 101.

7. Ibid., 103.

8. Frederick Buechner, *Wishful Thinking: A Theological ABC* (New York: Harper & Row, 1973), s.v. "Faith" and "Doubt."

9. Roy Hession, *The Calvary Road* (London: Christian Literature Crusade, 1950), 16, as quoted by Michael Cassidy, *Bursting the Wineskins: The Holy Spirit's Transforming Work in a Peacemaker and His World* (Wheaton, Ill: Harold Shaw, 1983), 173.

10. Paul G. Hiebert, "The Category 'Christian' in the Mission Task," *International Review of Missions* 72 (1983): 421–27, as cited by Abraham, 109.

11. Abraham, 109.

12. Abraham is an outspoken critic of this view that was popularized by Hiebert; see Abraham, 109–10.

13. Ibid., 109.

14. M. Scott Peck, *What Return Can I Make? Dimensions of the Christian Experience* (New York: Simon & Schuster, 1985), 12.

15. Ibid., 19–20.

16. Calvin Miller, *Spirit, Word, and Story: A Philosophy of Preaching* (Grand Rapids, Mich.: Baker Book House, 1996), 218.

17. Vincent J. Donovan, *Christianity Rediscovered*, 2d ed. (Maryknoll, N.Y.: Orbis, 1978), 108–9.

Chapter 7: Preaching Heart to Heart

1. Frederick Buechner, *Wishful Thinking: A Theological ABC* (San Francisco: Harper & Row, 1973), 86–87.

2. Dallas Willard, *The Divine Conspiracy: Rediscovering Our Hidden Life in God* (San Francisco: HarperSanFrancisco, 1998), 112.

3. Stanley Inouye, Arlene Inouye, and Sharon U. Fong, "Selected Data from the 1982 Survey of Primarily Japanese Churches in Los Angeles and Orange Counties," unpublished survey summary prepared by IWA, Inc., Glendale, California, 1983.

4. Eddie Gibbs, *Followed or Pushed?* (London: MARC Europe, 1987), 113–14.

5. Gregoir Lemercier, *Dialogues Avec Le Christ*, as quoted by M. Tanioka. (No other information was available.)

6. Calvin Miller, *Spirit, Word, and Story: A Philosophy of Preaching* (Grand Rapids, Mich.: Baker Book House, 1996), 18–19.

7. Ibid., 26, 44, 135.

8. M. Scott Peck, *What Return Can I Make? Dimensions of the Christian Experience* (New York: Simon & Schuster, 1985), 13–14.

9. Miller, 116.

10. Ibid., 69.

11. Ibid., 49–50.

12. Ibid., 70–71.

13. Inouye, Inouye, and Fong, 3 (27.6 percent).

14. According to the 1982 IWA survey, 44 percent (422 out of 963 surveyed) believe that humans are good, with only 13 percent believing that humans are evil. And this is from a group that identifies itself as being born-again Christians.

15. John Fischer, *Real Christians Don't Dance: Sorting the Truth from the Trappings in a Born-Again Culture* (Minneapolis: Bethany House, 1988), 29.

16. Inouye, Inouye, and Fong, 3.

17. Miller, 142–45.

18. Ibid., 148.

19. From a purely physiological standpoint, the heart is not capable of doing anything but pumping blood through our bodies. Although it has become identified in our culture as the seat of emotions, it may be physiologically more accurate to point to the right hemisphere of the brain as the organ in which nonrational experiences occur. While this may be true, for literary and traditional purposes, we will continue to use the term *heart*.

20. Miller, 153.

Chapter 8: Anticipating the Unconvinced

1. Eddie Gibbs, *Followed or Pushed?* (London: MARC Europe, 1987), 70.

2. Frederick Buechner, *Wishful Thinking: A Theological ABC* (New York: Harper & Row, 1973), 97–98.

3. See chapter 4.

4. John Fischer, *Real Christians Don't Dance: Sorting the Truth from the Trappings in a Born-Again Culture* (Minneapolis: Bethany House, 1988), 101–2.

5. A. P. Gibbs, *Worship: The Christian's Highest Occupation* (Kansas City: Walterick Publishers, n.d.), 62–64, cited by Calvin Miller, *Spirit, Word, and Story: A Philosophy of Preaching* (Grand Rapids, Mich.: Baker Book House, 1996), 48.

6. Fischer, 30.

7. James R. Coggins and Paul G. Hiebert, eds., *Wonders and the Word: An Examination of Issues Raised by John Wimber and the Vineyard Movement* (Hillsboro, Kans.: Kindred Press, 1989), 17.

8. C. Peter Wagner, *The Third Wave of the Holy Spirit: Encountering the Power of Signs and Wonders Today* (Ann Arbor, Mich.: Servant, 1988).

9. Coggins and Hiebert, 17.

10. Remember the discussion in chapter 5 about the lengthy initial premodern period of the church's history? I find it interesting how, in reaction to some of the excessiveness of modernity, some people (including some Christians) are reverting to premodern mysticism while another portion are plunging ahead to the mysteries of postmodernity.

11. Greg Ogden, "The Pastor as Change Agent," *Theology, News and Notes*, June 1990, 8.

12. Elton Trueblood, *The Incendiary Fellowship* (New York: Harper & Row, 1967), 41, as quoted by Ogden, 9.

13. Loren B. Mead, *The Once and Future Church: Reinventing the Congregation for a New Mission Frontier* (New York: The Alban Institute, 1991), 10.

14. Although Mead failed to note this, it was almost at this same point in history that the Armenians in Turkey nationalized Christianity, setting in motion a parallel movement that is still overlooked by Western scholars.

15. Mead, 18.

16. The Hebrew word in the Bible for righteousness or right relationships. When we speak of Sedaqah (pronounced tseh-dah-*kah*) Community we are looking to a future where people everywhere will live in right relationship to God and to one another. For those of us who believe in Jesus, it is his passion for right relationships that is our inspiration to live sedaqah everywhere.

Chapter 9: Rejuvenating Sick Bodies

1. Loren B. Mead, *The Once and Future Church: Reinventing the Congregation for a New Mission Frontier* (New York: The Alban Institute, 1991), 92.

2. Richard N. Ostling, "Those Mainline Blues: America's Old Guard Protestant Churches Confront an Unprecedented Decline," *Time*, May 22, 1989, 94.

3. Peter M. Morgan, *Story Weaving: Using Stories to Transform Your Congregation* (St. Louis, Mo.: CBP Press, 1986), 44.

4. Ibid. Evergreen Baptist Church of LA, EBC of San Gabriel Valley, and EBC–South Coast (Irvine), evangelical American Baptist churches, are perfect examples of this phenomena.

5. Joseph Wong, "Bridging the Gap," *About Face* 12 (February 1990): 2.

6. S. Chadwick, quoted by Jonathan Katagi, "Some Thoughts on the Need for Spiritual Renewal," *Grapevine*, San Gabriel Valley Japanese Christian Church, February 20, 1990, 1.

7. For more on this, see chapter 8 under the "Third Wave" section.

8. Admittedly, some interesting theological questions immediately spring up at this point, but we will have to leave the pursuit of them for another book or the classroom.

9. Isaiah 63:8–10,15,17–19. An alternate translation of verse 19 reads

"We are like those you have never ruled, like those never called by your name."

10. A. W. Tozer, as quoted by Katagi.

11. The propagation of ministries, both renewed and new, to reach the millions of postmodern, unconvinced, marginal Americanized Asian Americans for Christ is the unabashed intent of this book; however, this is not to suggest that it is the only way to accomplish this end. Proponents of the mono-Asian, multilingual paradigm should not feel threatened by the proposing of "new wineskins" to reach acculturated cod; there will always be a need for more homogeneous Asian churches in this country. However, even if those churches experience authentic renewal, they must understand that their paradigm, like all models, has its limitations. Those who identify with a blended subculture are more likely to select a ministry that better suits them. Thus, a plethora of healthy churches from different models will always be needed.

12. The Jews also have a chauvinistic culture. On a recent visit to the Holy Land, the marked separation at the Wailing Wall between the men and women spoke volumes about what the Jews believe about men and women. Men obviously had the inside track to God, while the women were left to be observers.

13. John Sculley, *Odyssey: From Pepsi to Apple* (New York: Harper & Row, 1987), 419.

14. Paul Wilkes, "The Hands That Would Shape Our Souls," *The Atlantic Monthly* (December 1990), 61–62.

15. Herb Miller, "What Can Church Leaders Expect in the 1990s?" *Net Results/UMC*, January 1989, 10.

16. Sculley, 96.

17. Bill Pannell, "A New Generation of Olds?" *World Vision*, December 1989–January 1990, 29.

18. Calvin Miller, *Spirit, Word, and Story: A Philosophy of Preaching* (Grand Rapids, Mich.: Baker Book House, 1996), 10.

19. Thomas A. Stewart, "Turning Around the Lord's Business," *Fortune*, September 25, 1989, 128.

20. Around 1994, on my trip to Korea to study Yoido Island Full Gospel Church (which then had a congregation numbering around 700,000), my host pastor asked me how large our church was in Los Angeles. "About 1,200 on a Sunday," I replied. Somewhat immodestly, he said, "In Korea, a small church is 20,000."

21. Fred Smith, quoted by Stewart, 128.

22. From 1987 to 1995, our average combined morning attendance rose from 450 to well over 1,200. At the time of the strategic church split (hive) in 1997, our combined attendance had slipped back to approximately 900. Two years later, the 600–plus who went with Evergreen-SGV had grown to about 750 and the 300–plus who stayed at Evergreen-LA had become at least 550. It is doubtful that either church would have experienced such rapid growth if they had started with fewer than 100 people.

23. John Childs, quoted by John Finney, *Understanding Leadership* (London: Daybreak, 1989), 5–6.

24. Sculley, 92–93.

25. Smith, quoted by Stewart, 128.

26. Miller, 51–52.

Chapter 10: What Will Asian America Look Like?

1. Michael Omi, a sociologist at University of California Berkeley, quoted in K. Connie Kang, "At a Crossroad," *Reaching Critical Mass: Asian Americans in California* series, *Los Angeles Times*, July 12, 1998.

2. Eric Liu, *The Accidental Asian: Notes from a Native Speaker* (New York: Random House, 1998), 82.

3. Calvin Miller, *Spirit, Word, and Story: A Philosophy of Preaching* (Grand Rapids, Mich.: Baker Book House, 1996), 172.

4. Jenifer Wana, "Confessions of a Student Activist,: *A. Magazine: Inside Asian America,* April/May 1998, 34.

5. More than twenty-five years ago, Evergreen-LA regular Dan Kuramoto felt led to organize a jazz fusion band called Hiroshima that would spawn a new American sound through the blending of traditional Japanese instruments and musical idioms with jazz. I was curious how the band has managed to accomplish this and has attracted such a multi-ethnic audience. Dan explained to me that "we first had to be cool with being Japanese before we were comfortable inserting our culture into the mainstream." In March of 1999, a group of American jazz musicians flew to Havana, Cuba, to partner in composing and playing with Cuban jazz artists for the first time in forty years. Unlike what happened when similar collaborations were held in Ireland, Romania, the former Soviet Union, and elsewhere, the American artists did not intimidate the Cuban musicians. The organizer remarked that this was the first time American musicians have come into contact with musicians who are just as strong, if not stronger, who know who they are and are proud of their culture. I believe that this is the same kind of dynamic that needs to occur if there are truly going to be multi-ethnic ministries that are pleasing to God. Each person in the fusion band must be comfortable with himself or herself in order to make the needed contributions.

6. Harry H. L. Kitano, Diane C. Fujino, and Jane Takahashi Sato, "Interracial Marriages: Where Are the Asian Americans and Where Are They Going?" in *Handbook of Asian American Psychology*, ed. Lee C. Lee and Nolan W. S. Zane (Thousand Oaks, Calif.: Sage Publications, 1998), 256–57.

7. Ibid., 257.

8. In October 1997 the Clinton administration passed a resolution that will allow people of mixed parentage to check off all ethnic categories that apply to them on the 2000 census. Thus, someone like Tiger Woods would not be forced to classify himself as just African American or just Thai American.

Instead, he will be able to check off all the categories that apply. This new ruling was made in response to growing pressure from groups of multiracial people who have felt that the previous system glossed over their true identities. Some African American groups are expressing grave concerns due to the probability that this change will encourage some people who would normally have to classify themselves as being black to take themselves out of that single category. The fear is that this will ultimately reduce the official percentage of African Americans, thus cutting into needed programs and funding.

9. Liu, 188.

10. Paul Ong and Suzanne J. Hee, "Growth of the Asian Pacific American Population: Twenty Million in 2020," in *The State of Asian Pacific America — A Public Policy Report: Policy Issues to the Year 2020* (Los Angeles: LEAP Asian Pacific American Public Policy Institute and UCLA Asian American Studies Center, 1993)

11. Paul Wilkes, "The Hands That Would Shape Our Souls," *The Atlantic Monthly* (December 1990), 62.

12. Mike Yaconelli, "Can We Talk?" *The Door*, September/October 1991, 36.

SELECT BIBLIOGRAPHY

Abraham, William J. *The Logic of Evangelism*. Grand Rapids, Mich.: Eerdmans, 1989.

Barker, Joel Arthur. *Future Edge: Discovering the New Paradigms of Success*. New York: William Morrow, 1992.

Buechner, Frederick. *Wishful Thinking: A Theological ABC*. New York: Harper & Row, 1973.

Busto, Rudy. "The Gospel According to the Model Minority? Hazarding an Interpretation of Asian American Evangelical College Students." *Amerasia Journal* 22, no. 1 (1996): 133–47.

Coggins, James R., and Paul G. Hiebert, eds. *Wonders and the Word: An Examination of Issues Raised by John Wimber and the Vineyard Movement*. Hillsboro, Kans.: Kindred Press, 1989.

Conner, John W. *Tradition and Change in Three Generations of Japanese Americans*. Chicago: Nelson-Hall, 1977.

Chua-Eoan, Howard G. "Strangers in Paradise." *Time*. April 9, 1990, 32–35.

Donovan, Vincent J. *Christianity Rediscovered*. 2d ed. Maryknoll, N.Y.: Orbis, 1978.

Fischer, John. *Real Christians Don't Dance: Sorting the Truth from the Trappings in a Born-Again Culture*. Minneapolis: Bethany House, 1988.

Gibbs, Eddie. *Followed or Pushed?* (London: MARC Europe, 1987).

Henry, William A., III. "Beyond the Melting Pot." *Time*. April 9, 1990, 28–31.

Hong, Peter Y. "Reaching Critical Mass: The Changing Face of Higher Education." *Los Angeles Times* special report, July 14, 1998.

Iwata, Edward. "Race Without Face: An Asian American Male Confronts the Cultural Demons of White America and His Own Psychic Surgery," *San Francisco FOCUS*. May 1991, 50–53, 128–32.

Kang, K. Connie. "At a Crossroad: Rising Numbers and Influence Bring Greater Success and Greater Problems for California's Asian Americans." *Reaching Critical Mass: Asian Americans in California* series, *Los Angeles Times*, July 12, 1998.

Kitano, Harry H. L. *Japanese Americans: The Evolution of a Subculture*. 2d ed. Englewood Cliffs, N.J.: Prentice-Hall, 1976.

Kitano, Harry H. L., and Roger Daniels. *Asian Americans: Emerging Minorities*. Englewood Cliffs, N.J.: Prentice-Hall, 1988.

Kitano, Harry H. L., Diane C. Fujino, and Jane Takahashi Sato. "Interracial Marriages: Where Are the Asian Americans and Where Are They Going?"

in *Handbook of Asian American Psychology*. Edited by Lee C. Lee and Nolan W. S. Zane. Thousand Oaks, Calif.: Sage Publications, 1998.

Liu, Eric. *The Accidental Asian: Notes of a Native Speaker*. New York: Random House, 1998.

McGavran, Donald A. *Understanding Church Growth*. Grand Rapids, Mich.: Eerdmans, 1970.

McGavran, Donald A., and Winfield C. Arn. *Ten Steps for Church Growth*. New York: Harper & Row, 1977.

Mark, Diane Mei Lin, and Ginger Chih. *A Place Called Chinese America*. Dubuque, Iowa: Kendall/Hunt, 1982.

Mead, Loren B. *The Once and Future Church: Reinventing the Congregation for a New Mission Frontier*. New York: The Alban Institute, 1991.

Miller, Calvin. *Spirit, Word, and Story: A Philosophy of Preaching* (Grand Rapids, Mich.: Baker Book House, 1996).

Peck, M. Scott. *What Return Can I Make? Dimensions of the Christian Experience*. New York: Simon & Schuster, 1985.

Regele, Mike, with Mark Schulz. *Death of the Church*. Grand Rapids, Mich.: Zondervan/HarperCollins, 1995.

Sowell, Thomas. *Ethnic America: A History*. New York: Basic Books, 1981.

Takaki, Ronald. *Strangers from a Different Shore: A History of Asian Americans*. Boston: Little, Brown, 1989.

Wagner, C. Peter. *Your Church Can Grow: Seven Vital Signs of a Healthy Church*. Ventura, Calif.: Regal, 1976.

———. *The Third Wave of the Holy Spirit: Encountering the Power of Signs and Wonders Today*. Ann Arbor, Mich.: Servant, 1988.

Willard, Dallas. *The Divine Conspiracy: Rediscovering Our Hidden Life in God*. San Francisco: HarperSanFrancisco, 1998.